THE INTERNAL AUDITOR AT WORK

A Practical Guide to Everyday Challenges

THE INTERNAL AUDITOR AT WORK

A Practical Guide to Everyday Challenges

K.H. SPENCER PICKETT

WILEY

John Wiley & Sons, Inc.

ISBN 0-471-45839-2

Printed in the United States of America

10 9 8 7 6 5 4 3 2 1

ABOUT THE INSTITUTE
OF INTERNAL AUDITORS

The Institute of Internal Auditors (IIA) is the primary international professional association, organized on a worldwide basis, dedicated to the promotion and development of the practice of internal auditing. The IIA is the recognized authority, chief educator, and acknowledged leader in standards, education, certification, and research for the profession worldwide. The Institute provides professional and executive development training, educational products, research studies, and guidance to more than 80,000 members in more than 100 countries. For additional information, visit the Web site at *www.theiia.org.*

*Special acknowledgement
to my wife,
Jennifer M. Pickett,
for her much appreciated assistance.*

*This book is dedicated with love
to our children,
Dexter and Laurel-Jade Pickett*

CONTENTS

LIST OF ABBREVIATIONS

ACFE	Association of Certified Fraud Examiners
ACL	Audit Command Language
AICPA	American Institute of Certified Public Accountants
CAE	Chief Audit Executive
CEO	Chief Executive Officer
CFE	Certified Fraud Examiner
CFIA	Competency Framework for Internal Auditing
CFO	Chief Finance Officer
CG	Corporate Governance
CIA	Certified Internal Auditor
CISA	Certified Information Systems Auditor
COSO	Committee of Sponsoring Organizations
CPA	Certified Public Accountant
CRSA	Control Risk Self-Assessment
CSA	Control Self-Assessment
ERM	Enterprise Risk Management
GAAP	Generally Accepted Accounting Principles
HR	Human Resource
ICE	Internal Control Evaluation
ICES	Internal Control Evaluation Schedule
ICQ	Internal Control Questionnaire
ID	Identification
IDEA	Interactive Data Extraction and Analysis
IIA	Institute of Internal Auditors
IS	Information Systems
IT	Information Technology
KPI	Key Performance Indicators
NYSE	New York Stock Exchange
OECD	Organisation for Economic Co-operation and Development
RBSA	Risk-Based Systems Auditing
SEC	Securities and Exchange Commission

1

INTRODUCTION

——— SECTION 1 ———
ABOUT THE BOOK

This new book provides a dynamic resource for business graduates and others entering the field of internal auditing as well as for seasoned auditors who are looking for ways to expand audit services. It acts as a concise guide to the role and responsibilities of the internal auditor within the context of the global themes of corporate governance, risk management, and control. The book addresses the challenges facing internal auditors in larger and medium-sized organizations in the private, not-for-profit, and wider public sectors. Although set in the U.S. economy, it is relevant throughout the developed and developing world—in line with the increasing reliance on internal auditing to promote integrity, accountability, and transparency in business and government. The book focuses on the context, role, and work of the internal auditor as an introductory text. It provides broad coverage of important concepts rather than just concentrating on the basic and detailed workbook exercises that some orientation guides contain. Internal auditing has many branches and specialist areas. The interpretation of the audit role will depend on the adopted perspective of the individual auditor and may consist of a combination of roles that includes:

- Basic internal auditing
- Retail and branch audits
- Information systems auditing
- Investigations and forensic examination
- Detailed analytical review
- Contract and large engineering project audits
- Internal audit management and quality assurance
- Corporate governance and top management reviews
- Specialist compliance, disclosures, and financial statement auditing

This orientation guide addresses the first item, basic internal auditing, and does not provide extensive details of the other more specialist areas of audit

1

work. There is a whole array of relevant material available to the budding internal auditor that provides an insight into these and many other specialist aspects of the job. Not least are the vast resources that appear on Internet Web sites using the key search words "internal auditing." The Institute of Internal Auditors (IIA), a global body that represents the interests of internal audit professionals and like-minded specialists, has developed a wealth of material that is both interesting and relevant. There are hundreds of specialist textbooks, study guides, videos, and CDs that address aspects of the internal auditor's work. The newly appointed auditor will doubtless visit these resources as his or her career develops.

This book limits reference material to the professional standards and practice advisories published by the IIA as a good starting place for the new auditor. As such, all references to standards and advisories throughout the book relate to the professional practices framework published by the IIA. Note that both the standards and practice advisories are in a constant state of development. Therefore, the reader is advised to track developments, as standards are updated and changed over the years. Most sections of the book conclude with ideas that the auditor could consider discussing with an audit colleague from the employing organization or anyone else who is associated with internal auditing in some shape or form. Each chapter closes with a set of exercises that should be tackled by the new auditor as part of his or her personal development plan.

> ### *For Further Discussion*
> *How has orientation training been covered in the past, and what other steps have new auditors taken to come to grips with the internal audit role?*

––––– SECTION 2 –––––

THE NEW INTERNAL AUDITOR

The growing emphasis on corporate accountability has led to a drive for more openness in the way private business and the public sector manage and communicate their performance to key stakeholders. This, in turn, has led to a search for mechanisms that may help promote the three linked concepts of integrity, accountability, and transparency, commonly known as good corporate governance. The *governance process* is defined by the IIA (Glossary) as:

> *The procedures utilized by the representatives of the organization's stakeholders (e.g., shareholders, etc.) to provide oversight of risk and control processes administered by management.*

One of the pillars of corporate governance relates to the establishment of sound systems of audit and accountability. Directors report to company owners and communicate with various stakeholders through the annual report, while independent auditors double-check the report and the associated accounts on behalf of these owners. This quite straightforward model is, however, dependent on effective internal systems to support the financial and corporate strategies of the organization. Moreover, the reality can be far from the theoretical model of ownership, stewardship, management, and accountability, because published information may not always be entirely reliable. There are many different types of risk that can undermine the search for success. The internal auditor appears on the horizon to help review the system of controls that address actual and perceived threats to an organization. Again, the auditor is an independent party who is able to stand back from apparently conflicting forces when performing its reviews. The formal definition of *internal auditing* is as follows:

> *Internal auditing is an independent, objective assurance and consulting activity designed to add value and improve an organization's operations. It helps an organization accomplish its objectives by bringing a systematic, disciplined approach to evaluate and improve the effectiveness of risk management, control, and governance processes.*

Free from Spin

The audit process has become increasingly relevant to successful businesses as there are fewer people around who are not engaged in the constant spin that clouds most reviews, reports, and published opinions. In turn, the internal audit process depends on a source of professional staff who are able to achieve the demanding goal of balancing the task of helping the customer develop good business systems with the need to provide an objective assessment of the same customer's systems. The internal auditor's role is that of assisting managers and their teams, while also working for the corporate body of the organization and often reporting to an independent audit committee. We will develop these dual themes of performing objective reviews and understanding the real pressures facing busy operational managers. Our main objective is to address these themes in the context of the changing role of internal auditing and how auditors can respond to new developments. The IIA defines an *internal audit activity* as:

> *a department, division, team of consultants, or other practitioner(s) that provide independent, objective assurance and consulting services designed to add value and improve an organization's operations. The internal audit activity helps an organization accomplish its objectives by bringing a*

*systematic, disciplined approach to evaluate and improve the effective-
ness of risk management, control, and governance processes.*

Three Aspects of Internal Auditing

Note that the three aspects of the audit role—*risk management, control, and
governance processes*—are referred to regularly throughout the entire book. No
apologies are offered for this approach, since it is important that there be constant reinforcement of the fundamentals of internal auditing.

> ### For Further Discussion
> *In what way has internal auditing changed over the years, and what
> are the highlights and downsides of these changes?*

―――― SECTION 3 ――――

THE CHALLENGES OF A CAREER IN INTERNAL AUDITING

It is a well-kept secret that in days gone by, many people found themselves
transferred to internal audit either by chance or because they were not really suited
to anything else. Over the last few decades, things have not only changed but
have also gone full circle. Now, instead of being "sent" to internal audit, many
staff members are prepared to fight for the chance to join the in-house audit
team. The prospects can be very good, and there is much scope for personal
development and excellent rewards from a career in internal auditing. Meanwhile, the challenges are quite unique. Balancing the auditor's consulting role
with the need to retain professional objectivity is quite an achievement. It takes
a certain type of individual to succeed in this task. A career in internal audit
involves acquiring more than just professional competence. It requires a
demeanor that is flexible and understanding but firm on important points of
principle. It requires someone who is able to listen, consider, and then make a
decision on a position even in the face of inconsistent and/or incomplete information. More than this, internal auditors need to see the "big picture," even
when aspects are missing or at times distorted. But the big picture must also
contain the little pieces that go together to make up the final image.

The Career Auditor

A career in internal auditing is not for the fainthearted. It is for those who are
prepared to go the distance and who do not mind the lack of glamour and gold
medals, but simply accept the challenge. This does not mean some people will

not benefit from a short spell in audit as part of a wider career development plan. Many in-house audit shops have been protected from external competitors because they provide an excellent facility for budding career managers on short transfers. For the career auditor, the topic of audit competencies is covered in some detail in Section 5 of Chapter 4. Here, we will simply note some of the personal attributes that go toward making a potentially successful career as an internal auditor:

1. *Focused.* The internal auditor needs to develop a clear focus on the audit objective. This entails an ability to rise above the office politics common to all work settings and stick to the main driver—for example, enhancing the ability of the organization to deliver as well as being able to account for this activity. Being able to see through the fog can be very difficult at times, because whenever a group of people come together there are tensions that pull in many different directions.

2. *Helpful.* Good auditors are able to adopt a helpful attitude toward busy managers. All managers have to recognize the significant risks that affect their operations and work out how best to manage these risks. They need as much help as possible with this task. Auditors who understand the causes of risk, who appreciate the relevant associated controls, and who are able to help management develop a suitable risk management strategy can provide a great deal of added value to an organization.

3. *Straight down the line.* A clear focus that helps management is a good start, but there are many pressures that could affect an individual's judgment. It can be tempting to assume the course of least resistance that is always present, but auditors are obliged to disclose all material facts and maintain their professional objectivity at all times.

4. *Determined.* The audit task is not always easy. It involves a dogged determination to see things through to the end, to ensure all key issues are understood and that all relevant evidence is obtained and documented. This attribute needs to be developed so that the auditor is able to drill down behind the facade and uncover the real picture painted by the substantive facts.

5. *Firm.* When the auditor needs to pursue a point, it should be explored regardless of the potential embarrassment to others. Being firm can be difficult at times, especially when this involves a message that people do not want to hear. Nevertheless, on important points of principle, the auditor must stand firm.

6. *Decisive.* All the above-mentioned attributes are of little use if the auditor's work has very little impact on what goes on in an organization. If the auditor sits on the fence and does not really have a view, then there is less

value from the audit role. The manager wants help in developing sound controls, while board members need to know about any risks that are not being addressed properly. The board and audit committee will want a firm view of controls from the in-house audit service. Good auditors do not simply report facts and move on; they also formulate a clear view on whether controls are sound or not and are able to explore the ensuing implications.

7. **Balanced.** Above all, the auditor must be fair—fair to the people being audited, fair to the senior management in question, and fair to the board who want to know that controls are in place and are being adhered to as well as the degree to which risk is being managed.

The budding internal auditor needs to acquire the above attributes to be successful. This is no mean feat, and for some individuals it may not be entirely possible. The apparent contradictions inherent within the attributes can create some discomfort. Being helpful is fine, but being determined can involve exploring the same issue until a sensible answer appears, even where the client may feel aggrieved by this search for the truth.

For Further Discussion
What makes a good auditor, and which of these attributes takes the most time to acquire?

——— SECTION 4 ———
POPULAR MISCONCEPTIONS

Many newly appointed auditors come to the job with a number of misconceptions. Some see the audit role as one of "procedure enforcement," where they police the way people are complying with procedures within an organization. Others see the role as one of pure consultancy, where the auditor simply does what the business unit manager in question asks. Among the most popular misconceptions are those listed below.

Risk Averse

Some see the audit role as revolving around recommending more and better controls. So auditors arrive at an office, review the controls that are in place, and work out what more needs to be done to reduce the level of risk. Meanwhile, managers want to push forward and secure more business, while the auditors want them to slow down and install more procedures wherever possible. The presumption is that the audit staff are essentially risk averse. This viewpoint is wrong, in that the new-look internal auditor has a balanced view of risk and only suggests controls where this makes good business sense. At times the auditor may feel that there are too many controls in place, as the following example illustrates:

EXAMPLE ➤ After reviewing a staff travel expense system, the auditor recommended that a finance officer who was currently spending his time checking each staff request be transferred to more useful duties. The travel expense system was redesigned to strengthen the role of the countersign-ing manager and reduce the finance checks to a random 10 percent (and discontinue checking 100 percent). The degree of risk in the redesigned system did not warrant the full-time involvement of the finance officer.

Audit Instructions

Another misconception is that auditors issue instructions concerning the way procedures are operated. As such, certain procedures such as filing arrange-ments, security checks, or document retention periods are not the responsibility of business unit managers but are simply basic audit routines. It is rare for inter-nal audit to issue instructions since the audit role is advisory, not executive in nature. Managers and their staff are responsible for setting a clear direction in all matters of accountability and procedure. The auditor is there to facilitate this task and ensure all material weaknesses are brought to light and addressed. An example brings home the potential for misunderstanding:

EXAMPLE ➤ A department manager called internal audit and asked whether he could send last year's files to the audit offices as he had little storage space and old files were mainly used by the auditors. The audit manager explained that the manager was responsible for his records, including storage, and it was more a question of considering the best way to archive important documents that could not yet be destroyed.

Design Controls

Many audit consultants expound the role of audit as helping busy managers get their systems of internal control focused and refined. This is a good way of "selling" the audit role, but one must take care. If not explained properly, people will get the impression that internal audit is simply there to design sound sys-tems of internal control. Once we allow managers to discard their responsibili-ties for this crucial task, the net result is that no one assumes this role. Again, it should be clear that auditors can help; they can advise, and they can facilitate the design of good controls, but this task properly sits with the business managers as a prime responsibility. An example follows:

> **EXAMPLE** ➤ A cashier's office manager asked the internal auditors to give some advice on the security of the office. The manager had in mind that the auditor would design a daily security routine that could be quickly installed. The auditor ended up recommending a visit by the local law enforcement officer, who gave advice on dealing with the threat of robberies. Also, the head of security was asked to devise a suitable procedure for opening and closing the office, and the internal auditor made several minor recommendations on addressing other security risks. The main recommendation revolved around initiating a series of risk workshops held with cashiering staff that focused on helping them develop better security arrangements.

Finger Pointer

Many still see the auditor as someone who represents senior management in terms of uncovering mistakes, misleading performance information, and poor decisions made at operational levels. This misconception is based on the view that audit staff are really informers, looking for bad supervisors and poor performers. The internal auditor does in fact point the finger, but only at areas where risk management arrangements can be improved, not at individual people within an organization. The auditor would be concerned over poor practices and high levels of error, but only so that problems can be resolved through better procedures, more staff training, or a focus on more effective teamworking. An example illustrates this fine distinction:

> **EXAMPLE** ➤ The audit manager met the transport manager to discuss problems identified during an audit whereby excessive vehicle downtime was causing late deliveries. The transport staff assumed that the maintenance people were not performing. However, the auditors had managed to isolate a problem with the computer system indicating maintenance scheduling dates were being notified to the workshop several weeks late. This fault was rectified without seeking to assign blame.

The Terminator

Another popular myth is that auditors have no emotions. This view has them operating much like the robot in the original *Terminator* movie, where the mission has to be accomplished, regardless of any human suffering or long-term stress. Each audit becomes a "hit" to knock out bad managers or reduce staffing levels or perhaps get rid of poor performers. In exceptional circumstances, an audit report may highlight control failings that eventually lead to outsourcing or the removal of a really poor staff member. The vast majority of audits merely lead to better ways of employing resources to manage risk or simply endorse the current risk management strategy in the area being audited. An example follows:

> **EXAMPLE** ➤ During an audit of the payroll section, there was some concern that the auditor would recommend that the function be outsourced to a specialist provider. In discussion with the payroll manager, the auditor suggested that measures to promote efficiency and good performance be part of the audit terms of reference, which in turn would help the payroll team meet the challenges presented by external providers.

Checker

Some people enter into internal auditing because they are quite good at checking things. At kindergarten, they were always chosen to collect and count the pencils after each class. As teens, they stacked shelves in the local grocery store during high school vacation time and were good at checking stock and lining boxes up in neat rows. Once fully grown, they would progress to checking figures in whatever schedule was presented to them in the office for accuracy and completeness. All of this was good training for a career in internal audit, or so it seems. The reality is that detailed checking is a very small part of the audit role and is only applied when absolutely necessary. The audit role is much more about high-level evaluations and providing helpful advice on dealing with operational risk:

> **EXAMPLE** ➤ In one inventory audit, the store's supervisor was surprised when the auditors said they were not going to count as much stock as possible during the time assigned to the audit. The audit focused on the way stock was held and supplies were being managed. A small amount of stock checking was performed but only to establish whether the inventory management system was working properly.

Corrector

One view of the auditor suggests that any problems concerning the records or account balances will be dealt with by the internal auditor. Here, the audit role is seen as finding errors in operational data and then making the necessary corrections. Again, this is a warped view in that management is responsible for the integrity of their information systems and underlying databases. Where these are at fault, the same managers need to put them right. Assigning this task to the auditor is inappropriate and in the long run will lead to further problems and a deskilled management team:

> **EXAMPLE** ➤ In one audit, the business unit manager declared that she was not bothered about a long-standing discrepancy in the returns made

to the head office, because the auditors would find the source of these errors when they arrived. It was explained that the manager is in charge of ensuring the integrity of the returns and should take steps to address problems immediately after they arose.

For Further Discussion
What did people think about the reputation of internal auditors before joining the audit profession?

—— SECTION 5 ——

A BRIEF HISTORY OF INTERNAL AUDITING

Internal audit has come a long way over the last two or three decades. In the past, internal audit was seen as a mechanism to double-check the many thousands of financial transactions that were posted to the accounts each week. In the 1950s and 60s, it pretty much consisted of basic tests of the accounts with a view to isolating errors and irregularities. Huge standardized audit work programs would be prepared that determined the steps that had to be taken to verify figures in the main accounting ledger and feeder systems. In contrast, today's internal auditor facilitates the development of suitable controls as part of a wider risk strategy as well as providing assurances on the reliability of these controls. The move from detailed low-level checks of huge volumes of mainly financial transactions, to high-level input into corporate risk strategies, has been tremendous. We can track this movement over the years in terms of shifting approaches, as illustrated in Exhibit 1.1.

1. **Check accounting records.** We have already argued that internal audit started out as a way of double-checking the accounting records. A small team would be set up in the accounts section to examine as many financial transactions as possible and determine whether they were correct or not. One key indication of the effectiveness of the internal audit was the number of errors that were uncovered during each audit (or accounting period); the more errors identified, the better the audit. In extreme cases, accounts staff would play cat and mouse, where they would try to hide as many errors as possible from the auditors. Meanwhile, the auditor would celebrate whenever an error was uncovered.

2. **Assess compliance.** Over the years, there has been some attempt to move away from a sole concern with the financial arena. Audit teams would also assess the extent to which operations staff were complying with financial and basic office procedures. This would typically be at a

Exhibit 1.1. Evolution of Internal Auditing

1. Check account records.	1950
2. Assess compliance.	1960
3. Examine procedure.	1970
4. Evaluate controls.	1980
5. Report on SIC.	1990
6. Assess risk management.	2000
7. Facilitate risk management.	2001
8. Assure risk/control.	2002
9. Add value.	2003
10. ???	2004/2005

remote site where rules on the receipt and banking of money, payment of vendors, staff claims, stock management, and petty cash would be checked by the visiting internal auditor. Again, the auditor would work through a detailed program of checks to determine whether set procedures were being followed. Many accounts staff doubled as auditors for these occasional visits, where they would review the way financial regulations were being applied. Some of the more robust audit teams assumed the reputation of being hit squads, who would turn up unannounced and pick through the records and assets held at each location, looking for instances of noncompliance with procedure.

3. *Examine procedures.* An interesting development came in around the 1960s, where more attention was placed on getting the procedures right. So the audit team would review files and records and, upon finding problems, would try to suggest improvements as well as list the errors for correction. Some more forward-looking auditors felt that errors and problems could result from a lack of clarity in the procedure manual or problems in the way head office procedures were being interpreted by users. The sight of internal auditors offering helpful advice to operations managers opened the door to a new interpretation of the audit role as something more than error spotters.

4. *Evaluate controls.* Further advancement was possible where the focus on procedures was broadened to the much more dynamic concept of

controls. Here, proper performance was seen to relate to more than simply following the procedures manual. Performance encompassed the interaction of all measures that ensure staff are equipped and able to set targets, perform, and measure the extent to which they have been successful. These factors all provide what can be described as controls to ensure objectives can be met. In this case, the internal auditor has been able to step outside the confines of rigid accounting routines and start to provide advice on the many and varied types of controls that should be in place.

5. *Report on systems of internal control.* The next stage of development appeared in the form of the auditor's providing an independent view on various systems of internal control employed by the organization. Here, the concept of overarching systems and structures comes to the fore. Generic systems that cross over the organization at a corporate and operational level can be reported on to the audit committee and board. The internal auditor then attempts the difficult task of giving a high-level view of the way controls are being developed and applied as a way of summing up the control environment. This vast leap from checking detailed transactions to delivering important messages on the state of controls represented quite a challenge during the 1980s and 1990s. Many internal audit outfits were pleased to announce their arrival at what was seen as a pinnacle in the growth of the audit process.

6. *Assess risk management.* Nothing stands still, and the 1990s saw the boom in risk management to stave off criticism of organizations that had been damaged or even destroyed by scandals, mismanagement, or events that had a major adverse impact on their business. The call for good systems of operational risk management underpinned the emphasis on corporate governance across all types of businesses and public-service-sector bodies. As a result of this development, many organizations looked to internal audit to take a lead in promoting risk management strategies and providing advice on ways to move forward in this respect. Internal auditors were being asked to assess the adequacy of risk management strategies and report on ways that structures, mechanisms, and practices could be improved in identifying and managing risk via suitable systems of internal control.

7. *Facilitate risk management.* Just when the auditor thought it was safe to go back to the comfort of standard systems audits, one further development has spread to many larger organizations. Here, the popularity of enterprise risk management meant much demand for people skilled in facilitating the identification, assessment, and proactive management

of risk in a way that embeds the process into adopted business strategies. Some internal audit shops have taken a lead on this, while others have suggested caution before turning the audit task into more of a consulting role. Still others have developed a hybrid approach to their audits whereby risk assessment is undertaken as an integral aspect of most audits on the basis of seamless participation of and cooperation between the auditors and the operations managers and work teams.

8. ***Report risk and assure controls.*** Notwithstanding the model applied above, there is still the need to officially report the results of all audit work to a high-level body within the organization. In turn, the board reports on its system of internal control in the annual report. The new-look internal auditor is able to tune into senior management's agenda and directly affect serious corporate issues in a meaningful manner.

9. ***Add value.*** We have more recently arrived at a new point in the internal auditor's role that is loosely described as adding value to the organization. Meanwhile, *adding value* has been described by the IIA in the following way:

> *Organizations exist to create value or benefit to their owners, other stakeholders, customers, and clients. This concept provides purpose for their existence. Value is provided through their development of products and services and their use of resources to promote those products and services. In the process of gathering data to understand and assess risk, internal auditors develop significant insight into operations and opportunities for improvement that can be extremely beneficial to their organization. This valuable information can be in the form of consultation, advice, written communications or through other products all of which should be properly communicated to the appropriate management or operating personnel.*

What Is *Value Add?* Rather than describe the services that fall under the value-add banner, it is more helpful to establish a basic policy that covers the concept of value-add. The policy could include the following key features:

- A value-add service (VAS) is based on getting the most impact from the budget allocated to the audit shop.
- VAS means supporting the board in meeting its obligation to ensure it is in control of their organization.
- VAS focuses on business managers' understanding of value in the sense of anything that helps them get the job done and be able to demonstrate how they performed.

- VAS forms the key platform on which the audit committee can base its oversight strategy and ensures committee members have a source of reliable advice.
- VAS relates to what is important in terms of current trends and directions.
- VAS means different things to different companies in different industries and different environments. Valuable activities will vary between performance and conformance stances depending on the level of confidence in global stock markets and whether the economy is growing or contracting.
- Audit shops that have not identified their approach to delivering VAS will run the risk of failing to succeed.

10. *What next?* This is an interesting question. As mentioned above, nothing stands still, and many new concepts are often hidden from sight just over the horizon. There will be something next, and this is likely to revolve around getting the business to succeed in a manner that meets both its narrow obligations to direct beneficiaries such as shareholders and also the wider duty to all those groups who are affected in some way by the business.

The movement in attitude, approach, and value from the internal audit process has developed rapidly over the years—from low-level checking to high-level consultancy and assurance work, from reviewing the petty cash to assessing risk from strategic alliances, from enforcing rules to being a management adviser. The problem, however, is that not all audit shops have moved at the same pace, and also, old reputations can be difficult to shake off. Newly appointed internal audit staff are well advised to focus on the new-look audit role and move this forward, and watch out for those who are still too immersed in old ways of thinking and behaving.

> ### For Further Discussion
> *Describe some of the work that the auditor was involved in many years ago and the contribution this work made to the organization.*

—— SECTION 6 ——

THE IMPORTANCE OF TRACKING NEW DEVELOPMENTS

The emergence of the new internal auditor has been plotted above, and we stopped at a level where the audit role revolved around providing guidance as well as assurances on risk management and internal control. But it does not really stop here. Things move on as new developments come to the fore. These developments are many and varied, including the use of business models for self-assessment purposes, and regulatory agencies who take a firm view on compliance issues. There are several reasons why new areas of interest should be carefully tracked, including the following:

- Today's headline is tomorrow's stale cheese. It is generally not a good idea to base the audit strategy on fads—that is, new initiatives that are not really sustainable in the long term. Having said this, there are new trends that replace older ones. A few years ago, value-for-money initiatives in the guise of one-off savings were popular, and audit teams did reviews looking for cost savings, and possible areas for budget cuts. Now if an organization wants to make quick savings, it will simply restructure and get rid of large numbers of staff. The internal auditor needs to scope the audit approach while taking into account current strategic themes.

- Society arguably swings between a laissez-faire and an enforcement culture. The old management perceptive of checking and double-checking staffs' activities has been replaced by the empowerment concept. But with staff downsizing and much more reliance on lowly paid contract staff who may have less allegiance to the organization, some managers are moving back into supervisory mode when managing their teams. Again, this changes the audit stance where it may be necessary to ensure that all evidence secured during an audit has been verified by the manager and not just accepted at face value.

- Individual scandals such as Enron and WorldCom can quickly break and often result in a major overhaul of existing regulatory practices. This is a main driver for changes in the audit approach. Dishonest employees, careless managers, and questionable accounting practices can impair the reputation of large companies and even entire industries such as financial services and banking. Most regulators react with a "how can we stop this from ever happening again?" position. The audit focus may well turn to concentrating on robust and perhaps somewhat old-fashioned controls to prevent similar problems' materializing again.

- Risk attitudes can change when a healthy economy lurches into recession and vice versa. Risk taking thrives where the economy is growing and there are many opportunities for expansion and diversification. Where, on the other hand, the economy is on the downturn, many organizations rationalize to mitigate the risk of being exposed in shrinking markets. The audit process should take a lead from the corporate business strategy and respond to whether managers are bolting things down or reaching out for more.

- Some trends simply go in cycles, where, for example, extensive compliance and fraud detection routines can become fashionable once again. When the audit process has turned into purist consultancy, there is oftentimes a gap in the overall mechanism of accountability. Over the years, this gap may be apparent in terms of increased fraud and irregularity that can become an embarrassment. Audit may be asked to plug this gap and, for example, turn back to performing more compliance-based work. Where this concentrates on financial transactions, aspects of the audit process may actually start to look a little like the old-fashioned model from the 1950s and 1960s.

- At times, successful strategies can lead to further demand for the services provided by the auditor. Where, for example, auditors are involved in promoting risk workshops for operational teams, this may become a major growth area. An original intention to kick start the initiative and then stand back from this activity after a while may well backfire. Successful new initiatives may lead to a demand for more facilitation-based services, and as auditors develop the appropriate skills base, that may lead to more such services being requested by clients.

- Global business opportunities can lead to new best practices arriving from abroad. The good chief audit executive (CAE) will have one eye on events within the organization and another eye on what is happening elsewhere, including abroad. Risk-based auditing is a global development and should be treated as such. When best practice is being finetuned and employed in one country, there is no reason why progressive ideas should not enhance the audit processes in other regions and countries. Tracking such practices is all part of benchmarking to improve a service.

- Corporate strategy can encourage change as the norm, as a way of reenergizing a business. One response to the question, "Why track new development?" lies in the problems that arise when we do not bother to keep up to date with changing events. An inward-looking audit team, which refuses to move with the times, may stagnate. In turn, the same team becomes vulnerable to criticism from people who need a robust and proactive audit process and who may therefore feel let down by the current incumbents. In extreme cases, a weak in-house team may face competition from external sources.

Changing Patterns of Internal Audit

The above points suggest the need to keep in touch with the changing patterns of internal audit services and approaches. There is no way out. The new auditor does not simply learn about auditing and then start doing the job. This is not enough. The new auditor would do better to embark on a journey through the world of internal auditing much as one joins a slow-moving train on a long voyage. The tracks diverge and at times converge much as a complicated maze of directions, speed, and form. Without this constant motion, the "sameness" factor creeps in, which unfortunately is normally accompanied by boredom and demotivated staff.

The final point to consider is that there is no single model of the audit task that can be held up as the accepted standard. Many new-look auditors may be seen as very helpful but a little superficial, while the more old-fashioned auditors discussed earlier may be seen as annoying but at the same time a reliable supplement to the control regime in place. Most organizations employ an audit resource that has evolved to suit the culture promoted by the senior management in place. There is no "one size fits all" standard that can be adopted universally. Fortunately, this diversity of approaches creates a rich blend of audit policies that make the job potentially much more rewarding.

> ### For Further Discussion
> How do auditors keep up to date with developments in the profession, and what are the best sources of information available?

----- SECTION 7 -----

THE AUDIT MODEL

In larger organizations, the shareholders and other stakeholders are separated from the executives who run the organization they have an interest in. The executives then appoint managers and staff to undertake the work carried out by the organization. The separation of ownership from management means some form of accountability must be established to ensure that the executives and staff discharge their responsibilities to the owners and stakeholders. This basic equation sets the premise for an audit and review process to support and enhance the accountability regimes needed to underpin the model. As a way of analyzing the role and practice of internal auditing, we have devised an appropriate model. This model will be developed throughout each chapter of the book and will culminate in a working tool for describing how the internal audit process may be positioned within an organization. The audit model starts out as shown in Exhibit 1.2.

Society and Stakeholders. The audit model is driven primarily by the needs and interests of society, that is, the need for good company performance that contributes to the economy, and both fair and transparent business practices.

Exhibit 1.2. Audit Model 1

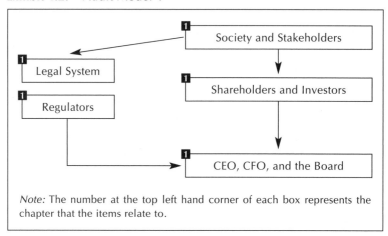

Note: The number at the top left hand corner of each box represents the chapter that the items relate to.

Stakeholders include all those who have a direct or indirect interest in the way business, commerce, and public services are conducted.

Shareholders and Investors.   Principal stakeholders are the people and institutions who hold shares in listed companies. Banks and investment companies may well have a direct interest that is represented in funds loaned to the company. Meanwhile, *The People* are principal stakeholders in public-sector organizations. Company shareholders should exercise their voting rights with due regard to the need to ensure there is ethical behavior and accountability from company officials.

Legal System.   There are a multitude of federal and state laws that relate to the way private- and public-sector organizations are established, maintained, and extinguished. Many larger organizations have responded by setting up compliance functions to address the variety and magnitude of such legal provisions. Company directors and officials can face severe penalties where specific laws are breached.

Regulators.   Most industries have an associated regulator that sets standards and represents the public in ensuring organizations behave properly. The SEC, American Stock Exchange, New York Stock Exchange, and NASDAQ regulations are some of the more well-known models.

CEO, CFO, and the Board.   Shareholders appoint a CEO and board of directors to direct and oversee the organization on their behalf. These officers have a responsibility to discharge their duties in a professional manner and account for the results to the shareholders. A management team will be appointed in public-sector bodies and have a similar responsibility to the government and general public. The board should adhere to the highest standards of ethics and ensure they conduct their business in an acceptable and documented manner. Moreover, the board should have in place suitable mechanisms through which they may judge their own performance and conduct.

—— SECTION 8 ——

SUMMARY: TOP TEN CONSIDERATIONS

A summary of the ten main points covered in the chapter follows:

1. The book represents a resource that should be used both by new and by less experienced internal auditors as part of their orientation/personal development. The reader should carefully work through the text material, discussion points, and set exercises to gain full value from the resource.

2. The book focuses on basic internal auditing and does not go into any detail regarding specialist and more involved topics such as retail and branch audits, information systems auditing, investigations and forensic examination, detailed analytical review, contract and large engineering project audits, internal audit management and quality assurance, corporate governance and top management reviews, and specialist compliance, disclosures, and financial statement auditing.

3. The role of the internal auditor is summed up in its formal definition: "Internal auditing is an independent, objective assurance and consulting activity designed to add value and improve an organization's operations. It helps an organization accomplish its objectives by bringing a systematic, disciplined approach to evaluate and improve the effectiveness of risk management, control, and governance processes." The three related concepts of risk management, control, and governance processes drive the new look audit process. Internal audit is one of the few parts of the organization that seeks to provide services to management, the board, and the audit committee that are free from spin and therefore reliable.

4. This new-look career auditor faces a real challenge in terms of living up to high expectations. That is, the auditor should be focused, helpful, straight down the line, decisive, determined, firm, and balanced.

5. There are several misconceptions about the internal audit role, many of which arise from its historical position as a "check and turn" process.[1] Some of these misconceptions include that internal audit is risk averse, issues audit instructions, designs controls, points the finger, acts as a Terminator, performs basic checking, and focuses on error identification and correction.

6. One version of the history of internal auditing from the 1950s to date can be plotted as follows:
   - Check accounting records.
   - Assess compliance.
   - Examine procedures.
   - Evaluate controls.
   - Report on systems of internal control.
   - Assess risk management.
   - Facilitate risk management.
   - Report risk and assure controls.
   - Add value.

7. Adding value to the organization is a major consideration of internal auditors. The IIA argues that: "value is provided through their development of products and services and their use of resources to promote those products and services." The features of a value-add audit service should be carefully identified, and this means delivering a service that helps the board, audit committee, and management meet their respective obligations.

8. All new and experienced audit staff should ensure they keep up to date with developments that impact the risk management, control, and governance processes. The value-add equation changes as new global trends emerge, and it is easy to get left behind.

9. The different interpretations of the internal audit role create a richness that should motivate and stimulate the auditor. The auditor's career becomes an exciting journey through the constant change and reinterpretation of this role.

10. A model of where internal audit fits into the organization can be constructed starting with the impact of society and stakeholders, shareholders and investors, legal system, regulators, CEO, CFO, and the Board.

—— SECTION 9 ——
YOUR PERSONAL DEVELOPMENT EXERCISES

There is much that can be gained from a study of internal auditing. There are also many years of development behind turning a budding new starter into a seasoned professional auditor. As a start into this journey, the new auditor may care to undertake the following tasks:

1. Ask people you know to give their understanding of the role of the internal auditor. Watch out for replies that harp back to the old-fashioned view

of "check and turn" auditing. Explain to each respondent the growth of the new-look internal auditor.

2. Talk to experienced audit colleagues about the types of work that auditors used to be engaged in. Relate the replies to the material in this chapter about the development of internal auditing.

3. Take the attributes of a good internal auditor that are noted in Section 3 and put them in order of importance, explaining the reasons behind your choices.

4. For the attributes mentioned in Section 3 above, prepare a commentary on the extent to which you are able to meet the relevant standards. Write out a personal action plan that may help you develop the competence to meet each of the attributes.

5. Visit your local library (community, university, college, or high school) and carry out the following tasks:

   • Ask your local library whether they would mind your doing an informal project on their services for the purpose of personal development. Make it clear that the review will not be reported to anyone externally and is simply part of your orientation program. Show the librarian a copy of this book and a letter from your university, college, or employer on the use of this exercise as part of your orientation program.

   • Find out what the key aims of the library service are, and determine whether these are clearly noted in brochures, published documents, and Web site material.

   • Ascertain the systems for storing books and other physical materials, checking in and out materials on loan, and establishing membership of the library. Also, consider other services such as Internet access and research facilities.

   • For each of the above processes, think about the risks that mean the system fails to achieve its objective.

   • Consider the extent to which these risks are being managed by the system in question. For example, how is the risk of false ID managed when becoming a member of the library? How is the risk of the theft of books managed? How is the risk of failure to return books managed? How is the risk of failing to meet customer needs managed?

   • Note any occasion where procedures are skipped or where they are apparently poor. For example, are receipts given for fines paid on overdue books, or are audio books checked on return to make sure the tapes are okay?

- Prepare a list of potential strengths and weaknesses in the library systems in use and ask the chief librarian whether he or she would be interested in receiving informal comments from a customer (i.e., yourself).
- Note the need for sensitivity when giving advice or an opinion and how tact and care can be used to build a positive relationship with the recipient of this advice.
- Ask the chief librarian to give you feedback on your approach to the brief review and whether the attributes from Section 3 have been demonstrated.

NOTE

1. "Check and turn" is an old-fashioned method of checking a document against another source and checking them off if they agree.

2

THE AUDIT CONTEXT

—— SECTION 1 ——
THE GROWTH OF CORPORATE GOVERNANCE

It is clear that the definition of internal audit is aligned to the governance agenda. Moreover, the newly appointed auditor should acquire a good understanding of corporate governance and its ramifications. Corporate governance is now a global concept that impacts all countries and all sectors of business, commerce, and public services. Most agree that corporate governance is about the way an organization is directed and controlled. It is about the way business performance is achieved and the way risks to an organization's success and reputation in the marketplace are managed, including the need to conduct business in a proper and acceptable manner.

The growth of corporate governance stems from a push-pull process that on the one hand involves driving the business forward to reach strategic targets. On the other hand, it also involves pulling back from unacceptable risk and improper (or illegal) practices. Good systems of corporate governance have in place fundamental components that help ensure business success is supported by:

- Effective arrangements of board functioning and oversight
- Audit
- Accounting
- Accountability
- Performance management
- Risk management

Moreover, the board should be able to issue published statements about these arrangements in terms of having an effective system of internal control.

> ### For Further Discussion
> What pressures result from balancing the push-pull process, that is, driving strategy forward while at the same time as conducting business in an acceptable manner?

—— SECTION 2 ——

UNDERSTANDING SOCIETAL EXPECTATIONS

The growing concern about the arrangements for proper corporate governance has its roots in the demands and expectations of society itself. Corporate bodies and federal and state government organizations are run on behalf of people who have a stake in the organization. These stakeholders want to see a return on their investment, sustainable growth, strong leadership, and reliable reports on corporate performance and business practices. The board, meanwhile, or public-sector management team will respond to the various performance targets and pressures exerted by voting shareholders and financial analysts.

The task of matching the interests and aspirations of these two sets of people—stakeholders and board members—causes tremendous difficulties that are partly addressed by the efforts of various regulators and examining authorities. Corporate governance codes are likewise issued to help ease these tensions and ensure each organization is able to perform well and adhere to appropriate regulations, laws, and principles of acceptable business practices. Meanwhile, these codes are in a constant state of development as new problems emerge from failings in the direction, accounting, and audit practices applied to corporate business and not-for-profit services. A brief examination of the issues arising from the Enron and WorldCom cases from 2002 demonstrates the need to continually update corporate accountabilities and keep watch for suspect practices.

Enron

Background

Enron, the multinational energy trading company, bought and sold gas. With deregulation of the energy business in the 1980s, and new suppliers on the deregulated market, energy prices became less stable. Enron took the opportunity to make profit in the new deregulated futures market. Buyers and sellers use futures markets to get a better deal on commodities than they would do ordinarily on the open market. Enron's role in the new market was to act as middleman and buy and sell gas for potential customers in the futures market at a fixed price. So, for instance, Enron would buy tomorrow's energy and sell it at a fixed price today. Enron's strategy worked to keep prices relatively stable and minimize fluctuations in the market. Meanwhile, Enron was able to make money from these transactions, as the company was able to charge for its role in this process. At one stage, Enron controlled almost a quarter of all gas in the U.S. market. The company also moved into other areas, such as offering companies the opportunity to hedge against the risk of price increases in other commodities like coal and steel, as well as external factors such as weather risk. By the year 2000, Enron planned to move into broadband Internet networks to reflect the success of the dot.com economy. The company's share price grew as it began Internet trading and offering investors a free service, resulting in increased customers.

Accounting Practices

To maintain the impression that the company was making money, Enron used complicated accounting methods to keep its share price high. These techniques included removing losses from its books and legally passing them on to an independent partnership as "assets." Another accounting ploy was to treat as profits investment money linked to particular business enterprises coming into the company, although those projects had not yet started.

The Crisis

Enron's share price in Summer 2000 was $90, but there was also speculation that the company had profited by reselling gas it had purchased in the futures market at a much higher cost to the consumer. The company denied this was the case, and its 2000 annual report showed income had increased by some 40 percent in three years. In August 2001, Enron's chief executive resigned. This unnerved investors, who sold millions of shares, which cut $4 off the share price by the end of that week. By October 2001, Enron was unable to recover its losses, while the share price continued to fall, because it had hedged against its own stock. On November 8, 2001, Enron decided to restate its profits for the previous four years.

In effect, Enron admitted to inflating profits by concealing the extent of its debt through complicated accounting methods—that is, removing losses from its books and legally passing them on to an independent partnership as "assets." This method of reporting profits gave investors the impression that the company was worth more than it actually was. By then, Enron had overstated its profits by about $600 million. The company went from being worth more than $60 billion to bankruptcy in 2001. The share price eventually fell from more than $90 to less than $1.

WorldCom

Background

Similarly to Enron, WorldCom, a large U.S. telecommunications company, also admitted overstating its profits for 15 months from the beginning of 2001. Compared to Enron, which had overstated its profits by $600 million, WorldCom's overstatement was approximately six times greater.

Accounting Practices

To maintain the impression that the company was generating larger profits than it actually was, and inflate its share price between 2001 and 2002, the company treated about $3.8 billion in general everyday office operating expenses as investments. By doing this, the accountants were able to avoid accounting for these expenses immediately and were able to spread them over several years.

The Crisis

WorldCom went from a billion dollar company to bankruptcy almost overnight. The share price fell from $60 to about 20 cents. Thousands of WorldCom employees lost their jobs as a result of the crisis, and shareholders suffered as the value of their shares plummeted.

The Winds of Change

The concerns arising from the above-mentioned cases have led to a tightening up of the arrangements for listed companies. Enhanced legislation and regulations are designed to ensure another WorldCom-type scandal could not happen again. One of the most important developments was the 2002 Sarbanes-Oxley Act and the resulting amendments to the SEC regulations. The Sarbanes-Oxley Act was enacted on July 30, 2002, alongside a fanfare of media publicity and a presidential speech from New York—extracts of which include the following sentiments:[1]

> The lure of heady profits of the late 1990s spawned abuses and excesses. . . . My accountability plan also requires CEOs to personally vouch for their firms' annual financial statements. Currently, a CEO signs a nominal certificate, and does so merely on behalf of the company. In the future, the signature of the CEO should also be his or her personal certification of the veracity and fairness of the financial disclosures. When you sign a statement, you're pledging your word, and you should stand behind it. . . . I've also called on the SEC to adopt new rules to ensure that auditors will be independent and not compromised by conflicts of interest. . . . Tougher laws and stricter requirements will help. . . . Yet, ultimately, the ethics of American business depend on the conscience of America's business leaders. We need men and women of character, who know the difference between ambition and destructive greed, between justified risk and irresponsibility, between enterprise and fraud.

Sarbanes-Oxley

The Sarbanes-Oxley Act added sections to the Securities Exchange Act of 1934, leading to changes in the SEC rules applied to listed companies. The main aim of the revised rules was to enhance the perceived value of the final accounts, and so increase overall confidence in the securities market, including the veracity of the external audit process. The audit committee is given a pivotal role in ensuring the reliability of the external audit and that non-audit fees are properly disclosed and do not interfere with the auditor's independence. The SEC has published its final rules, which are noted below in summary:

- Revise the Commission's regulations related to the non-audit services that, if provided to an audit client, would result in the accounting firm's being deemed to lack independence with respect to the audit client.
- Require that an issuer's audit committee preapprove all audit and non-audit services provided to the issuer by the independent accountant.
- Prohibit certain partners on the audit engagement team from providing audit services to the issuer for more than five or seven consecutive years, depending on the partner's involvement in the audit (smaller accounting firms may be exempted from this requirement).
- Prohibit an accounting firm from auditing an issuer's financial statements if a person in a financial reporting oversight role of that issuer had been a member of the accounting firm's audit engagement team within the one-year period preceding the commencement of audit procedures.
- Require that the auditor of an issuer's financial statements report certain matters to the issuer's audit committee, including "critical" accounting policies and practices used by the issuer.
- Require disclosures to investors of information related to audit and non-audit services provided by, and fees paid by the issuer to, the auditor of the issuer's financial statements.

Further SEC rules that add to the Sarbanes-Oxley Act include:

- Applying the partner rotation rules to additional "audit partners."
- Applying the one-year cooling-off period to persons in a financial reporting oversight role with the issuer.
- Prohibiting an accounting firm from compensating an audit partner for directly selling non-audit services to an audit client.

There are now firm restrictions on the provision of non-audit services by the company's external auditor, including services that mean auditors would be auditing their own work, acting as managers or advocates for the company. These services may be added to if necessary but currently include:

- Bookkeeping or other services related to the accounting records or financial statements of the audit client.
- Financial information systems design and implementation.

- Appraisal or valuation services, fairness opinions, or contribution-in-kind reports.
- Actuarial services.
- Internal audit outsourcing services.
- Management functions or human resources.
- Broker-dealer, investment adviser, or investment banking services.
- Legal services.
- Expert services unrelated to the audit.

Additional Features

Certain types of services such as tax compliance and, in relation to the audit fee, small amounts of non-audit work approved by the audit committee may be allowed. There are also rules concerning the retention of records by audit firms, with severe penalties for failure to observe the five-year retention periods. In fact, the destruction of documents that impedes a federal or agency investigation can lead to a twenty-year prison sentence. Destruction of corporate audit records can lead to ten years' imprisonment. The self-regulation concept that has been developed by the accountancy profession over many years has been complemented by a new independent Public Accounting Oversight Board under the auspices of the SEC.

The new board acts as a form of additional quality assurance and quality control over the accounting firms that are registered to perform audits of public companies. Meanwhile, the penalties for corporate fraud have been increased to reflect the serious threat that fraud and abuse pose to the economy. One important feature of the 2003 accounting and audit regime is the significant responsibilities on principal executives and the accounting officer who must personally certify the annual accounts and take responsibility for internal controls. False certifications can lead to long prison sentences. Disclosure has become increasingly stringent, with regulations covering areas such as off-balance-sheet transactions, pro forma financial numbers, annual assessment of financial controls, whether there is a code of ethics for key finance officers, and a requirement that there be at least one "financial expert" on the audit committee. Ethics form the basis for the proper conduct of business, and this effort must be fully resourced.

Corporate America is engaged in a struggle to ensure the free flow of funds in an unimpaired market economy. The basis of business, and for that matter federal and state government functioning, is trust—trust that corporate investors are set on a level playing field; trust that financial and business performance is correctly portrayed in published reports; and trust that directors, officials, managers, staff, and business associates behave in an honest and open manner.

Where there is less faith placed in these principles of trust, financial markets become less reliable and in fact less trustworthy.

> **For Further Discussion**
>
> What weaknesses in corporate governance arrangements were exposed by the Enron and WorldCom scandals?

—— SECTION 3 ——

THE GLOBAL DIMENSION

The struggle for good corporate governance is a global development. Achieving proper and efficient business, commerce, and public services is an aspiration that has eluded many developed and emerging economies. Each new governance code brings together work done in earlier editions across the world. Publicly quoted companies are common in the West, while family-run concerns are more popular in Asia and beyond. Most governments now contract out many services to private enterprises or work in joint ventures with the private sector. A brief visit to some of the other corporate governance codes quickly brings home the commonality in thinking, aspiration, and practical application that is found in these codes.

United Kingdom—The Turnbull Report

The Turnbull Committee brought together the previous work on corporate governance for companies listed on the London Stock Exchange and was reported in 1999. Among the areas that now form part of these listing rules are the following:

- The board should maintain a sound system of internal control to safeguard shareholders' investments and the company's assets.
- The directors should, at least annually, conduct a review of the effectiveness of the group's system of internal control and should report to shareholders that they have done so. The review should cover all controls, including financial, operational, and compliance controls, and risk management.
- Companies that do not have an internal audit function should from time to time review the need for one.
- Each company should draft a narrative statement of how it has applied the principles set out in the Combined Code, providing explanation that enables its shareholders to evaluate how the principles have been applied.

- Each company should draft a statement as to whether it has complied throughout the accounting period with the provisions set out in the Combined Code.

- The intention is that companies should have a free hand to explain their governance policies in the light of the principles, including any special circumstances that have led to their adopting a particular approach.

Since this code was published, there have been ongoing reviews in the United Kingdom of specific aspects of corporate governance covering external audit independence, nonexecutive directors, and audit committees. A new Combined Code was issued in 2003.

South Africa—The King Report

This 2002 update of the 1994 King Report is considered by many to be an example of international best practice in corporate governance and contains a wealth of guidance. The report provided the following seven characteristics of corporate governance:

1. Discipline—correct and proper behavior

2. Transparency—true picture of what is happening

3. Independence—no undue influences

4. Accountability—actions of the board may be assessed

5. Responsibility—to all stakeholders

6. Fairness—rights of various groups respected

7. Social responsibility—good corporate citizen

Canada—The Dey Report

Building on the 1994 Dey Report, the 2001 version, *Beyond Compliance: Building a Governance Culture,* by the Canadian Institute of Chartered Accountants, provides another useful framework for corporate governance, as shown by these extracts:

- *The objective of corporate governance is to promote strong, viable and competitive corporations. Boards of directors are stewards of the corporation's assets, and their behavior should be focused on adding value to those assets by working with management to build a successful corporation and enhance shareholder value.*

- *Not only is disclosure preferable to regulation as a tool to change behavior, it is also appropriate. The evolution of capital markets has clearly shown that disclosure instills discipline and increases efficiency. With regards to corporate governance, we see two important benefits of disclosure. First, disclosure can provide examples of good practices that can assist boards that are looking for ways to become more effective. Second, a requirement to disclose against guidelines ways to become more effective by forcing boards to focus explicitly on their roles and responsibilities and how they are being discharged.*

- *Boards should actively look beyond traditional sources in seeking men and women with the right mix of experience and competencies. Diversity of background and experience can add value to boardroom deliberations. . . .*

- *If boards are to add value, they must involve themselves actively and regularly in the function of strategic planning and risk management. We believe that these functions need to be closely integrated: strategic planning should be based upon an identification of opportunities and the full range of business risks that will condition which of those opportunities are most worth pursuing. Strategic planning is an ongoing process that must be responsive to changes in the external environment and the internal developments. Flexibility and responsiveness are critical. In this sense, strategic planning is a much broader concept than developing a business plan and should include assessments of opportunities and risks across a range of areas.*

- *They [effective boards] will oversee the processes that management has in place to identify business opportunities and risks. They will consider the extent and types of risk that is [sic] acceptable for the company to bear. They will monitor management's systems and processes for managing the broad range of business risk. And most important, on an ongoing basis, they will review with management how the strategic environment is changing, what key business risks and opportunities are appearing, how they are being managed, and what, if any, modifications in strategic direction should be adopted.*

OECD Code

The corporate governance (CG) code of the Organization for Economic Co-operation and Development (OECD), a representative body, has to be somewhat general to fit the different contexts and circumstances it is meant to cover. However, it has developed five key principles of corporate governance:

1. **Rights of shareholders.** *CG framework should protect shareholders' rights.*

2. **The equitable treatment of shareholders.** *CG framework should ensure the equitable treatment of all shareholders, including minority and foreign shareholders.*

3. **The role of stakeholders in corporate governance.** *CG framework should ensure that timely and accurate disclosure is made of all material*

matters regarding the corporation, including the financial situation, performance, ownership and governance of the company.

4. **Disclosure and transparency.** *CG framework should ensure that timely and accurate disclosure is made on all material matters regarding the corporation, including the financial situation, performance, ownership and governance of the company—includes financial and operational results, company objectives, share ownership and voting, board membership and remuneration, material foreseeable risk factors, governance structures and policies and annual audit and access to information by users.*

5. **Responsibility of the board.** *CG framework should ensure the strategic guidance of the company, the effective monitoring of management by the board, the board's accountability to the company and the shareholders. The board should be fully informed, fairly treat shareholders, ensure compliance with laws etc., review performance and risk policy etc. also ensuring that appropriate systems of internal control are in place, in particular, systems for monitoring risk, financial control and compliance with the law and disclosure and communications. Board should consider using nonexecutive directors and have access to accurate, relevant and timely information (and access to key managers such as company secretary, and the internal auditor and recourse to independent external advice).*

Malaysian Code—Internal Audit Aspects

We close this section with a look at the 2002 code adopted by the Malaysian stock exchange, focusing on the references to internal auditing and the value it can bring to all parties:

- *Reviewing objectives and activities—review with management the operational activities and ensure the principal objectives are aligned to overall company's objectives.*
- *Evaluating risk—identify all auditable activities and relevant risk factors, and to assess their significance.*
- *Confirming information—research and gather information that is competent, factual and complete.*
- *Analyzing operation—analyze and examine that operations are effective.*
- *Providing assurance on compliance—provide assurance on compliance to statutory requirements, laws, company policies and guidelines.*
- *Recommending internal controls—recommend appropriate controls to overcome deficiencies and to enhance company operations.*
- *Assuring safeguards—evaluate procedures in place to safeguard company assets.*

- *Consulting and facilitating — assist management in establishing a proper risk management framework, assessing risks and monitoring the effectiveness of the risk management program . . . and ensuring the adequacy of the internal control system.*

Other Countries

If we turn to Australia, New Zealand, Mexico, Brazil, and India and consider France, Germany, and other advanced and developing countries throughout the world, we will find similar codes that fit their individual environments. Corporate governance brings ideas, concepts, measures, and many specific provisions to turn ideas into ideals, and then into actual corporate practices, all aimed at increasing stakeholder confidence and promoting growing but sustainable economies.

For Further Discussion

What common areas are found in most corporate governance codes around the world, and will there come a time when all such codes more or less coincide?

––––– SECTION 4 –––––
IMPACT ON THE BOARD AND SENIOR MANAGEMENT

The task of reporting on internal controls and attesting to the reliability of published financial statements causes much concern for executives, in particular the principal executive and chief finance officer (CFO). The corporate governance arrangements locate responsibility at the very top of the organization. The audit committee, meanwhile, provides a further oversight mechanism to promote ethical and compliant behavior by corporate bodies. The natural reaction where boards are confronted by increased regulation is to appoint an appropriate responsible officer who would lead on the subject in question. However, the essence of corporate governance is the reporting process and public declarations that as far as practicable, all reasonable steps have been taken to ensure risks are managed, including the risk of failing to adhere to laws, generally accepted accounting standards, and regulations.

This new requirement, in turn, calls for support from professionals who specialize in supporting the reporting process and who can help the corporate body establish and implement the underpinning arrangements: a job for internal audit? There are some commentators who believe that in the past, boards had conspired with their external auditor's senior reporting partners to apply whatever accounting arrangements suited their needs, regardless of whether they were appropriate or not. Mutual back scratching in the form of bonuses, consulting contracts, and the promise of a "future position" was seen as an inevitable aspect of such a corporate culture. The expectations from a new breed of investors, who demanded quick and large returns in booming industries, have led to tremendous pressures for creative accounting that, so long as it got past the corporate lawyers and independent auditors, was fair game. To make matters worse, shareholders were seen as a group of undisciplined and fragmented personalities who simply wanted these quick and impressive returns, as did the board.

Governance Codes

The governance codes attaching to the NYSE and NASDAQ have created a different but equally severe pressure on boards to ensure performance is matched with conformance, not only to the letter of the law but also to the overall spirit of fair play and propriety. This is not an easy task. The external auditors must be independent and be seen as independent, and the board has to establish committees that ensure this happens. At the same time, the many returns that have to be filed with the SEC and others demonstrate to the watching world that all is well, or if not, any problems are being properly addressed by the company. Breach of SEC regulations and the associated legislation can lead to serious implications for all those associated with this act. In the past, executives worried most about hitting their key corporate targets. Nowadays, they are equally concerned about making sure all public returns, statements, and reports are reliable and defensible. Moreover, the board has significant responsibilities to supervise the external audit process and can be reviewed by the SEC and asked to explain decisions they have made.

For Further Discussion

What pressures are being placed on the board through the development of stricter corporate governance codes?

----- SECTION 5 -----

THE ROLE OF THE AUDIT COMMITTEE

One main component of corporate governance arrangements relates to the appointment of an audit committee within the organization. Section 205 of the Sarbanes-Oxley Act defines an *audit committee* as "a committee (or equivalent body) established by and amongst the board of directors of an issuer for the purpose of overseeing the accounting and financial reporting processes of the issuer and audits of the financial statements of the issuer." If there is no audit committee, then the entire board becomes one.

The SEC suggests that: "the audit committee serves as an important body, serving the interests of investors, to help ensure that the registrant and its accountants fulfil their responsibilities under the securities laws. Because the definition of an audit committee can include the entire board of directors if no such committee of the board exists, these rules do not require registrants to establish audit committees. Likewise, the auditor independence rules do not require that the committee be composed of independent members of the board."

Meanwhile, IIA Standard 2060, on independence and objectivity, makes it clear that:

> *The chief audit executive should report periodically to the board and senior management on the internal audit activity's purpose, authority, responsibility, and performance relative to its plan. Reporting should also include significant risk exposures and control issues, corporate gover-nance issues, and other matters needed or requested by the board and senior management.*

For larger organizations, the internal audit plans and reports will tend to be presented to the audit committee. The IIA has its own definition of the audit committee in Practice Advisory 2060-2, which runs as follows: "The term 'audit committee,' as used in this document, refers to the governance body that is charged with oversight of the organization's audit and control functions. Although these fiduciary duties are often delegated to an audit committee of the board of directors, the information in this Practice Advisory is also intended to apply to other oversight groups with equivalent authority and responsibility, such as trustees, legislative bodies, owners of an owner-managed entity, internal control committees, or full boards of directors."

Responsibilities of the Audit Committee

The role and responsibilities of the audit committee as part of the corporate gov-ernance jigsaw has accelerated in recent years outside all recognition. The old view that the committee was made up of friends and acquaintances on reciprocal grounds has now all but disappeared. The position of the audit committee is now firmly embedded in legislation and SEC regulations, along with federal and state government codes of practice. The new-look audit committee has tremen-dous responsibilities in conjunction with its pivotal role in corporate governance arrangements and oversights. Responsibilities of the audit committee, many of which have been touched on earlier, include:

- Ensure that the audit committee members meet the criteria for independence and that they do not receive fees or bonuses for, say, consulting work to the company, or be associated with any such party.
- Ensure there is at least one appropriate so-called "Financial Expert" who sits on the audit committee and who understands the accounts, accounting standards, internal controls, financial reporting, and workings of the audit committee.
- Oversee the appointment, compensation, performance, and retention of the external auditor and ensure any problems involving the audit service are addressed and resolved; furthermore, ensure there is proper rotation of the lead audit partner and others as required by relevant regulations.
- Approve admissible non-audit services provided by the external auditor.
- Receive reports from the external auditor concerning the use of material GAAPs and alternative policies, the management letter, and other correspondence such as the independence and engagement letters.
- Ensure that there is a suitable whistleblower's facility covering audit and accounting matters.
- Engage suitable experts, which may include the external auditor, to conduct investigations into accounting impropriety when required and appropriate.
- Oversee the internal audit process.

This short list masks the huge workload that falls on the shoulders of a team of part-time independents, who assume the full weight of detailed provisions that can result in substantial legal exposures that are scaring lawyers, insurers, and company boards alike. Many legal firms are providing support with the detailed returns and compliance aspects of the new regime, alongside external consultants who all provide input into coming up with corporate solutions. The internal auditor has also entered the fray by supporting the board and audit committee, but without the vested interest of chargeable fees. Note that the remainder of this book is based on this simple concept. The potential contribution from internal audit is recognized by the IIA, which makes it clear in Practice Advisory 2060-2 that:

> The Institute of Internal Auditors recognizes that audit committees and internal auditors have interlocking goals. A strong working relationship with the audit committee is essential for each to fulfill its responsibilities to senior management, board of directors, shareholders, and other outside parties.

An illustration of an audit committee comes from General Electric, whose Audit Committee Charter reads:[2]

The audit committee of the board of directors of General Electric Company shall consist of a minimum of four directors. Members of the committee shall be appointed by the board of directors upon the recommendation of the nominating and corporate governance committee and may be removed by the board of directors in its discretion. All members of the committee shall be independent directors under the standard proposed by the New York Stock Exchange, and shall also satisfy the New York Stock Exchange's more rigorous independence requirement for members of the audit committee. All members shall have sufficient financial experience and ability to enable them to discharge their responsibilities and at least one member shall be a financial expert. The purpose of the committee shall be to assist the board in its oversight of the integrity of the financial statements of the company, of the company's compliance with legal and regulatory requirements, of the independence and qualifications of the independent auditor, and of the performance of the company's internal audit function and independent auditors. In furtherance of the purpose, the committee shall have the following authority and responsibilities:

1. *To discuss with management and the independent auditor the annual audited financial statements and quarterly financial statements, including matters required to be reviewed under applicable legal, regulatory or New York Stock Exchange requirements.*

2. *To discuss with management and the independent auditor, as appropriate, earnings press releases and financial information and earnings guidance provided to analysts and to rating agencies.*

3. *To recommend, for shareowner approval, the independent auditor to examine the company's accounts, controls and financial statements. The committee shall have the sole authority and responsibility to select, evaluate and if necessary replace the independent auditor. The committee shall have the sole authority to approve all audit engagement fees and terms and the committee, or a member of the committee, must preapprove any non-audit service provided to the company by the company's independent auditor.*

4. *To discuss with management and the independent auditor, as appropriate, any audit problems or difficulties and management's response, and the company's risk assessment and risk management policies, including the company's major financial risk exposure and steps taken by management to monitor and mitigate such exposure.*

5. *To review the company's financial reporting and accounting standards and principles, significant changes in such standards or principles or in their application and the key accounting decisions*

affecting the company's financial statements, including alternatives to, and the rationale for, the decisions made.

6. *To review and approve the internal corporate audit staff functions, including: (i) purpose, authority and organizational reporting lines; (ii) annual audit plan, budget and staffing; and (iii) concurrence in the appointment, compensation and rotation of the vice president–corporate audit staff.*

7. *To review, with the senior vice president–finance, the vice president–corporate audit staff, or such others as the committee deems appropriate, the company's internal system of audit and financial controls and the results of internal audits.*

8. *To obtain and review at least annually a formal written report from the independent auditor delineating: the auditing firm's internal quality-control procedures; any material issues raised within the preceding five years by the auditing firm's internal quality-control reviews, by peer reviews of the firm, or by any governmental or other inquiry or investigation relating to any audit conducted by the firm. The committee will also review steps taken by the auditing firm to address any findings in any of the foregoing reviews. Also, in order to assess auditor independence, the committee will review at least annually all relationships between the independent auditor and the company.*

9. *To prepare and publish an annual committee report in the company's proxy statement.*

10. *To set policies for the hiring of employees or former employees of the company's independent auditor.*

11. *To review and investigate any matters pertaining to the integrity of management, including conflicts of interest, or adherence to standards of business conduct as required in the policies of the company. This should include regular reviews of the compliance processes in general and the corporate ombudsman process in particular. In connection with these reviews, the committee will meet, as deemed appropriate, with the general counsel and other company officers or employees.*

The committee shall meet separately at least quarterly with management, with the corporate audit staff and also with the company's independent auditors.

The committee shall have authority to retain such outside counsel, experts and other advisors as the committee may deem appropriate in its sole discretion. The committee shall have sole authority to approve related fees and retention terms.

The committee shall report its recommendations to the board after each committee meeting and shall conduct and present to the board an annual performance evaluation of the committee. The committee shall review at least annually the adequacy of this charter and recommend any proposed changes to the board for approval.

For Further Discussion

What makes for a good audit committee, and what types of competencies should audit committee members possess?

—— SECTION 6 ——

RISK MANAGEMENT: THE KEY TO SUCCESS

Risk management is a distinct part of the internal auditor's remit, which is to help promote effective risk management within the organization and to provide assurances on this matter to the board. Good organizations understand risks to their business lines and are able to keep the relevant regulators happy with their methods for managing risk. Good organizations also understand their risk profile and how risk is spread and addressed across the business in different ways that nonetheless feed into a "big picture" road map that makes sense to all the various business units, product lines, work units, project teams, and support staff. Decisions at all levels in an organization should be made in conjunction with an integrated risk management process that ensures all key existing and emerging risks are analyzed and mitigated where appropriate. The IIA defines risk as:

The uncertainty of an event occurring that could have an impact on the achievement of objectives. Risk is measured in terms of consequences and likelihood.

The Risk Management Cycle

The risk management cycle is fairly straightforward, and one version is illustrated in Exhibit 2.1.

Each key stage is briefly described below:

1. *Objectives.* Risk management starts and stops with helping an organization achieve its objectives. This includes high-level corporate objectives and the lower-level operational objectives that derive from an overall strategic plan. Risks are any uncertainties that impact the business objectives in terms of actual and perceived threats and missed opportunities. Efforts to set up a system of risk management often start with revisiting the set objectives and ensuring that they are clearly defined and properly understood by everyone.

Exhibit 2.1.   Risk Management Cycle

2. **Risk policy.** One aspect of risk management that comes to the fore when developing suitable arrangements relates to commonality and consistency—that is, consistency in terminology, clarity of respective roles within the organization, an accepted assessment methodology, and a willingness to develop a culture that supports risk management and accountability rather than blame assignment. People need to talk the same language and have a shared understanding of what's important and what's less relevant to the business focus. In other words, there needs to be a clear policy in place that addresses the issues mentioned above and other aspects of risk management.

3. **Risk identification.** The risk cycle asks that there be a formal process in place for identifying risks to the business. This may be through research, business analysis, risk workshops, audit and review, industry benchmarking schemes, or regular staff surveys. Whatever the format, the chosen method or methods should ensure all relevant risks are captured. One way of facilitating the identification stage is to set a series of risk categories in the risk policy. It is important to avoid extended discussion about what category a risk may fall in, and focus on the need to address all relevant risks. However, set categories may act as a lens to focus the range of risks that interfere with the drive toward success.

Each enterprise will have a different focus. Banks will be concerned with risks that have an impact on liquidity, loans, regulators, automation, product lines, treasury management, and so on. An oil company may be focused on risks that affect production setup, safety issues, environmental concerns, mergers, and overseas joint ventures. A government agency may view risks in categories such as funding, regularity, service standards, complaints, best practice, and staff retention. Control risk self-assessment (CSRA), discussed later, is a technique that provides a powerful mechanism for isolating business risk across all parts of the organization.

4. *Risk assessment.* Once all known risks are documented, there needs to be a mechanism to put them into context, to sort out what is important and crucial to address and those risks that can be sidelined for the time being. The idea is that an organization can allocate its base resources to areas of high risk with a view to mitigation and meanwhile assign venture capital to areas of low risk that can be further exploited. It is also possible to reassess business lines in terms of whether the projected returns secured are worth the costs of managing risks inherent in the business. Moreover, the risks that cannot be controlled within the available budget might be so volatile as to make a product line unattractive in the long term.

Risk assessment is about assigning values to the risks that have been identified and weighing their respective priorities. Traditionally, this has been done by assessing the potential impact of the risk if it were to materialize, and then assessing the likelihood that this risk will in fact materialize. Best practice calls for people closest to the operation, or project, to be involved in assessing risks to achieving the set goals. It is also felt that each risk should be owned by the person most responsible for the areas affected by the risk in question.

5. *Risk mitigation.* High levels of unacceptable risk have to be tackled. That is, they need to be mitigated to bring them to an exposure that fits the organization's risk appetite. Mitigation revolves around installing controls where required. Controls increase the certainty that risks will be addressed, and therefore, objectives have more chance of being achieved. Some controls, such as liquidity ratios, are required by regulators as part of the compliance program for the industry or sector in question. Breach of these regulatory rules will fall under the guise of compliance risk, and like all other material risks, they must be contained.

6. *Risk management.* The overall response to risk across an organization will be found at this stage: the adoption of a risk management strategy. The response to risk depends on the nature of the risk and whether it is high, medium, or low priority. Some risks have to be accepted because there is little that can be done to mitigate them, or the cost of such mitigation is prohibitive. Here, the risk management strategy may revolve around damage limitation and contingency plans. Other risks may be so remote that they can be disregarded and simply insured against. Still other

risks may be tackled by extra control routines such as increased security or rigorous hiring procedures or detailed reconciliations. An overall risk strategy that reaches all levels and parts of an organization is known as enterprisewide risk management (some call this ERM, for enterprise risk management). Here, all threats to the business, including product, operations, support services, and project risk as well as financial reporting aspects, fall under the remit of the risk management approach.

7. *Review.* Risk assessment exercises may result in risk maps and registers that align documented risks against the relevant processes, products, programs, projects, or units that are used to define the business. The risk registers result in documented controls that are focused and relevant and so enable the executives to report each year on their internal controls. There is a temptation to view the risk cycle as an annual event that fits into the annual business planning, performance review, and published reports. In practice, the risk cycle should be revisited as often as necessary. This may be quarterly, monthly, weekly, or in response to significant changes and joint ventures.

The review process relates more to developing the right culture than just a requirement to simply update past risk assessments. This means, for example, that all important decisions are supported by a formal assessment of risk and that all new ventures, projects, and strategic changes are likewise risk assessed. It also means staff have risk assessment and management built into their job profiles and that key performance measures include the results from risk assessment exercises. The risk review process should not only be part of corporate regulations but also be seen more as the way people and associates work in an organization.

8. *Reports.* Many risk management cycles fail because they generate masses of data but very little real information. Others fail because they result in a set of complex risk metrics that stand outside the real business planning and performance management system that staff understand and accept. The recommended approach is to build risk management into the main business management practices while seeking some refocus to assimilate new risk concepts into current thinking amongst employees. Risk management simply provides the lens through which management and staff can focus and coordinate their energies and resources. Many risk-reporting systems revolve around risk registers that are compiled during team workshops set up to review risk and controls in various operational areas across the organization. The registers will comprise important documents—say, spreadsheets—that capture information such as:

- Operation
- Key objective

- Responsible manager
- Workshop date
- Participants
- Facilitator
- Risk assessment details—risks, scores for impact and likelihood, rating, review of existing controls
- Action, and controls required to improve risk management that is assigned to appropriate risk and process owners
- Review points and updates

Risk management has been adopted by most large concerns, and as far as possible, risks are being managed through suitable strategies, including internal controls—which is the subject of the next section. Extracts from the Merrill Lynch 2002 annual report on risk management illustrate the type of response that companies are adopting:[3]

Risk Management

Growth, consistent returns and capital are jeopardized if risk is not controlled. Merrill Lynch's market, credit and operating risk management framework seeks to reduce volatility in our operating performance and lower our cost of equity by managing risks both within and across businesses. We limit our risk profile by diversifying risk and revenue sources, growing fee-based and recurring revenues, and minimizing the break-even point by carefully managing fixed costs. Other risk management objectives include focusing our trading activities on client-driven business, limiting proprietary risk-taking, and closely monitoring our long-term exposure to illiquid assets. We continuously look for opportunities to strengthen our worldwide market and credit risk controls, with particular attention to avoiding undue concentrations. At all levels of the organization, Merrill Lynch recognizes that sound corporate governance and oversight policies are critical to effectively managing risk and protecting the interests of shareholders.

For Further Discussion

There is one view of risk management that suggests it is mainly about changing organizational culture to incorporate a consideration of risk into current business practice.

If risk is embedded into the way people think and behave, does this mean organizations will not necessarily have a separate "system of risk management" in the future, as risk will be implicit in all business systems anyway?

—— SECTION 7 ——
UNDERSTANDING INTERNAL CONTROLS

We can start our consideration of internal controls by setting out the IIA definition of *control* as follows:

> *Any action taken by management, the board, and other parties to enhance risk management and increase the likelihood that established objectives and goals will be achieved. Management plans, organizes, and directs the performance of sufficient actions to provide reasonable assurance that objectives and goals will be achieved.*

This is a wide-ranging concept that takes on board all efforts by an organization to ensure it is successful. That is, it is able to anticipate and meet all foreseeable risks that interfere with its ability to be successful. This point is further developed by the IIA, which argues that control processes are:

> *The policies, procedures, and activities that are part of a control framework, designed to ensure that risks are contained within the risk tolerances established by the risk management process.*

Internal control is a fundamental concept that drives the audit process and that is now part of the reporting requirements for listed companies. Individual controls fit into the risk cycle that was described above under "mitigation," where risks have been identified and assessed. Mitigation is essentially about ways and means of controlling risk so that the impact on the business is reduced to acceptable levels. Controls are then measures put in place to contain risk, while being in control is a state that equates to meeting stakeholders' expectations. Control depends on controls, and we can only build good controls where there is a firm foundation within the organization to support a culture of good performance and accountability, all of which form the basis of good corporate governance. The foundation for control may be referred to as the *control environment,* which is defined by the IIA as:

> *The attitude and actions of the board and management regarding the significance of control within the organization. The control environment provides the discipline and structure for the achievement of the primary objectives of the system of internal control. The control environment includes the following elements:*
>
> - *Integrity and ethical value.*
> - *Management's philosophy and operating style.*
> - *Organizational structure.*
> - *Assignment of authority and responsibility.*
> - *Human resource policies and practices.*
> - *Competence of personnel.*

It is these attitudes and actions that are important to guide the organization through the maze of moral judgments that mean the difference between plain sailing and reckless risk taking. The control environment is also the platform for the COSO model of control that was developed by the Committee of Sponsoring Organizations of the Treadway Commission back in 1992, as the first real attempt to define a robust control model. The COSO model is made up of the following five components:

1. **Control environment.** This element, described above, forms the ethical platform upon which to build good systems of internal control.

2. **Risk assessment.** The next stage is to ensure there is an effective process for recognizing and weighing the various internal and external risks that face an organization and that may stop it from meeting or exceeding stakeholder expectations.

3. **Control procedures.** Having prioritized risk to the business, various appropriate measures can be adopted to control these risks. Procedures may therefore be based around aspects of the business that cannot be left without direction because of the need to instill some degree of certainty to ensure success.

4. **Communication and information.** The glue that binds the system of internal control together comes next. The control environment and need to install effective risk management is communicated to staff, and the resulting control activities provide information on whether risks are being managed properly. Communication flows through, around, and across an organization and ensures people who work for or do business with it understand the way things are done. Flaws in this aspect of the control model may lead to misunderstanding or breach of procedure and may possibly lead to inappropriate levels of unmitigated risk.

5. **Monitoring.** The final component of the control model relates to the arrangements for overseeing the way the model works in practice, that is, monitoring by the board, audit committee, senior management, and audit and review teams. It also relates to the way business managers review their risk registers to ensure they are capturing and addressing key risks to their areas of responsibility. The monitoring process is mainly dependent on information concerning working practices, performance, near misses, and the overall risk management strategy.

Together, these five components form a dynamic framework for assessing and reporting on controls. In fact, many observers feel that it is not possible to report on internal controls without establishing an appropriate control model that suits the organization concerned. Risks to the business come in many shapes and sizes, and a high-tech company may be most concerned about the speed of getting new products to the market. A transport company, on the other hand, may concentrate on risks that affect reliability and safety. In contrast, a retail chain may focus on risks to the low procurement cost that is needed to earn decent returns from small profit margins. One control theory runs that there is a fundamental conflict between the three concepts of time, cost, and quality. Because it is difficult to maintain systems that are able to achieve all three criteria, that risk and, therefore, the relevant controls will be assessed having regard to whichever of the three criteria is most important at this time.

In the past, standard controls were set by management, and all operations were assessed by considering how far the adopted controls were being applied. Nowadays, businesses focus on the way risks may interfere with their progress and then build controls to address the more significant risks. However, there are many well-known control concepts that are available to management, and as an example, five such concepts are noted below:

1. *Supervision.* Staff should be supervised unless there is little chance that risks will materialize with no supervision. The extent of this supervision depends on the type of work, type of staff, and whether there is a culture of empowerment in place. Where an operation has a high risk of failure, supervision and review is a good tool to ensure employees know what they are doing and perform to the required standard. For example, a supervisor at a fast-food outlet will help reduce the risk of substandard work, breach of hygiene standards, customer complaints, and excessive time away from the job.

2. *Authorization.* This control concept helps ensure activities and transactions fall in line with set standards. Authorization practices should reflect the accountability arrangements and relate to higher risk transactions that have more effect on the bottom line or on transactions that are susceptible to fraud and irregularity. Orders for office equipment over a certain value may have to be authorized by the budget holder as a way of minimizing the risk of inappropriate or irregular procurements. Likewise, the finance manager may need to authorize the write-off of uncollectible accounts on production of a clear business case, as a way of minimizing the risk of fraud and inefficiency.

3. *Segregation of duties.* This is an important control concept to guard against the risk of staff collusion, error, and breach of procedure. The control can also go hand in hand with authorization policies. An example may be staff recruitment being organized by the human resource (HR) section, while compensation checks are handled by a separate payroll team. In this way, an employee can only be paid if set up by HR and actioned by Payroll. Systems that involve the movement of funds, cash, assets, or benefits should be split across several sections to ensure propriety.

4. *Procedures.* Where an operation or business activity is complicated or has to meet specified regulatory requirements, or is particularly sensitive in terms of decisions that need to be made, there should be clear procedures in place. Procedures are needed to address the risk of confusion, abuse, inefficiency, and breach of regulation or obligations, and they will be as comprehensive as called for to manage these risks. For example, where an organization needs to shed staff in one business unit, there should be formal procedures in place to ensure the task is carried out fairly, efficiently, and in accordance with relevant legislation.

5. *Reconciliations.* Accounting systems are based on assets equating to liabilities so that the year-end balance sheet adds up. Movement between accounts and sections is based on a giving and receiving action that is accounted for in company ledgers. Reconciliation between these accounts and between records and physical counts is a useful control for ensuring nothing is missing or is incorrectly recorded or stored. A basic example is that the cash received from a retail sales point will be counted and reconciled to the record of cash entered on the cash system. Meanwhile, the cash receipting system will be reconciled to the banking system for cash banked in the same period.

The list goes on and on, and so long as there is a significant risk that is likely to have an impact on objectives, suitable measures should be established for dealing with the implications of this risk. Whatever best works to contain the risk to acceptable levels should be considered. Internal control needs to have a focus on the management process, and it is partly about getting business done successfully and partly about doing this business in a proper manner. This means controls need to guard against risk to the management process. The IIA Practice Advisory 2100-1 (Nature of Work), which sets out clear criteria that underpin the management process, includes the following comments:

Broadly, management is responsible for the sustainability of the whole organization and accountability for the organization's actions, conduct, and performance to the owners, other stakeholders, regulators, and general public. Specifically, the primary objectives of the overall management process are to achieve:

- *Relevant, reliable, and credible financial and operating information.*
- *Effective and efficient use of the organization's resources.*
- *Safeguarding of the organization's assets.*
- *Compliance with laws, regulations, ethical and business norms, and contracts.*
- *Identification of risk exposures and use of effective strategies to control them.*
- *Established objectives and goals for operations or programs.*

These six elements form a useful framework for assessing control structures. The question to ask is, "Do controls help ensure good information, value for money, protection of corporate resources, and compliance with relevant obligations?" If the answer to this question is yes, we have the basis for a good system of internal control. A control should only be applied if it meets the following criteria:

- The control is worthwhile in that the benefits outweigh the costs. Metal detectors at entrance points should only be used where there is a significant risk that undesirable and armed persons may seek to enter the facility, or that the fallout from such an event would be significant because of the nature of the facility, even if the event is unlikely to occur.

- Control theory recognizes that there is no such thing as 100 percent certainty in most business operations. There are some risks that cannot be foreseen and that may have been assessed as unlikely but may still happen. An operational site may experience a power failure, and the back-up power supply may crash at the exact same time.

- Most controls are only as good as the people who operate them. An exception report that documents all transactions that fail to meet a standard criteria is only of use if the person who receives the report takes action to investigate and deal with possible problems.

- Inflexible controls slow down the business and fail to respond to changes in the risk profiles that affect an organization. Where a local office has to get head office approval for bulk purchases, but local vendors are offering to sell off surplus stock on a first-come basis, the slow approval system may mean special offers may not be taken advantage of.

- Controls should fit the culture and the way people work. In an empowered organization, excessive supervisory checks may lead to a defensive workforce, with employees who mistrust their team leaders and leaders who in turn mistrust their staff.

The SEC internal control reporting requirements are similar to disclosure requirements for state and federal bodies and agencies. Many such requirements suggest that controls need to be adequate, and the IIA has suggested that adequate control is:

> *present if management has planned and organized (designed) in a manner that provides reasonable assurance that the organization's risks have been managed effectively and that the organization's goals and objectives will be achieved efficiently and economically.*

An understanding of internal control and how controls work in practice is fundamental to achieving good corporate governance and risk management. The main issue is the way the control concept has moved from basic accounting controls and compliance checks, to controls being viewed as the wider concept of the entire business being in control of its destiny, as far as it is able. Corporate governance depends on the organization's being able to appreciate the risks that affect its business and therefore impact the shareholders, and the way these risks are managed depends on a sound system of internal control, based on a robust control framework and reliable specific controls. In this way, corporate governance, risk management, and control are three interdependencies that have to be considered together to make any sense.

Cable and Wireless

The extracts below, from the U.K. company Cable and Wireless's *Annual Report 2002, Directors' Report—Corporate Governance,* demonstrate the link between risk management and internal control:[4]

Internal Control and Risk Management

The Board is ultimately responsible for the Group's system of internal control and for reviewing its effectiveness. However, such a system is designed to manage rather than eliminate the risk of failure to achieve business objectives, and can provide only reasonable and not absolute assurance against material mis-statement or loss. The Directors have reviewed the effectiveness of internal controls.

The Directors regularly review the effectiveness of all internal controls, including operational controls.

Risk assessment and evaluation takes place as an integral part of the annual strategic planning cycle. Having identified the risks to achievement of their strategic objectives, each business is required to document the management and mitigating actions in place and proposed in respect of each significant risk.

Risk Review Boards comprising the Chief Executive, Chief Financial Officer and one other senior executive have been formed within the Group's major trading units.

These Boards meet throughout the year and have responsibility for ensuring that risks to the business are identified and evaluated and that effective responses are developed for their management.

A structure of control self-assessment and hierarchical reporting has been established which provides for a documented and auditable trail of accountability. This structure, which has been applied throughout the Group's operations, is facilitated by Group Risk Management and provides for successive assurances to be given at increasingly higher levels of management and, ultimately, to the Board. This structure, which accords with the Turnbull guidance, has been in place for the full financial year and up to the date the financial statements were approved.

The Group's Internal Audit function has a formal charter approved by the Board which describes its purpose, authority and responsibility. It supports the Directors in assessing key internal controls through a structured review program. . . .

The finance and general management of operating units are required to acknowledge in writing that their financial reporting is based on sound data. They are also required to acknowledge, in writing, that they are fully aware of their responsibility to operate internal control systems and that their results are properly stated in accordance with Group and statutory requirements.

Additionally, a structure has been developed to assess the Group's corporate social responsibility including social, environmental and ethical matters and this is covered in the Social, Environmental and Ethical Report.

By order of the Board of Directors

For Further Discussion

What are the attributes that make for a good system of internal control?

—— SECTION 8 ——

DEFINING THE INTERNAL AUDIT ROLE

The traditional internal auditor fought for propriety against all comers. The battle involved extensive checks over transactions and assets to make sure everything was in order. The new-look internal auditor spends a great deal of time considering the organization's approach to corporate governance, risk management, and control. It is only after this consideration that the chief audit executive (CAE) can start to define the internal audit role. This straightforward approach is further complicated when defining the internal audit role, and reference should be made to:

- Actual corporate audit practices
- Best international auditing standards
- Expectations of stakeholders and the marketplace

The organization's corporate governance, risk management, and control arrangements, along with the formulation of the internal auditors' contribution to these challenges, may be compared to best practice and to what key players would like to see from their internal audit shop. We have described the context of the audit role and can now repeat the formal definition of *internal auditing*:

Internal auditing is an independent, objective assurance and consulting activity designed to add value and improve an organization's operations. It helps an organization accomplish its objectives by bringing a systematic, disciplined approach to evaluate and improve the effectiveness of risk management, control, and governance processes.

The challenges are immense. The internal audit shop promises to help set up systems of governance, risk management, and control. At the same time, it promises to provide an objective view on whether these systems are in place and working, something that is now right at the helm of the executive agenda for all types of organizations. There are several aspects of the internal audit concept that need to be mentioned before we launch into the audit process itself, including:

- The audit charter
- Audit independence
- Assurance and consulting services

The Audit Charter

The charter is a key document that sums up the audit role and responsibilities within an organization. The IIA suggests:

The charter of the internal audit activity is a formal written document that defines the activity's purpose, authority, and responsibility. The charter should (a) establish the internal audit activity's position; (b) authorize access to records, personnel, and physical properties relevant to the performance of engagements; and (c) define the scope of internal audit activities.

In practice, the charter will reflect the nature of the balance between assurance and consulting work and the fit between internal audit and the governance, risk, and control systems. The charter itself will be approved by the board and endorsed by the audit committee. In days past, the audit charter would be a standing document that remained on the company "books" as a permanent fixture once signed by the board. Nowadays, just as all organizations are in a state of continual change in an effort to keep in touch with their markets, most internal audit teams are trying to refocus their efforts to meet the challenges we have discussed earlier. The audit charter is now a living document that is revised as and when necessary, and Practice Advisory 1000-1 suggests:

The chief audit executive should periodically assess whether the purpose, authority, and responsibility, as defined in the charter, continue to be adequate to enable the internal audit activity to accomplish its objectives. The result of this periodic assessment should be communicated to senior management and the board.

The Practice Advisory also argues: "If a question should arise, the charter also provides a formal, written agreement with management and the board about the role and responsibilities of the internal audit activity within the organization."

Audit Independence

The concept of independence is built into the definition of internal auditing. It means the work performed and reports issued by the auditors can be viewed as reliable, with no vested interests. Objectivity is an attribute that does not always apply to views expressed by other teams in the organization. Independence also means the auditors have unimpaired access to all relevant sources of information, and their work and reports have sufficient status to make a difference. The need for sufficient independence is enshrined in the IIA's Attribute Standard 1100, which states:

> *The internal audit activity should be independent, and internal auditors should be objective in performing their work.*

The Seven Ps of Independence

Standard 1100 highlights the two main planks of independence: a well-positioned audit shop and auditors who are able to apply a degree of objectivity to their work. Much depends on the audit shop's achieving seven "Ps":

1. *Position* and reporting lines of adequate status within the organization.
2. *Planning* profile and unrestricted access to all aspects of the organization, with sufficient resources to deliver a risk-based strategy.
3. *Performance* standards that mean auditors are able to work systematically and without impediment.
4. *Professional* audit staff who are equipped to do a good job with no obvious conflicts of interest or divided loyalties from previous (or future) positions. IIA Standard 1130.A1 says that auditing an activity within one year of being responsible for the same activity is presumed to impair objectivity. This provision does not apply to consulting services (as made clear in Standard 1130.C1).
5. *Presentation* of findings without fear or favor, or unreasonable time restrictions.
6. *Persistence,* where any points of principle arising from the audit will be followed up until they are properly addressed.
7. *Proficient* reconciliation of the assurance and consulting roles so as to retain an adequate degree of objectivity in the provision of audit assurances.

If the CAE feels unable to provide an adequate degree of independence in the audit product, that fact should be documented. This requirement is built into IIA Attribute Standard 1130:

> *If independence or objectivity is impaired in fact or appearance, the details of the impairment should be disclosed to appropriate parties. The nature of the disclosure will depend upon the impairment.*

Not only must audit assurance work be independent, but also it must be seen to be so. And if this is not the case, this fact must be formally revealed. No one can be a judge in his or her own case. Where the CAE has additional responsibilities as well as the internal audit role, it becomes difficult to provide an audit coverage of these other areas. Attribute Standard 1130.A2 comes to the rescue by requiring:

> *Assurance engagements for functions over which the CAE has responsibility should be overseen by a party outside the internal audit activity. Where there is a potential impairment to independence for a consulting engagement, this fact should be revealed to the client before the engagement is accepted (1130.C2).*

In the past, some auditors viewed independence as an absolute position that had to be achieved and held on to. Having as little contact as possible with the "auditee" was seen as important, and a distant, icy persona became the norm for staff in many an audit shop. These days, independence is seen more in terms of being able to do a good job and have the results taken seriously by senior executives and management alike. Being close to the "client" as a way of understanding what is happening in each part of the organization is now the norm, so long as a professional demeanor is retained at all times.

Unfortunately, this message has not always gotten back to everyone, and the old viewpoint still attaches to the internal auditor in the eyes of people who have no recent experience of the audit process and how it has developed. The perceived need to secure absolute independence from the "auditee" gets in the way of doing good audit work. At the same time, there is some need to retain a professional dignity even when working alongside the "client." As with all things, a sensible balance and sound judgment is more important than detailed rules.

Assurance and Consulting Services

We have made reference to the fact that internal audit shops provide both assurance and consulting services. While the overall IIA standards apply to both roles, there are separate implementation standards that address each type of role. Assurance services constitute the principal role of the internal auditor, and this involves giving an objective view of the state of governance processes, risk management, and control within the organization. The formal IIA definition of *assurances services* follows:

> An objective examination of evidence for the purpose of providing an independent assessment of risk management, control, or governance processes for the organization. Examples may include financial, compliance, systems security, and due diligence engagements.

This is what most people think of when considering the role of internal auditing. In practice, auditors have thrown themselves into various parts of the organization to help solve problems, to give advice on risk and control issues, and often, to conduct special projects at the request of senior management. This type of work tended to be done whenever there was time left over after planned systems reviews were performed. The provision of consulting services is now formally recognized in the IIA standards as an important aspect of the audit role. *Consulting services* appear in the definition of internal auditing and are defined as:

> Advisory and related client service activities, the nature and scope of which are agreed upon with the client and which are intended to add value and improve an organization's operations. Examples include counsel, advice, facilitation, process design, and training.

The relationship between assurance and consulting services is fundamental to the future of internal auditing. The balance and flavor of audit services will determine whether the CAE is able to meet the heightened expectations from society for all players in the corporate governance equation to contribute fully to a successful economy. The internal audit provides a reliable insight into what is really happening in terms of whether there is adequate propriety and sound controls over a business. Moreover, auditors apply their special insights into risk and control to help managers wherever possible to establish risk management and deal with the fallout where risks have materialized and cause problems. The latter aspect is consulting work, and this revolves around the need to add as much value as possible to the business. Consulting work opens many doors for the internal auditor and means a whole raft of high-level, advice-based projects may be carried out, as and when required.

> ### For Further Discussion
> How should the internal auditor balance the assurance and consulting roles, bearing in mind there are limited audit resources?

───── SECTION 9 ─────
EXTERNAL AUDIT

We have said that internal audit was seen as an extension of external audit in days gone by. Extensive checking and testing of accounting data carried out by the internal auditor enabled the external auditor to reduce the latter's own testing and rely, in part, on the work already carried out on the accounting data. Things have moved on from this, and the distinction between the two audit functions becomes increasingly relevant. Internal audit is now a fully accepted professional discipline and, as such, stands alongside the external counterparts as an equally important force in the drive toward better governance and accountability. There is some need for coordination, and IIA Performance Standard 2050 requires that:

> *the CAE should share information and coordinate activities with other internal and external providers of relevant assurance and consulting services to ensure proper coverage and minimize duplication of efforts.*

There are also other external and internal review functions that have some similarity to internal audit. It is necessary to make sure there is some alignment of the audit services to ensure there is no excessive duplication of effort. An *external services provider* is defined by the IIA as:

> *A person or firm, independent of the organization, who has special knowledge, skill, and experience in a particular discipline. Outside service providers include, among others, actuaries, accountants, appraisers, environmental specialists, fraud investigators, lawyers, engineers, geologists, security specialists, statisticians, information technology specialists, external auditors, and other auditing organizations. The board, senior management, or the CAE may engage an outside service provider.*

External Audit in the Front Line

External auditors are in the front line of the corporate governance equation. They are key to verifying the financial information provided to shareholders by the CEO, CFO, and the main board. The external auditor examines the financial statements that are prepared by the organization and provides an independent opinion on whether the statements show a true and fair view of the company's affairs for the year in question. It is essential that the work performed by the external auditor be unimpaired by any actual or potential conflicts of interest, and so can be relied on by shareholders and other interested parties. This dynamic has come under considerable strain over the years as large audit firms have provided a mix of audit and consulting work for huge amounts that for all intents and purposes have been approved by the board, or public-sector executive group. Government directives, legislation, accounting standards, SEC filing requirements, and various associated rules and regulations that affect both government and commerce provide an abundance of rules covering the external audit process. Over the years, these rules have become increasingly demanding in an attempt to address weaknesses highlighted by the corporate scandals à la Enron and WorldCom that appear on a regular basis. The various SEC filing and other regulations are designed to ensure:

- There is a full external audit of the published final accounts.
- The external auditors are free from undue pressures due to having a disproportionate level of income from any one major client.
- There is no conflict of interest resulting from the pursuit of large consulting fees earned by the external auditor.
- The audit staff are well trained to professional standards and are able to perform to the requisite standard. This depends mainly on charging full market rates for audit contracts.
- The senior audit partner is able to retain professional skepticism despite promoting good working relationships with the senior executives, and in particular the CFO.
- The audit committee provides an adequate oversight of the audit process and ensures the external auditor represents shareholder interests properly.
- The external auditors' role in relation to employee fraud and irregularity is clearly defined and discharged.
- The external auditor is able to recognize and disclose any material misstatement of the final accounts that is perpetrated by senior executives.

There are many existing, new, and proposed regulations to address the above. In one sense, it is pointless trying to capture the rules at any point in time, as they are in continual flux, changing and evolving. In turn, the IIA has published guidance that addresses issues such as SEC reporting requirements, notwithstanding the constant updating that is now the norm. Essentially, the external audit requirements are about securing independence and professionalism so that the separation of ownership and management that we mentioned earlier is underpinned by robust accounting, attestation, and audit routines. The principles behind this model are sound; it is the practical application that can be fraught with difficulties. The struggle to ensure the rules are applied in a sensible and honest manner is made difficult by the tremendous pressure to either succeed in the marketplace or give the impression that the business (or public service) is successful. The internal audit position has changed immensely over recent years. Nowadays, internal auditors are being asked to act as an additional layer of assurance over the entire corporate governance arrangements, including the external audit process. In defining the relationship between internal and external audit, it is interesting to note and comment on some of the areas of contact that are mentioned in IIA guidance as follows:

- Practice Advisory 2210.A1-1 deals with risk assessment in engagement planning and suggests that part of gathering background information on the activity to be reviewed and the results of other engagements includes considering the work of external auditors, completed or in progress. In terms of reporting on risk and control, Practice Advisory 1110-2 (para. 8) says that: *"CAEs should also consider their relationships with other control and monitoring functions (risk management, compliance, security, legal, ethics, environmental, external audit) and facilitate the reporting of material risk and control issues to the audit committee."*

- The external auditor may be given a copy of internal audit reports to assist effective communications and coordination. Since the external auditor may wish to place reliance on internal audit work, any internal reviews of internal audit will be of interest to them. Practice Advisory 1311-1 clarifies this point, advising that: "the CAE should share the results of internal assessments and necessary action plans with appropriate persons outside the activity, such as senior management, the board, and external auditors."

- There is further scope to utilize the external auditor's work when planning the follow-up of previous internal audit engagements. Practice Advisory 2500.A1-1 notes this point by providing that "follow-up by internal auditors is defined as a process by which they determine the adequacy, effectiveness, and timeliness of actions taken by management on reported engagement observations and recommendations, including those made by external auditors and others."

- Finally, official IIA guidance also recognizes the need to allow the external auditor to access internal audit working papers, and Practice Advisory 2330.A1-1 addresses this and other related issues by stating that: "It is common practice for internal and external auditors to grant access to each other's audit working papers. Access to audit working papers by external auditors should be subject to the approval of the chief audit executive."

Internal and external audit should achieve a mutually acceptable working relationship that recognizes areas of similarity and difference. The external auditor is concerned with the financial accounts that are published by the organization and with the reliability of these accounts. This reliability depends on the financial systems that support the production of the final accounts, and the application of generally accepted accounting standards in a fair and proper manner. Internal auditors are concerned about governance, risk management, and control as a broader concept that incorporates the adequacy of financial reporting as only one of the principal concerns. External audit should ask whether there is any work that has been completed by internal audit that might help them form an opinion on the financial statements issued by the organization.

Meanwhile, internal audit will want to see a robust external audit process to support the quest for good corporate governance, and that there is no duplication of work as a result of poor communications between the two disciplines. This point cannot be stressed too much. The audit committee has tremendous new responsibilities for ensuring that the corporate arrangements for accounting, accountability, and audit make sense. Committee members will not be impressed by the two types of audit functions acting in a fragmented and uncoordinated manner. Practice Advisory 2060-2 deals with the relationship with the audit committee and requires that any such inefficiencies be reported. Extracts from the advisory read:

> *Confirm there is effective and efficient work coordination of activities between internal and external auditors. Determine if there is any duplication between the work of the internal and external auditors and give the reasons for such duplication.*

There is much to be gained from an efficient working relationship with external audit and much scope for embarrassment for the CAE where this is not the case. This principle is much the same for relationships with other review teams such as consultants, financial control, compliance sections, and the chief risk officer's team. The audit committee would like to sense some form of harmony from all those voices that have something to say about corporate governance and risk management. The rules covering registered firms of accountants that audit the companies covered by the SEC are becoming increasingly demanding.

AICPA Guidance

The American Institute of Certified Public Accountants (AICPA) has provided a brief history of self-regulation, dated February 20, 2002:[5]

> *In the modern financial era, self-regulation by the accounting profession can be traced to just after the Securities and Exchange Commission (SEC) was established by the Securities Act of 1933 and the Securities Exchange Act of 1934. These new laws were passed by Congress in response to the vast sums lost by investors in the stock market crash of 1929 and the subsequent financial depression. At the outset, there were serious discussions in Washington about whether the federal government should establish standards for preparing and auditing financial statements of publicly held companies. The SEC was given statutory authority to set accounting standards and oversight over the activities of auditors. The role of establishing auditing standards was left to the accounting*

profession. . . . The Public Oversight Board (POB) was created in 1977 and oversees the peer review and quality control inquiry processes of the SECPS, as well as the SECPS' other activities and the Auditing Standards Board. The POB has maintained its independence from both the profession and the regulatory process by being self-perpetuating. Although funded by SECPS member firm dues, the POB elects its own board members, hires its own staff, and sets its own budget without challenge from the SECPS. . . . The SEC is now in the process of making its own proposals to create a new oversight body made up of a majority of public members and operating outside the AICPA. At the same time, the AICPA, Big Five, and the 1,200 firms that are members of the SECPS are forging ahead on implementing improved audit standards for detecting fraud and new measures for deterring fraud such as expanded internal control procedures for management, boards, and audit committees. Reforms also need to be made in the financial reporting model, the analyst community, boards of directors and audit committees, and in the corporate culture of companies.

For Further Discussion

In what ways can external auditors ensure they are independent when performing their work?

––––– SECTION 10 –––––

THE VALUE-ADD PROPOSITION

In the past, internal audit tended to exist because it was required in a directive, act, or regulation, particularly for public-sector bodies, while more recently, it has become a requirement for companies regulated by the SEC. Organizations with an audit committee were seen as incomplete without an internal audit shop that reported in to the committee on their work plan and resulting reports. This state of affairs meant that the audit presence was tolerated because it was one of the few organizational teams that were protected by various rules that meant it had to exist. The new pressures on corporate America and government services, alongside the additional responsibilities placed on audit committees, have rebounded on the internal auditor. Having a concern for governance, risk management, and control has pushed the work of the internal auditor onto the executive boardroom agenda in terms of helping define solutions to the push for better governance. Meanwhile, the internal auditor is called on to support the audit committee oversight of these very same solutions through the provision of reliable assurances. Large organizations no longer see internal audit as something that is simply part of the regulations but more as a key component in its corporate growth, success, and position in the marketplace. In other words, the internal auditor is called upon to add value to the business. This concept is enshrined in Performance Standard 2000 on Managing the Internal Audit Activity, which states:

> *The CAE should effectively manage the internal audit activity to ensure it adds value to the organization.*

These simple words reflect an important new dynamic for the internal auditor, one that may take several years to fully appreciate. It means the audit shop must help grow the business and use the considerable expertise of its staff and unique position in the organization to help deliver a successful performance and a respected reputation. *Value-add* is defined in different ways by different entities in different countries. Not only must the audit shop add value but also it must be seen as doing so. The external review of internal audit that must be completed at least every five years includes a consideration of this factor, as made clear in an extract from Practice Advisory 1312-1 on external assessments:

> *The determination whether the audit activity adds value and improves the organization's operations.*

While assurance work adds value to the efforts an organization makes to attest to the state of its internal controls, consulting work may also add value to the organization's ability to deliver results. To reinforce this point, IIA Performance Standard 2010.C1 argues:

> *The CAE should consider accepting proposed consulting engagements based on the engagement's potential to improve management of risks, add value, and improve the organization's operations. Those engagements that have been accepted should be included in the plan.*

If a consulting engagement is valuable to an organization, it should be considered in formulating audit plans. Meanwhile, if an internal audit shop is unable to demonstrate that it makes a valuable contribution to the business, there are several possible repercussions:

- Internal audit will have little credibility and therefore a limited status within the organization.
- Executives will turn to others for input into their efforts to enhance risk management and control.
- In-house shops may be disbanded and the internal audit service outsourced to external providers.
- Audit staff may feel demotivated by the lack of impact they have on the growth of the organization. In turn, potential new recruits (including internal staff) may feel less inclined to join the team.

- The CAE may become defensive and spend much time trying to convince others that the internal audit process is worthwhile.
- The budget held by the CAE may become targeted for reduction. This may mean less audit staff or lower pay rates for existing audit staff.
- The audit committee may fail to receive a dynamic service from internal audit and may be unable to discharge all their responsibilities properly.

We have said that it is important to add value and have noted the implications of any failures on this front. Building on our comments in Chapter 1, Section 5, we can discuss adding value further. Help is at hand through the IIA, and we can repeat the opening extract from their description of the concept of adding value:

> *Organizations exist to create value or benefit to their owners, other stakeholders, customers, and clients. This concept provides purpose for their existence. Value is provided through their development of products and services and their use of resources to promote those products and services.*

It is the expertise that the auditor has in respect of risk management and internal controls that is so important. In the past, this expertise was held as a well-kept secret. Nowadays, the same expertise is being used to develop models and techniques such as CSA workshops, control awareness seminars, and risk-reporting tools that help busy managers come to grips with the development of suitable risk-focused internal controls. The assurance role of internal audit helps protect the reputation of the organization, while the consulting role helps enhance the business of the organization. If done well, these two dimensions become part of the value chain that sees basic inputs transformed into valuable outputs for the customer. Moreover, stakeholders may have confidence in the reported results issued by the entity's management. The internal auditor has assumed a pivotal role in many large organizations, as the CAE tends to have a reporting line into the board. In addition, and as recommended by Practice Advisory 1110-2, the CAE should report into the audit committee, and there should be private meetings between the CAE and audit committee. The audit committee should have a final say in the annual audit plan, and the CAE's administrative reporting lines should not lead to interference with the work of the internal audit activity. Note that value-add is dealt with in more detail in Chapter 6.

For Further Discussion

Give examples of some of the ways that internal audit has added value to the organization.

—— SECTION 11 ——

THE AUDIT MODEL

The audit model can now be developed to incorporate business objectives setting, financial accountability, audit committees, audit (both external and internal), risk management, and control. Exhibit 2.2 shows how these features have been added to the basic owner-manager split covered in Chapter 1.

Society and Stakeholders. The audit model is driven primarily by the needs and interests of society, that is, the need for good company performance that contributes to the economy, and both fair and transparent business practices. Stakeholders include all those who have a direct or indirect interest in the way business, commerce, and public services are conducted.

Shareholders and Investors. Principal stakeholders are the people and institutions who hold shares in listed companies. Banks and investment companies

Exhibit 2.2. Audit Model 2

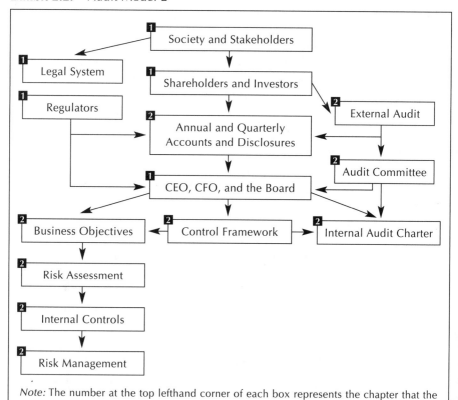

Note: The number at the top lefthand corner of each box represents the chapter that the items relate to.

may well have a direct interest that is represented in funds loaned to the company. Meanwhile, *The People* are principal stakeholders in public-sector organizations. Company shareholders should exercise their voting rights with due regard to the need to ensure there is ethical behavior and accountability from company officials.

Legal System. There are a multitude of federal and state laws that relate to the way private- and public-sector organizations are established, maintained, and extinguished. Many larger organizations have responded by setting up compliance functions to address the variety and magnitude of such legal provisions. Company directors and officials can face severe penalties where specific laws are breached.

Regulators. Most industries have an associated regulator that sets standards and represents the public in ensuring organizations behave properly. The SEC, American Stock Exchange, New York Stock Exchange, and NASDAQ regulations are some of the more well-known models.

CEO, CFO, and the Board. Shareholders appoint a CEO and board of directors to direct and oversee the organization on their behalf. These officers have a responsibility to discharge their duties in a professional manner and account for the results to the shareholders. A management team will be appointed in public-sector bodies and have a similar responsibility to the government and general public. The board should adhere to the highest standards of ethics and ensure they conduct their business in an acceptable and documented manner. Moreover, the board should have in place suitable mechanisms through which they may judge their own performance and conduct.

Annual Accounts and Disclosures. The organization reports to its stakeholders through published financial and performance statements. These reports act as a window to the outside world, and business analysts spend a great deal of time examining the detailed facts and figures in company accounts on behalf of their clients. Listed companies, along with many other organizations, have to make various disclosures on an annual and quarterly basis, in particular resulting from the Sarbanes-Oxley Act. The published accounts should be reliable and now have to be personally certified by the principal executive and CFO.

External Audit. The external auditors are appointed by the shareholders to make sure the board has provided a full and reliable account of the company's financial performance over the previous year. The financial statements will be checked by the external auditors before the statements are formally published. External auditors should ensure they are independent in their audit work and are able to exercise an appropriate degree of professional skepticism at all times.

This part of the audit model is a major contribution to governance, as material published by the organization is independently verified.

Audit Committee.   A further layer of governance that is growing in importance is the audit committee. This forum, established by the board, comprises independent directors who provide an additional oversight role, focusing on the specialist areas of financial accounting, ethics, audit, accountability, risk management, and control. The audit committee is not there to undermine the board but rather to provide advice and support regarding the specialist areas in question. Moreover, the committee should ask challenging questions of the board, on the premise that it is better that these tough questions come from an in-house audit committee than from external regulators.

Internal Audit Charter.   The internal auditor's role and position in the organization is set by the audit charter that is agreed to by the board and audit committee. To be of any real use, this charter should be set firmly within the governance, risk management, and control arenas.

Business Objectives.   The next stage of the model relates to the setting of formal corporate objectives that document the mission of the organization and what it is there to achieve.

Risk Assessment.   Anything that has an impact on business objectives can be seen as a potential risk. These risks need to be understood, isolated, and weighed in terms of significance. Formal risk assessment gives an organization a head start in understanding where its vulnerabilities lie and where it has scope for advancement. The bottom line is that risks that affect the organization's ability to deliver and achieve its objectives have to be addressed for there to be any real chance of success. Control risk self-assessment and regular risk surveys are good ways of promoting risk assessment throughout the organization.

Internal Control.   Controls should be in place to address risks that have been assessed as significant. The current climate stresses the importance of controls over financial reporting and disclosures as well as compliance with various standard regulations. The systems of internal control need to be maintained, updated, and made right as part of the way employees work.

Risk Management.   Controls fit into the wider remit of risk management, and managers and their teams need to build risk mitigation into their overall strategies. There are many different potential responses to risks, depending on the nature, significance, and cost of controls. The organization needs to weigh the available measures on a regular basis and ensure the adopted response meets the expectations of the board and stakeholders. In other words, the response to risk needs to fit the risk tolerance levels that have been defined by the board in its risk and control policy.

Control Framework. The entire risk management and control policy should be incorporated within the adopted control framework. Standard models such as COSO sit on a foundation of ethical values and propriety, which may be seen as the "tone at the top" that is set by the board and top executives.

—— SECTION 12 ——

SUMMARY: TOP TEN CONSIDERATIONS

A summary of the ten main points covered in the chapter follows:

1. Corporate governance is a main driver for the internal audit process. It is based on business success and effective arrangements for board functioning and oversight, audit, accounting, accountability, and performance management.

2. The Enron and WorldCom scandals of 2002 have brought home the need for more effective systems of corporate governance and in particular the financial reporting aspects of corporate accountability.

3. One response to corporate scandals was the wide-ranging Sarbanes-Oxley Act. Among other things, this new legislation seeks to strengthen the independence of external audit and role of the audit committee in ensuring appropriate reports and disclosures are made by listed companies.

4. Corporate governance codes and associated regulations are a global development, and there are many examples of good practice from around the world. The Organization for Economic Co-operation and Development has attempted the task of setting an international code that can be applied in a variety of different contexts and circumstances.

5. Governance codes are having a major impact on company and organization boards, and in particular, the new requirements to report on internal controls have led to significant challenges for many large and complicated organizations. Most corporations now recognize that adhering to the spirit of the law is more important than minimal compliance with specific rules.

6. The audit committee has now assumed a pivotal role in overseeing the corporate governance systems and disclosure arrangements. If there is no audit committee, the entire board becomes one.

7. Another important part of the corporate governance jigsaw is suitable systems of risk management within each organization. The IIA defines *risk* as "the uncertainty of an event occurring that could have an impact

on the achievement of objectives. Risk is measured in terms of consequences and likelihood." Most accept that there is a basic risk management cycle that can be written as a series of set stages, and one version covers:

- Objective setting
- Risk policy
- Risk identification
- Risk assessment
- Risk mitigation
- Risk management
- Review
- Reports

8. Another important aspect of corporate governance is internal control frameworks and specific internal controls. The IIA views control as "any action taken by management, the board, and other parties to enhance risk management and increase the likelihood that established objectives and goals will be achieved." The Committee of Sponsoring Organizations of the Treadway Commission developed a control model back in 1992 that incorporates the following key components:

- Control environment
- Risk assessment
- Control procedures
- Communication and information
- Monitoring

Internal controls may be applied to mitigate risks. Some general examples of key controls include:

- Supervision
- Authorization
- Segregation of duties
- Procedures
- Reconciliations

9. It is only by understanding the entire governance process, and where audit fits into the picture, that the internal and external audit roles can then be properly appreciated and coordinated. The internal audit role should be established having regard to the need to define:

- The audit charter
- Audit independence
- Assurance and consulting services

Meanwhile, the external audit role is key to verifying the financial information provided to shareholders by the CEO, the CFO, and the main board. The new governance regime emphasizes the importance of independence and professionalism from the external auditor. The risk to external audit independence was exposed by the Enron and WorldCom scandals, with obvious repercussions.

10. The audit model may be further developed to incorporate additional factors such as the following:

- Annual accounts and disclosures
- External audit
- Audit committees
- Internal audit charter
- Business objectives
- Risk assessment
- Internal control
- Risk management
- Control frameworks

—— SECTION 13 ——

YOUR PERSONAL DEVELOPMENT EXERCISES

1. Obtain a copy of the corporate governance policy document or any policy covering accountability, ethics, and audit arrangements for your university/college. Using the concepts found in this chapter, appraise the good features and possible weaknesses in this policy and prepare a 1,000-word report setting out your findings.

2. Think about the last time you purchased an expensive consumer product (e.g., a car, bike, or laptop), and for this product, define the following:

- Your objectives in terms of your time, costs, and quality features of the product.
- The risks that you encountered when buying this product as they affect your ability to achieve the objectives as set out earlier.
- An assessment of which risks are significant and which risks are likely to materialize if nothing is done about them.
- The measures that may be adopted to deal with the risks that should be addressed.
- A risk management strategy, taking on board all suitable measures that should be in place to promote the achievement of the set objectives in purchasing the item in question.

- The benefits of taking the above systematic approach to assessing and managing risk as compared to your original approach to making the purchase.

3. Prepare a list of key considerations for the internal audit function for performing audit assurance work and a similar list for performing internal consulting services.

4. Prepare a presentation on how internal audit shops can be considered independent when they tend to be located within an organization.

5. Write a note on each of the attribute and performance standards mentioned in this chapter, explaining for each standard why it is important and why it is needed as a mandatory requirement for internal audit teams.

6. Scan the World Wide Web, and look at various internal audit charters that are documented in organizations' Web sites. List the areas that tend to appear in the audit charters of most published Web sites.

7. Prepare a brief presentation explaining the concept of added value, and describe ways that an internal audit shop can add value to an organization.

8. Write a short paper explaining the challenges presented by the Sarbanes-Oxley Act of 2002.

9. Prepare a speech explaining why internal controls are so important to a business and the need for senior executives to provide and publish a formal report on internal controls.

NOTES

1. Speech by President George W. Bush, at the Regent Wall Street Hotel, New York, July 9, 2002, *www.whitehouse.gov* (accessed March 2003).
2. GE Proxy Statement 2003, *www.ge.com* (accessed March 24, 2003).
3. *www.ml.com* (accessed March 24, 2003).
4. *www.cw.com* (accessed March 24, 2003).
5. *www.aicpa.com* (accessed March 2003).

3

THE STRATEGIC DIMENSION

——— SECTION 1 ———
APPROACHES TO INTERNAL AUDIT WORK

We have set the context for the internal audit role and a working definition that is founded on the threefold platform of governance, risk management, and control. The audit role is supported by a detailed set of standards and guidance that provides a direction and focus and, more than this, a challenge for all audit shops. This chapter considers the way the audit role is discharged as we move closer to the actual performance of audit work itself. Note that risk-based strategic planning is dealt with in Chapter 5, Section 2. The audit context is clear and is repeated in Performance Standard 2100, which covers the nature of audit work, stating:

> The internal audit activity should assist the organization by identifying and evaluating significant exposures to risk and contributing to the improvement of risk management and control systems.

It is good to hold the above firmly in mind when considering what internal auditors do at work. Most roads lead back to the risk management and control arena. Even where the auditor is stuck on a project that involves lots of compliance testing and examination of basic data, it is still helpful to rise above the detail and consider where the results fit into the way risks are being managed, and the reliability of internal controls that mitigate risk in the operation in question. When a fraud is being investigated, again the failure of controls needs to be kept in mind at the same time. Computer audits and reviews of complicated contracts and projects all involve the need to identify, assess, and deal with risk to business performance. Practice Advisory 2100-1 provides further guidance on the nature of internal auditing work. The advisory acknowledges the dual nature of internal auditing, which involves providing reasonable assurances on the organization's existing risk management, control, and governance processes and providing recommendations for improving the organization's operations, in terms of both efficient and effective performance. It also suggests that executives and the board may be involved in providing some input into the planned scope of audit work. Internal auditors are concerned with appraising the overall management process, and the Advisory makes the point:

> *All business systems, processes, operations, functions, and activities within the organization are subject to the internal auditors' evaluations. The comprehensive scope of work of internal auditing should provide reasonable assurance that management's:*
>
> - *Risk management system is effective.*
> - *System of internal control is effective and efficient.*
> - *Governance process is effective by establishing and preserving values, setting goals, monitoring activities and performance, and defining the measures of accountability.*

This is a pretty wide remit that turns the internal audit task into a real challenge. The nature of audit work remains that of evaluation, assessment, and review. But the subject matter of this review encompasses the core processes that are key to any successful business. Internal audit is also concerned with performance within an organization. Where performance is strong, the organization has a better chance of achieving its objectives now and in the future. Practice Advisory 2100-1 encourages a forward-looking approach where auditors are concerned about what is being planned as well as what is actually happening that may affect performance by arguing:

> *Internal auditors should be alert to actual or potential changes in internal or external conditions that affect the ability to provide assurance from a forward-looking perspective. In those cases, internal auditors should address the risk that performance may deteriorate.*

There are many commentators who feel that the audit process should not become immersed in reviewing past events. The audit role is seen as more about considering future strategy and ensuring there are controls in place to take the business successfully into the future, despite the uncertainty that comes hand in hand with looking ahead. As with all uncertainty, it is a matter of anticipating the risks and designing workable solutions as far as practicable. Giving assurances about this process and also helping out individual managers wherever possible are the cornerstones of internal auditing.

For Further Discussion

What main approach is applied to performing audit work, and how has this developed over the years?

RISK-BASED SYSTEMS APPROACH

Systems auditing has been applied by internal auditors for many years. Although the principles remain the same, a risk-based focus has developed in more recent years. The basic assurance review takes an audit area and analyzes the system to determine whether risks to the business objectives are being adequately addressed by suitable controls. Practice Advisory 2100-1 brings home the importance of controls by suggesting:

> *Control is any action taken by management to enhance the likelihood that established objectives and goals will be achieved. Controls may be preventive (to deter undesirable events from occurring), detective (to detect and correct undesirable events which have occurred), or directive (to cause or encourage a desirable event to occur). The concept of* **a system of control** *is the integrated collection of control components and activities that are used by an organization to achieve its objectives and goals.*

The Systems Approach

It is the phrase *system of control* that provides a hint at the importance of adopting a systems viewpoint when assessing risk and controls during the audit process. The audit work based on reviewing systems of internal control in turn feeds into the corporate reporting system used for the board's published annual report on internal control. Having isolated an audit area, it is then viewed by the internal auditor as a system that has a basic objective, inputs, a process, and outputs. Using this framework, the auditor may assess risks to the objectives and appraise the measures used to mitigate or otherwise manage these risks. The systems-based approach concentrates on the high-level concept of the operation being audited, rather than simply checking transactions from the system as used to be the case in times past. Conceptualizing the system under review is an intellectual task that brings out the best from the auditor. It also requires a close liaison with the client to obtain and agree on a suitable understanding of the "system." For example, a payroll system may include links with:

- The personnel section
- The new starters' routine
- Verification of personal data
- Security measures for the database
- Operational procedures

- Deductions and tax accounting
- Overtime claims and other staff claiming systems
- Payments and bank transfers
- Staff budgets and coding
- Staff compensation returns
- And many other subsystems

It is important to assess the relative risk in each part of the overall system, and then focus on aspects that present the greatest inherent risks to the business. One version of a ten-point, risk-based systems approach is set out in Exhibit 3.1.

Each stage is briefly explained below (further details on audit fieldwork can be found in Chapter 5):

1. *Plan the engagement.* The audit assignment should be planned to establish the aim of the audit and scope of work to be performed, along with various practical matters concerning the audit team, timing, budgets, and so on.

2. *Ascertain systems objective.* The actual objectives of the system under review should be clarified and documented.

3. *Identify inherent risks.* There are risks that affect the achievement of system objectives, and these should be identified through analysis and discussion with the client management and their teams.

4. *Assess risks for impact and likelihood.* For the risks identified in stage three above, each one should be assessed for its potential impact on the business objectives and whether it is likely to occur. Significant risks (high impact/high likelihood) will become the focus of the audit.

Exhibit 3.1.   Ten-Point Risk-Based Approach

1. Plan engagement.
2. Ascertain systems objective.
3. Identify inherent risks.
4. Assess risks for impact and likelihood.
5. Evaluate current risk management and internal controls.
6. Isolate areas where internal controls are crucial.
7. Test for evidence of risk exposures due to control weakness.
8. Discuss and agree on action on internal controls.
9. Report results.
10. Follow up.

5. *Evaluate current risk management and internal controls.* Set against the risks that have been deemed significant if left unguarded, the current measures to address these risks should be reviewed.

6. *Isolate areas where internal controls are crucial.* The next stage involves determining where controls (and the wider risk management strategy) are fundamental to addressing key risks. Risks that are not adequately controlled, or where controls are excessive and/or redundant, should become apparent from the analysis at this stage of the audit.

7. *Test for evidence of risk exposures due to control weakness.* All material views on control adequacy should be confirmed through formal testing procedures applied to the controls (compliance tests) and performance (substantive tests) of the system.

8. *Discuss and come to an agreement regarding action on internal controls.* Suitable controls may be firmly in place but not applied by staff, or there may be gaps in the control regime that lead to unmitigated (or insufficient) levels of risk. Measures to remedy this situation should be discussed with the client and form the basis of an agreed action plan.

9. *Report results.* The results of the audit should be reported in draft to the client manager for comment and feedback before becoming a final report along with the agreed action plan. The results of all audits may be summarized and form part of a general report to the audit committee at its next meeting.

10. *Follow up.* After a suitable period, the agreed action plan should be considered by internal audit to determine whether it has been fully implemented by the client.

The risk-based systems approach brings a systematic and disciplined approach to the audit process and in so doing meets the requirements of the IIA standards. In assessing whether the controls in place make sense and work, reference may be had to the way the organization sets control standards. Where there are well-developed control standards in place, the auditor needs to check that they are working. Where these standards have not been well developed, the auditor may focus on helping management make progress in this respect.

For Further Discussion

What are the stages of risk-based systems auditing used in the audit shop, and how should each of the stages be applied to audit assurance work?

—— SECTION 3 ——
CONSULTING SERVICES

One service that has been provided by internal auditors for many years relates to consulting work. The typical internal audit shop tends to be staffed with people who have specialist skills in many important areas, including expertise in:

- Understanding how financial and operational systems fit together and contain core processes relating to inputs, process, and outputs.
- Ability to capture a system in a suitable documented format that illustrates key features.
- Understanding risk and how risks affect performance and relate to underlying root causes.
- Appreciation of control frameworks and corporate governance arrangements that help ensure business success.
- Knowledge of general control concepts such as authorization and specific control routines such as error tolerance levels set for individual business operations.
- Appreciation of compliance issues where regulations, laws, obligations, and policies provide an official direction, that may or may not be adhered to in practice.
- Experience at identifying and gathering evidence that is reliable and available, and used in conjunction with extensive access rights attaching to the audit activity.
- Ability to perform complicated projects that involve planning, fieldwork, and reporting.
- Expertise in special techniques such as interviewing, analyzing, appraising, examining, and assessing facts, data, and systems.
- Deep-rooted acceptance of the need for objectivity and sound judgment when performing review work.
- Ability to apply problem-solving techniques and develop responses that are workable, risk-based, and cost-effective.
- Ability to work within challenging environments where there may be some resistance to any required changes.

Because the above skills have been taken for granted, it is only over the last decade that the internal auditor has been seen as potentially an excellent internal consultant. The consulting role should be set in the context of corporate governance, risk management, and control that were described in Chapter 2. Moreover, consulting should be contrasted with the audit assurance role. Assurances tell the board, audit committee, and ultimately the general public that a business is being conducted properly, in line with published standards. Consulting, on the other hand, starts with the question, "How can we help you conduct your business?" and also deals with problems that are inevitable in any organization as it strives to meet its targets. Consulting work can range from brief and informal advice over the phone to a line manager, to involvement in a major project that runs across the organization. Chapter 2, Section 8, mentioned the assurance and consulting roles of internal audit. The IIA's definition of *consulting* is repeated here:

> *Advisory and related client service activities, the nature and scope of which are agreed upon with the client and which are intended to add value and improve an organization's operations. Examples include counsel, advice, facilitation, process design, and training.*

The consulting role of internal audit should be firmly located in the audit charter and made clear to clients within the organization who use this service, including the criteria for accepting formal consulting engagements. Practice Advisory 1000.C1-1 recognizes the links between assurance and consulting work and the fact that each may lead to the other. For example, an assurance review of a new process may report that there are significant risks that still need to be addressed by the management team. Meanwhile, the management team may ask the internal audit shop to help them set up the risk management system as part of a separate consulting exercise. The reverse situation, where a reportable concern comes from a consulting project, needs to be handled carefully, as it may appear to "blow the whistle" (for example, in respect of serious risk exposures) on the client management. To get around this point, the link between assurance and consulting should be made clear when agreeing to take on any such project. Any decisions made as a result of an audit consulting assignment should be made by management, and internal audit should not assume any managerial responsibilities, as it only has an advisory capacity. This point is made clear in the Practice Advisory, along with the need to apply a systematic approach to all types of audit work. One useful statement included in the Advisory for "resolving conflicts or evolving issues" runs along the following lines: "An internal auditor is first and foremost an internal auditor."

One basic model for performing formal consulting engagements is set out below:

1. *Entry.* Hold an initial contact meeting with the client to determine the problem and identify the matters that are uppermost on the minds of the client and stakeholders.

2. *Terms of reference.* Develop an agreed reference for the work and how the results will be reported. Practice Advisory 1000.C1-2 suggests: "As observed above, internal auditors should reach an understanding about the objectives and scope of the consulting engagement with those receiving

the service. Any reservations about the value, benefit, or possible negative implications of the consulting engagement should be communicated to those receiving the service. Internal auditors should design the scope of work to ensure that professionalism, integrity, credibility, and reputation of the internal audit activity will be maintained."

3. **Contract.** This formal document reflects the terms of reference and constitutes agreement on respective roles and responsibilities for all parties involved. It should also cover quality assurance arrangements to ensure the terms of reference are fully achieved. Where there are matters that audit feel should be addressed in terms of significant risk exposures but that have been left out of the assignment's scope, there are two courses of action suggested in Advisory 1000.C1-2:

- *Persuade management to include the additional objectives in the consulting engagement.*
  or
- *Document the fact that the objectives were not pursued and disclose that observation in the final communication of consulting engagement results; and include the objectives in a separate and subsequent assurance engagement.*

4. **Analysis.** Undertake an analysis that covers:

- Diagnosis of problems and possible solutions
- Planning for action based on consulted recommendations
- Implementation timetables setting out which managers are responsible for the implementation of selected solutions

Refer once more to Practice Advisory 1000.CI-2, which suggests:

The objectives, scope, and terms of the engagement should be periodically reassessed and adjusted during the course of the work.

5. **Release.** Release the auditor and client from the contract.

Consulting engagements are reported to the client commissioning the work, while assurance audits are reported to the responsible manager and the board (and/or audit committee). Only the overall results from consulting work will go to the audit committee. There are still standards to be observed in reporting consulting work, and where there have been limitations or restrictions in the work performed by the auditor, this fact should be recorded in the final report. Official guidance in the guise of Advisory 1000.C1-2 goes on to make clear that when consulting reports need to go further than the commissioning client, there are a number of steps that may be considered by the internal auditor, including:

- *First, determine what direction is provided in the agreement concerning the consulting engagement and related communications.*

- *Second, attempt to convince those receiving or requesting the service to expand voluntarily the communication to the appropriate parties.*
- *Third, determine what guidance is provided in the internal audit charter or audit activity's policies and procedures concerning consulting communications.*
- *Fourth, determine what guidance is provided in the organization's code of conduct, code of ethics, and other relative policies, administrative directives, or procedures.*
- *Fifth, determine what guidance is provided by The IIA's Standards and Code of Ethics, other standards or codes applicable to the auditor, and any legal or regulatory requirements that relate to the matter under consideration.*

Another point relevant to consulting work is that documentation standards need not be as rigid as that applied to assurance audits. Consulting work should not be confused with the assumption of management responsibilities for a particular operation, and IIA standards make it clear that this situation should be avoided wherever possible. Where the internal audit shop is responsible for an aspect of the business, say within the official duties of the CAE, there are steps that can be taken to manage this unfortunate situation, as suggested by Practice Advisory 1130.A1-2:

- *Impairment to independence and objectivity are* [sic] *required to be disclosed to appropriate parties, and the nature of the disclosure depends upon the impairment.*
- *Objectivity is presumed to be impaired if an auditor provides assurance services for an activity for which the auditor had responsibility within the previous year.*
- *If on occasion management directs internal auditors to perform non-audit work, it should be understood that they are not functioning as internal auditors.*
- *Expectations of stakeholders, including regulatory or legal requirements, should be evaluated and assessed in relation to the potential impairment.*
- *Assessment—The results of the assessment should be discussed with management, the Audit Committee, and/or other appropriate stakeholders. A determination should be made regarding a number of issues, some of which effect* [sic] *one another:*
  - *The significance of the operational function to the organization (in terms of revenue, expenses, reputation, and influence) should be evaluated.*
  - *The length or duration of the assignment and scope of responsibility should be evaluated.*

○ *Adequacy of separation of duties should be evaluated.*

○ *The potential impairment to objectivity or independence or the appearance of such impairment should be considered when reporting audit results.*

• *Audit of the Function and Disclosure—Given that the internal audit activity has operational responsibilities and that operation is part of the audit plan, there are several avenues for the auditor to consider:*

(a) *The audit may be performed by a contracted, third party entity, by external auditors, or by the internal audit function. In the first two situations, impairment of objectivity is minimized by the use of auditors outside of the organization. In the latter case, objectivity would be impaired.*

(b) *Individual auditors with operational responsibility should not participate in the audit of the operation. If possible, auditors conducting the assessment should be supervised by, and report the results of the assessment to those whose independence or objectivity is not impaired.*

(c) *Disclosure should be made regarding the operational responsibilities of the auditor for the function, the significance of the operation to the organization (in terms of revenue, expenses, or other pertinent information) and the relationship of those who audited the function to the auditor.*

(d) *Disclosure of the auditor's operational responsibilities should be made in the related audit report and in the auditor's standard communication to the Audit Committee or other governing body.*

There are formal engagements and other aspects of audit work that fall under the definition of consulting work. The facilitated control and risk self-assessment workshops and internal control awareness seminars that are now popular in many organizations may be led by internal audit under the consulting banner. Helping managers formulate their risk management strategy and internal control reporting systems may be legitimate audit tasks outside the more traditional assurance role. Assurance adds value to the organization's ability to inspire confidence in their stakeholders. Consulting work, on the other hand, enables internal auditors to apply their unique skills and experience to add value to the business. But each consulting engagement must be performed with due professional care, and Attribute Standard 1220.C1 sees this involving a consideration of the:

• *Needs and expectations of clients, including the nature, timing, and communication of engagement results.*

- *Relative complexity and extent of work needed to achieve the engagement's objectives.*
- *Cost of the consulting engagement in relation to potential benefits.*

It is only after a careful assessment of costs and benefits that formal consulting projects should be resourced and carried out.

For Further Discussion

How are formal consulting engagements performed by internal audit, and how are these different from assurance audits?

—— SECTION 4 ——

COMPLIANCE

Compliance is an interesting concept for the internal auditor. It is defined by the IIA as:

> *The ability to reasonably ensure conformity and adherence to organization policies, plans, procedures, laws, regulations, and contracts.*

The IIA Attribute Standard 1220.A1 states that the internal auditor should exercise due professional care by considering the:

- *Extent of work needed to achieve the engagement's objectives.*
- *Relative complexity, materiality, or significance of matters to which assurance procedures are applied.*
- *Adequacy and effectiveness of risk management, control, and governance processes.*
- *Probability of significant errors, irregularities, or **noncompliance*** (emphasis added).
- *Cost of assurance in relation to potential benefits.*

It is clear that compliance (or the absence of) is a key feature in the scope of internal auditing, and is also an important component of the corporate governance process. When plotting the development of internal auditing over the years, many commentators feel that the profession has moved on from basic compliance checking, to corporate-level assurance and consulting. This quantum leap is explained as a move toward risk-based auditing against the background of improving the governance process in corporate and government organizations. Unfortunately, this is a too simplistic view, as there are many complicated factors that impact the compliance debate. Some of the key issues relating to corporate compliance incorporate the following points listed below.

Compliance-Based Internal Auditing

Many internal audit shops are located on the compliance agenda, where their main role is to perform or review the compliance process. Banks and insurance and investment companies operate in highly regulated environments, and these organizations recognize that breach of rules, solvency provisions, regulations, laws, directives, and policies are seen as major risks to their business. Retail organizations will fund change programs, joint ventures, market shifts, and strategic performance reviews, but their main concern is to ensure all local operations (e.g., stores) operate in line with set standards and procedures. Compliance with relevant standards is key to success in these types of enterprises. Likewise the internal audit coverage may concentrate on compliance routines and perform some of the compliance work itself as a way of adding value to the business.

Compliance Programs

Many organizations have a separate compliance function that covers key areas relating to, for example, environmental regulations, corporate disclosures, and health and safety matters in conjunction with a special compliance audit program. Most industries have specific federal and state laws and regulations that relate to its products, practices, and complaints. These compliance review teams check on working practices, incentives to encourage compliance, and the kind of help and advice that may be provided in difficult areas and they may provide sanctions where there are ongoing problems. The rigorous SEC accounting, disclosure, and filing requirements add a new dimension to this effort, where compliance and review teams are being set up to ensure all corporate returns are properly prepared and filed and that no legal exposures result from late, wrong, or inappropriate documentation. In this environment, the internal auditor will see the compliance effort as part of the audit universe and will review the arrangements and, under the consulting role, may help ensure they are put in place where necessary. A visit from external regulatory inspectors will tend to start with the question, "What does your compliance program look like, and how effective is it?" This matter is so important that the IIA has issued a Practice Advisory 2100-5 (Legal Considerations in Evaluating Regulatory Compliance Programs), which may be used in conjunction with legal counsel when considering the corporate compliance program and which is summarized below:

- The organization should establish compliance standards and procedures and a written user-friendly code of conduct.

- Roles and responsibilities in respect of the compliance program should be firmly established at the board level and below. A specific individual should oversee the compliance program using high-level personnel and involvement from the CEO. The program may also be operated at a business-unit level.

- Reward systems should not encourage unethical behavior. For example, in one vehicle-recovering company, bonuses and targets were set for each team to sell new batteries to people whose vehicle had been rescued. The result was that many recovery teams adopted a widespread practice of informing drivers that their car batteries needed to be replaced, when in truth they were perfectly capable of being recharged.

- Global compliance programs should reflect local laws and regulations.

- Staff recruitment practices should involve an appropriate system of staff screening.

- Standards and procedures should be properly communicated to staff in a practical and high-impact manner (e.g., interactive workshops). Ongoing communication (e.g., via the intranet) with employees and agents should be a feature of the program. An annual return to the board should be made on this process.

- All reasonable steps should be taken to achieve compliance with standards, including a suitably designed and protected hotline where staff can notify internal audit regarding problems. Ethics questionnaires returned by staff is another useful assessment tool.

- The compliance program should have a direct link into the staff disciplinary procedures, where appropriate sanctions may result from activities that involve noncompliance with standards. Offenses should result in steps to deal with the offender and to improve the compliance program.

The Advisory goes on to suggest that internal audit should spend some time reviewing compliance programs, and, in conjunction with views from employees, should seek to improve the arrangements where possible. The position set by the IIA guidance promotes a useful interpretation of the audit role, where rather than perform compliance programs en masse, internal audit review the corporate arrangements in place to achieve effective compliance.

Compliance Testing

The systems-based approach that has already been referred to is based on assessing the overall system of risk management in place and reviewing the adequacy of specific controls that support risk mitigation. As part of this process, audit will need to form a view on the extent to which key controls are working in practice. If a site is deemed high risk in terms of the need to provide twenty-four-hour guarded protection, then a suitable arrangement may have been designed and implemented. Any audit of physical security will probably include some testing of the twenty-four-hour protection and whether this is actually happening. If, on visiting the building at night, the auditor finds that security staff have left the site unattended to spend the night at a local hotel bar, the control has been circumvented. In other words, there is noncompliance, leaving a hole in the official risk management strategy. In another example, if a government agency is required to establish a whistleblowing hotline as part of state regulations, this control is designed to mitigate the risk of ongoing inappropriate behavior (e.g., abuse of facilities) that is not being reported. An audit of the hotline system may find that staff are not told about the facility, and those staff who make tentative inquiries are told by senior management that any use of this hotline would mean their careers are dead (or worse). The hotline, in this instance, will not act in the manner originally intended, and as a control over the risks of abuse, it is a failure. Compliance is an important issue in any system of internal control, and a good internal auditor will want to explore the reasons why compliance is poor and link this to the overall control environment. A culture of noncompliance undermines the corporate control framework and should be reported to the board and audit committee. There is no reason why the ten-point systems-based approach cannot be applied to an audit of compliance within an organization. Working through the ten-point approach, we would simply concentrate on the compliance program as the main internal control over the risk of noncompliance.

> ### For Further Discussion
> *How is compliance viewed in the audit shop in terms of building this factor into the audit process?*

—— SECTION 5 ——
FRAUD AND ABUSE

The IIA Attribute Standard 1220.A1, mentioned in Section 4 above, includes the following line in terms of what should be considered when performing internal audits with due professional care:

*Probability of significant errors, **irregularities**, or noncompliance.*

We are concerned here with irregularity, which in serious cases involves fraud, as this matter also concerns the internal auditor. *Fraud* is defined by the IIA as:

> *Any illegal acts characterized by deceit, concealment or violation of trust. These acts are not dependent upon the application of threats of violence or physical force. Frauds are perpetrated by individuals, and organizations to obtain money, property or services; to avoid payment or loss of services; or to secure personal or business advantage.*

Fraud can be against the organization, such as an embezzlement by a senior manager. Or it can be perpetrated to benefit the organization, such as paying a bribe to win a contract or a tax fraud scheme. Many of the scandals that have occurred over recent years relate to corporate fraud, and many of the provisions regulating business, commerce, and government agencies are aimed at tackling fraud and abuse. The Association of Certified Fraud Examiners' Report to the Nation has estimated employee fraud in 2002 as involving up to $600 billion, an increase over previous years. The survey goes on to suggest that around 80 percent of frauds involve asset misappropriation, including cash, which accounted for 90 percent of this figure. They remarked that financial misstatement was the most damaging type of fraud for companies, and this is borne out by the problems found at Enron and WorldCom. Fraud is big business, and there are many specialist legal firms and forensic investigators who are able to provide expert services on request. An employee fraud affects a business and if not identified, investigated, and put right may damage the reputation of an organization, whether public- or private-sector based. There is also legal culpability where an organization has failed to establish suitable measures to manage the risk of fraud among their staff, agents, and associates. The question of roles and responsibilities has been a vexing issue for many years and particularly affects the external auditor, who may face lawsuits if a material internal fraud has been allowed to continue unnoticed in an organization. Likewise, the internal auditor must face up to the issue of role definition in respect of fraud, abuse, and irregularity, and ensure that this role is fully understood by senior management. We can start with the viewpoint that the internal auditor is not a specialist fraud investigator, and IIA Standard 1210.A2 makes this clear by saying:

> *The internal auditor should have sufficient knowledge to identify the indicators of fraud but is not expected to have the expertise of a person whose primary responsibility is detecting and investigating fraud.*

But at the same time, the internal auditor does fit into the fraud prevention, detection, and investigation jigsaw, as does everyone else who works for or is associated with the organization. Help is available through Practice Advisory

1210.A2-2, which provides some direction on defining internal audit's responsibilities. Management is responsible for detecting fraud, and it is one of those risks to the business that should be managed through effective risk management and controls. If there are inadequate controls that guard against the possibility of fraud, the organization is vulnerable to attack and there is likely to be an actual or attempted fraud. Advisory 1210.A2-2 highlights audit's advisory role with the following words:

> *The objective of internal auditing in fraud detection is to assist members of the organization in the effective discharge of their responsibilities by furnishing them with analyses, appraisals, recommendations, counsel, and information concerning the activities reviewed.*

We have mentioned Standard 1220, which requires the auditor to keep an eye open for the possibility of fraud, and whether further investigation needs to be commissioned in the event of suspicions. The systems approach we mentioned earlier argues that if the system is sound, it will achieve its objectives, and efforts to develop good controls over the system will promote a successful business. Audit effort on the systems in place that mitigate the risk of fraud is supported by Practices Advisory 1210.A2-1, which suggests the following audit coverage in assessing this system:

- *The organizational environment fosters control consciousness.*
- *Realistic organizational goals and objectives are set.*
- *Written policies (e.g., code of conduct) exist that describe prohibited activities and the action required whenever violations are discovered.*
- *Appropriate authorization policies for transactions are established and maintained.*
- *Policies, practices, procedures, reports, and other mechanisms are developed to monitor activities and safeguard assets, particularly in high-risk areas.*
- *Communication channels provide management with adequate and reliable information.*
- *Recommendations need to be made for the establishment or enhancement of cost-effective controls to help deter fraud.*

The internal auditor should understand the factors that may suggest there is a fraud happening in the organization and be prepared to extend the audit testing to probe weakness in the system of control that may lead to fraud. If, for example, authorization procedures are poor and a knowledgeable person could obtain goods from a vendor for personal use, this weakness should be explored to find out whether this may have happened or may still be happening. In other words, although the internal auditor's primary responsibility is not that of fraud detection, the auditor should still be alert to the possibility of fraud. If during an audit the internal auditor suspects there is something suspicious, the appropriate persons should be notified.

Ideally, the corporate fraud policy should define roles and responsibilities and should also refer to a fraud response plan that applies when there is a suspicion of wrongdoing. The Practice Advisory argues that many parties have a role in dealing with a reported allegation of fraud, including internal auditors, lawyers, investigators, security personnel, and internal or external specialists. The IIA advisories recognize that some internal audit shops undertake formal investigations into fraud in their organizations, and there is guidance on the process of accumulating evidence and reporting the results of such an investigation. If internal audit carry out fraud investigation in conjunction with the appointed attorney, even though each fraud is unique, it is nonetheless possible to document a basic staged approach to this task, as shown in Exhibit 3.2.

Each stage is briefly explained:

1. *Allegation.* This is where the fraud or attempted fraud comes to light through audit tests, a whistleblower's hotline, internal control reports, unusual losses, manager suspicions, or other means. The fraud response plan should give guidance on dealing with allegations and suspicions. The board, counsel, and public relations should be informed of the allegation at an early stage.

2. *Background research.* This stage involves working out whether the allegation warrants further consideration and if so, the outline shape and form of such work.

Exhibit 3.2. Fraud Investigation Process

1. Allegation
2. Background research
3. Preliminary report
4. Investigation plan
5. Support
6. Definition of barriers
7. Strategy
8. Full investigation
9. Interim reports
10. Witness statements
11. Suspect interview
12. Final report
13. Action
14. Review

3. **Preliminary report.** All parties set out in the fraud response plan should be notified of a possible fraud, and the report should seek authorization for an investigation if required.

4. **Investigation plan.** The plan will define resources, initial approach, assigned attorney reporting lines, and lead officer.

5. **Support.** Support from the CEO, board, and company attorney should be secured at an early stage in the assignment.

6. **Definition of barriers.** It is a good idea to work through any sensitivities and potential problems, including legal restrictions in obtaining the evidence required for the investigation.

7. **Strategy.** The investigation team need to get together and decide exactly how they will proceed with their inquiries via a formal strategy for the investigation. The internal audit resource (if they are given the job) would need to reflect the experience and expertise required to deal with the alleged fraud. It is important to identify suspects and possible conspirators at an early stage, and whether any evidence (including witnesses) may be at risk.

8. **Full investigation.** This is mainly about gathering sufficient and reliable evidence to support the allegation and indicate a suspect, in an admissible and cost-effective manner. The chain of custody and preservation of evidence are important matters to consider during the investigation.

9. **Interim reports.** These should appear at intervals during the investigation either at set periods, on request from executives (or law enforcement agencies), when there are developments to report, or when board authorizations are needed for further inquiries.

10. **Witness statements.** These should be gathered throughout the investigation, along with an indication of the reliability of each witness.

11. **Suspect interview.** Where there is enough evidence to present to the main suspect, this should be done, taking legal advice and ensuring the local police are kept informed. The individual's legal rights should be observed at all times.

12. **Final report.** This document may be presented to external parties and should be prepared with care under the direction of the company attorney.

13. **Action.** The investigation should lead to establishing the fraud and extent of losses, charging the suspect for the defined offenses (and disciplining the suspect if an employee), determining a damage limitation strategy in recovering losses and repairing the corporate reputation, and strengthening controls to ensure a similar problem does not arise in future.

14. **Review.** This should involve ensuring all necessary action has been taken and that the investigation was carried out to quality standards, and improved controls have been properly implemented.

The above represents a brief introduction to the complex topic of fraud and forensic investigations. For newly appointed auditors, the best approach would be to talk to the audit manager if they come across anything suspicious.

> ### For Further Discussion
> *What fraud work has been performed in the past by internal audit, and what is the agreed audit role with respect to fraud detection?*

—— SECTION 6 ——
INFORMATION SYSTEMS

There are internal auditors who specialize in reviewing information systems and the technical aspects of information technology that drives all progressive organizations. In fact, the IIA recognizes the need to consider information systems (IS) issues as part of the overall audit process. Draft Implementation Standard 1210.A3 makes this point clear by saying:

> *Internal auditors should have general knowledge of key information technology risks and controls and available technology-based audit techniques. However, not all internal auditors are expected to have the expertise of an internal auditor whose primary responsibility is information technology auditing.*

A good understanding of computer systems and the additional risks that come with automated processing is part of the internal auditors' skills base. Specialist and more advanced expertise relating to network security, Internet technology, database management, operating systems, and other technology that supports the development of e-business may be expected from the specialist IS auditor. Most business processes are supported by a networked information system that will use as much advanced technology as necessary to ensure the efficient and effective processing of data and the production of useful information. Specialist IS auditors should have a good understanding of at least the following matters:

- Applications risk and associated input, process, and output controls
- IS design
- Project management

- Information technology (IT) security, including Internet security, virus control, and firewalls
- Network design and support technology
- Database management
- Operating systems
- Data privacy rights and regulations
- Automated document management
- End-user computing
- Outsourced IT facilities
- IS/IT strategies
- Software piracy
- Program control procedures
- Data interrogation using specialist software

The problem is that general auditors should also have some understanding of these matters, albeit to a lesser extent. Whenever an auditor is reviewing an operation, there needs to be a consideration of whether the information processed and used to manage this operation makes sense, is secure, and serves the needs of the business. To do this, the auditor needs to get inside the system and extract data to judge whether the information passes the above-mentioned tests. Information is at risk if it is not properly protected, and effective information security is the main response to these risks. The IIA has prepared guidance on IS security in the guise of Practice Advisory 2100-2, which in summary suggests that internal audit should:

- Have access to (or possess) sufficient competence to evaluate information security.
- Ensure that the board and audit committee should be appraised of IS breaches and possible threats by management and given information on corrective measures.
- Assess the effectiveness of IS risk mitigation.
- Periodically assess the IS practices and issue assurance reports to the board and audit committee.

The Advisory goes on to accept that the auditor can conduct specific reviews of IS security across the organization and look at risks and the way that these risks are being managed. Conversely, the auditor may consider IS security arrangements as a component of many of the audits that are carried out during the year. Again, assurances can be provided as to whether IS security is working well in pockets of the organization, and as a general policy throughout the business units and support services.

The ten-stage risk-based approach shown earlier in Exhibit 3.1 on page 72 can be adapted to relate to audits of information systems. Below we explain each stage in the context of IS auditing. (Note that further detail on audit fieldwork can be found in Chapter 6):

1. **Engagement planning.** Define the information system and process owner and work out the extent to which IS expertise is required on the audit.

2. **Ascertain systems objective.** Determine the system aim and interfaces with other systems. The information should be secure, complete, accurate, timely, not irregular, meaningful, and not excessive for the purpose.

3. **Identify inherent risks.** Materiality levels may be set at to what is acceptable in terms of data processing and what falls outside these limits. Assess the extent to which the risks to the information impacts the ability to meet business goals.

4. **Assess risks for impact and likelihood.** Risks should be prioritized in terms of how long the business could continue and thrive without the information system in question, and to what extent fraud, abuse, and error are mitigated.

5. **Evaluate current risk management and internal controls.** Assess the extent to which input, process, and output controls ensure the integrity of the information.

6. **Isolate areas where internal controls are crucial.** Determine key aspects of the information system that need to be controlled to ensure the system meets its objectives.

7. **Test for evidence of risk exposures due to control weakness.** Extract and download a representative sample of data to perform interrogations to assess the integrity of the data. Determine whether key controls such as access restrictions, verification routines, data encryption, duplicate transaction checks, file control totals, exception reports, and so on are applied in an appropriate manner. Accessibility of data (in terms of auditor rights and practical considerations) and use of specialist IS interrogation software such as IDEA and ACL are important considerations here.

8. **Discuss and agree on action on internal controls.** Check with the process owner to ensure that improvements are feasible, and involve security staff in wider issues relating to systems protection, backup, and contingency plans.

9. **Report results.** Report results to the manager and IS support staff to ensure all key players are involved. Some controls relate to the application under review, say a new performance measurement information

system, while there are other controls that apply to information systems generally. These are known as general controls (in contrast to application controls) and relate to the environment for developing and running the various applications. Project management, program change control, IT staff support, contingency planning arrangements, IT security, and so on all contribute to the overall IS control environment.

10. *Follow up.* Follow-up may involve further examination of extracted data downloads.

Information Systems Consulting Work

A further issue that confronts the IS auditor relates to the consulting and assurance roles. Experienced IS auditors can make a huge impact on solving IS problems where systems are being set up, or a newly merged business needs to be assimilated into the existing facilities, or a joint venture has to be reported in integrated published statements. When the IS auditor is involved in detailed non-audit work, this person is not able to audit and provide assurances on these same areas of the business. Arrangements need to be in place to avoid a conflict of interest and to ensure that all interested parties, such as the audit committee, are aware of the situation. Independent assurances on information systems contribute to the IT governance of an organization, which in turn is part of the overall corporate governance arrangements.

Information That Supports Control

Note that efficient and reliable information systems across the organization are also an important part of control frameworks such as that developed by COSO. There is a view that no application will be reliable if there is a poor IS environment in place, much as COSO suggests that no system of control will work alongside a poor control environment, where people in an organization do not care about ethical standards and quality performance. The internal auditor will be concerned that the IS system supports the business that it relates to and that raw data becomes information which then becomes knowledge for the business.

When operational managers are involved in developing the IS and understand the importance of security arrangements and IS controls, there is a better chance of success. As such, the IS auditor needs also to understand the business that the information serves, to make a real value-add contribution during the audit. This is why many audit shops ensure a close working relationship between the general auditors and specialist IS auditors. Moreover, manual controls are just as important as automated controls when considering an information system.

An automatically generated exception report has little impact if the reader does not intervene to respond to the matter highlighted by the report. But if the auditor fails to explore the computer program that causes the exception to be reported and cannot verify whether this control is working, the audit will be substandard.

One further point to note when reviewing information systems is that many IT support facilities are outsourced, and this can cause practical problems in assessing automated controls over the system. The internal auditor need not be an IT expert but will need sufficient expertise to ensure any audit that is performed takes on board the risks attaching to the information processed, maintained, and used by the business under review. The future of many business and government concerns lies in Web site–based interfaces, and the auditor will have to keep up with or ideally be ahead of the game to ensure the internal audit service remains effective and worthwhile.

For Further Discussion

What kinds of work does the IS auditor get involved in, and how does the IS auditor interface with field auditors?

SECTION 7

CSA WORKSHOPS

Control self-assessment (CSA—some call this CRSA, for control risk self-assessment) has been variously described as an audit approach, a management tool, and a general technique that can be used by anyone who can see a benefit from applying it. CSA is simply the process of getting people together to assess risks and work out how best to control those risks that need to be addressed. CSA is an extremely useful concept because:

- It gets people together to discuss ways of improving the work area.
- It is based around the team objectives and so links the discussion into actual aims of the team or group.
- It encourages a shared understanding of risk and control issues and is therefore a good development tool.
- It supports the development of a sound system for managing risk.
- It promotes bottom-down communication (through risk policies), upward communication (results of the CSA events), and sideways communication (through team discussion and consistency across the teams and business units).

- It provides a way of gathering information to inform the board about the state of controls and that they have been reviewed.

- It encourages better performance by ensuring significant risks to achievements are addressed.

- It encourages compliance with regulations that call for effective risk management and sound internal controls.

The CSA approach tends to involve work teams getting together in a workshop to make their way through a process that may appear as shown in Exhibit 3.3.

Stages 1 through 9 shown in Exhibit 3.3 may be facilitated by a suitable person and the results captured on a reporting system that feeds into the overall information on the state of the organization's system of internal control. The auditors at Gulf Canada who developed the CSA technique have seen many versions and interpretations of their original ideas, as each version will suit the organization, section, or team in question. The ideals and perceptions inspired by the CSA concept come close to the aspirations of many internal auditors whose role revolves around reviewing risk and controls. Many managers, associates, and work teams have turned to the internal auditor for help in setting up CSA, as they realize the auditor tends to have a real understanding of control frameworks, risk assessment, and detailed control mechanisms.

At the same time, the consulting role of internal audit allows the auditor to step outside the review role and disclose the secrets of establishing good risk management practices, how to assess controls, and how to test for compliance. This has breathed life into many an auditor who has found a new role as friend and advisor to audit "clients" rather than being seen as an outside verifier by the

Exhibit 3.3.   CSA Approach

1. Design and introduce the CSA concept.
2. Identify their objectives.
3. Discuss key issues and plans.
4. Identify risks that impact the ability to achieve their objectives.
5. Work out which risks need to be addressed.
6. Consider current arrangements for addressing key risks.
7. Determine what needs to be built into the current strategy to ensure risks may be properly managed.
8. Consider the extent to which new measures give the team a better chance of achieving their objectives.
9. Report the results and action plans in a meaningful manner.

"auditee." Meanwhile, there are others who argue that too much involvement in setting up CSA programs stops the auditor from objectively reviewing this "management process," as it is not possible to objectively assess a system developed by the assessor. Practice Advisory 2100-3 makes clear the audit role in the risk management process:

> *Risk management is a key responsibility of management. To achieve its business objectives, management should ensure that sound risk management processes are in place and functioning. Boards and audit committees have an oversight role to determine that appropriate risk management processes are in place and that these processes are adequate and effective. Internal auditors should assist both management and the audit committee by examining, evaluating, reporting, and recommending improvements on the adequacy and effectiveness of management's risk processes. Management and the board are responsible for their organization's risk management and control processes. However, internal auditors acting in a consulting role can assist the organization in identifying, evaluating, and implementing risk management methodologies and controls to address those risks.*

The internal auditor then has several possible roles in reporting on the risk management process and whether it is working well, and perhaps helping management get the risk management process up and running. The balance and format of these roles should be noted in the audit charter and is determined by executive management, the CAE, and the audit committee. The Practice Advisory goes on to describe this balance in terms of a continuum that ranges from:

- *No role.*
  to
- *Auditing the risk management process as part of the internal audit plan, to active, continuous support and involvement in the risk management process such as participation on oversight committees, monitoring activities, and status reporting.*
  to
- *Managing and coordinating the risk management process.*

The actual role will depend on many factors, and where an organization has not gotten far with establishing risk management, Practice Advisory 2100-4 suggests that internal audit encourage management to get started. In this scenario, internal auditors may offer proactive help in the task so long as they do not assume *ownership of risks*. The assurance role is redundant where there is nothing much to report on, and the fact that the auditor is acting as risk management consultant should be appropriately disclosed. The general stages for CSA workshops mentioned earlier and shown in Exhibit 3.3 are briefly explained below:

1. *Design and introduce the CSA concept.* The workshops will not work if people in the organization do not know about them, or can see no benefit from getting involved. Launch seminars and pre-event checklists may be useful in stimulating interest. The workshop aims should be made clear at the outset. If there is a nonblame culture in the organization (or section), it may be an idea to open the events with a keynote message from one of the senior executives.

2. *Identify their objectives.* Discussions with the team leader, process owner, or project manager can make clear the formal objectives of the work team. Determine whether the CSA policy is to include or exclude the process manager. It is possible to gauge the extent to which the team understand and support the set work objectives. Make it clear that CSA is about having a better chance of being successful and not just another set of boxes to tick for the executives. Workshop numbers may range from twelve to eighteen, if possible.

3. *Discuss key issues and plans.* Issues such as change programs, performance measures, decision-making style, strategies developed by senior management, a history of failed initiatives, and so on all help open discussions on operational risk. These issues should be brought out from the team and noted. The corporate risk policy should be explained at some stage and a note made as to where CSA fits in.

4. *Identify risks that impact the ability to achieve their objectives.* Most workshops build on stage 3 and involve brainstorming risks (or whatever equivalent format) using visual techniques for getting full contributions from the group. The results should be captured and presented back to the group.

5. *Work out which risks need to be addressed.* This stage involves categorizing those risks that fit together and then getting the group to arrive at a rating of the potential impact, and the likelihood of its happening, for each risk identified in stage 4. Some workshops use an electronic voting system such as OptionFinder to ensure anonymity and visual effect.

6. *Consider current arrangements for addressing key risks.* Arrangements for addressing risks mainly relate to defining suitable controls. At this stage, it may be an idea to describe the control framework adopted by the organization and the way internal control is defined along with a few simple examples. The need to form a statement on internal control should have been mentioned earlier. The group should weigh up the controls that

are in place and whether they are working as well as expected and perhaps ways that they could be further checked.

7. *Determine what needs to be built into the current strategy to ensure risks may be properly managed.* The current control arrangements may be weighed against the risk assessment that has been carried out. The group can arrive at a view on what needs to be done to existing controls and additional measures to address outstanding risks.

8. *Consider the extent to which new measures give the team a better chance of achieving their objectives.* At this stage the objectives may be revisited, to consider how the current strategy can be updated to take on board the measures and plans that result from the workshop. This should result in a suitable action plan built into the current planning and performance mechanisms used by the team. The process manager may be involved in this stage, if excluded from earlier stages of the workshop.

9. *Report the results and action plans in a meaningful manner.* The above should be recorded (some workshops employ a scribe to record the outputs on a PC). The information should really be assimilated into the system for reporting on internal controls, the planning system, and the performance measurement system. The targets from the agreed action plan should be followed up and reviewed as part of the usual planning and review process used in the organization. Excessive use of new reporting systems may be seen by staff as just another layer of bureaucracy.

CSA is based on promoting a better awareness of risk, defining responsibility for dealing with unacceptable levels of risk, and being able to report the resulting action to interested parties. Many organizations do much the same in a fragmented and informal manner, but CSA provides a systematic and transparent mechanism for formalizing this task, and also provides a record (e.g., the risk register) that may be independently examined. It is an ideal tool for managers as they start to appreciate their responsibilities for designing and implementing internal controls that help manage excessive risk. It provides a self-audit process that in turn may complement the internal audit process. Note that the IIA has developed a certification program for CSA practitioners that can be viewed on its Web site, *www.theiia.org.*

For Further Discussion

What experience does internal audit have with CSA, and what makes for a good facilitator where CSA workshops are in use?

—— SECTION 8 ——

DEVELOPING AN INTEGRATED APPROACH

We have touched on some of the approaches to internal audit work and briefly described how each approach may be carried out. When starting in a new internal audit shop, the appointee may be tempted to ask, "What approach do you take to your audit work?" In the past, a one-line answer would have sufficed. This may be that a compliance approach is assumed, or that we review risk and controls in various systems across the organization, or we concentrate on information systems and security arrangements. Other audit shops get involved in detailed fraud investigations and perform detection routines to isolate any abuse that may not be obvious. However, we are now moving toward a "blended approach" to internal auditing where, equipped with a wide range of available approaches and tools, internal auditors may simply apply the most appropriate mix of such tools to the work at hand. To explore this idea, we need to reconsider the nature of internal auditing work that was referred to at the start of the chapter in Practice Advisory 2100-1:

> *All business systems, processes, operations, functions, and activities within the organization are subject to the internal auditors' evaluations. The comprehensive scope of work of internal auditing should provide reasonable assurance that management's:*
>
> - *Risk management system is effective.*
> - *System of internal control is effective and efficient.*
>
> *Governance process is effective by establishing and preserving values, setting goals, monitoring activities and performance, and defining the measures of accountability.*

The idea is to achieve the above in the best way possible, with the most efficient use of the audit resource. Moreover, for sound risk management and controls to be in place, there needs to be compliance with procedures, reliable information and financial reporting systems, good antifraud measures, and a reasonable assurance that corporate and business objectives will be achieved. Risk-based systems work involves reviewing these matters and ensuring the system comes together to protect the organization, drive it forward, and deliver sound public reports. Compliance reviews can be used to check that what should be happening is actually happening, as part of systems auditing or as a special program directed at high-risk areas. Fraud work is useful in searching out irregularity, and keeping an eye out for red flags, as well as investigating problems in conjunction with specialists. IS audits are crucial to the new business context where an information strategy can mean the difference between success and complete failure.

Meanwhile, CSA and consulting projects shift the audit process into pure value-add services, where internal auditors apply their expertise in helping the business succeed. Together this vast armory of approaches, tools, and techniques can be applied by the auditor in the most appropriate way. When asked about the audit approach adopted by the audit shop, one useful response may be: "It all depends on what is needed in the area in question." For example, some simple criteria to help make this decision may run along these lines:

1. *Are there clear operational standards in place that have been recently reviewed and updated for a highly regulated local operation?* Here the auditor may be concerned about the arrangements for ensuring compliance with the set procedures, and audit the compliance system. Some compliance testing may be undertaken to check that the compliance and supervision routines are actually working in practice.

2. *Is there a highly developed risk management system in place that results in the design of robust controls to address risks that are assessed on an ongoing basis?* In this environment, the auditor may wish to verify the risk management arrangements and help the process managers make improvement where possible. Most of the audit drive may be assurance based, where a clear view may be provided on whether the risk management setup is working well to improve the business and provides reliable reports on the state of internal controls.

3. *Are there known problems regarding regularity in an operation such as cashiers, inventory management, and payments where attractive portable items may be at risk?* Here the auditor may focus on anti-fraud strategies and employ fraud detection routines to make sure there are no actual frauds or abuse happening.

4. *Is the operation based around key information systems and new IS projects?* This may call for the internal auditor to employ IS audit approaches and techniques to test the integrity of the information inputs, processing, and outputs, along with IT security reviews. Meanwhile, the auditor may wish to get involved with some of the more significant IS projects with a view to advising on risk assessment within the project, and risk and control issues relating to the new or enhanced application being developed.

5. *Is the operation undergoing any major changes, such as a merger or de-merger that are causing numerous problems to the business managers?* A fast-moving change strategy may lead internal audit to focus on consulting input to help the management team implement their strategy and get the business on track. The auditor may carry out short reviews of aspects of the change strategy, provide advice on planned changes to the control routines, and help management stay in line with corporate policies and external regulations.

6. *Does the operation have a history of a poor control culture?* One audit service that is becoming increasingly popular is the provision of risk and control awareness workshops and seminars. There is a view that good controls cannot be developed where managers, supervisor, and staff have no real understanding of risk and control concepts. Seminars and learning events can be used to promote the organization's control and self-assessment programs and can be delivered by internal auditors under their consulting arm.

7. *Is there a need for CSA workshops to be developed and run?* Internal audit staff may initiate the CSA program and facilitate the first few workshops, or develop a small team from the operational area so that they might facilitate workshops in their area of work. Again, this role would be provided under the consulting services of internal audit.

8. *Do the board, audit committee, or individual executives have particular concerns about parts of the organization that mean they seek targeted assurances from internal audit?* The pure assurance role tends to involve the systems approach we mentioned above, where the auditor will ascertain the system under review, assess the inherent risks and controls put in place, and then test these controls, as well as aspects of the business where there is poor control. The audit report will be an objective representation of the work carried out and recommendation made. Alternatively, the board or audit committee may ask internal audit to carry out a special investigation into an area where there are concerns, and this work will take these concerns and examine the extent to which they can be verified, determine the underlying causes, and suggest appropriate actions in light of the findings. These suggestions will relate to improving systems, solving problems, and may involve considering action against any persons who have failed to discharge their responsibilities properly.

9. *Is there a request from a business unit manager for help from internal audit?* Where the business manager wants help that requires the skills that audit possesses, the resulting consulting project will be based on the terms of reference agreed with the client and may follow the approach we mentioned when discussing formal consultancy engagements.

10. *What would provide the best value add for the organization and its management?*

The list could go on and on. In fact, it is not as simple as this, as within an individual audit it may be possible to employ the "blended approach" to internal auditing by using a mix of styles and techniques. For example, the auditor may start the engagement by talking to the client about any specific concerns the client may have and try to build the provision of ongoing advice and assistance into the terms of reference for the assignment. When working through the system objectives, risks, and required controls, the auditor may convene a workshop with representatives from the client's team and facilitate a CSA event to get to key risks and associated key controls. The results may be used to drive the rest of the audit as the auditor focuses on risks that the work team have identified. Control evaluation and testing will be carried out as usual, and then the results can be presented back to the workshop forum so the team can come to an agreement on ways to go forward, which become part of the management action plan reported in the audit report. If, during the audit, the controls are found to be well designed and derived from, for example, detailed environmental regulations, the auditor may focus on the compliance process and retest the extent to which staff are adhering to the standards. The audit could move on and change when it is found that staff have a poor understanding of the importance of following set standards and cannot see the implications of this failing. Here the internal auditor, rather than simply report routine noncompliance, could offer to help the business manager set up staff development seminars to spread the message regarding compliance and the substantial fines that could result from failure to adhere to the rules. In a part of the business where there is extensive abuse of company resources, audit could conduct special investigations as part of the assurance role. But the auditor can also help set up ethical awareness training for management and staff under the consulting role, with a view to changing hearts and minds where possible. A further move may be to carry out a project to assess the feasibility of employing an ethics officer and developing a corporate ethics program across the organization. Where the internal auditor finds common problems in areas such as suspect ethical practices, unreliable information systems, history of noncompliance, inefficient operations, no risk management, and so on, rather than simply reporting these failings, it may be better to look at corporate solutions. The internal auditor can report the lack of assurances over key aspects of the business, recommend appropriate solutions, and where there is a governance, risk, and control implication the auditor can offer to help develop good solutions.

A Blend of Services

It is the rich blend of available services that has made the new-look internal auditor so important to an organization, and there is little that falls outside the remit of the audit service so long as:

- The auditor possesses the requisite skills.
- It is supported by the board and audit committee.
- The work constitutes a worthwhile allocation of audit resources.

And the work must pass one further test: that it does not represent a conflict of interest in that (in IIA parlance) it is not:

> *any relationship that is or appears to be not in the best interest of the organization. A conflict of interest would prejudice an individual's ability to perform his or her duties and responsibilities objectively.*

For Further Discussion

Have consulting skills been applied to audit assurance work and in what way might facilitation skills improve the assurance product?

——— SECTION 9 ———
THE AUDIT MODEL

The audit model may be enhanced by the inclusion of a further component—the audit strategy. This strategy will flow from the governance framework that is in place in the organization, as shown in Exhibit 3.4.

Society and Stakeholders. The audit model is driven primarily by the needs and interests of society, that is, the need for good company performance that contributes to the economy, and both fair and transparent business practices. Stakeholders include all those who have a direct or indirect interest in the way business, commerce, and public services are conducted.

Shareholders and Investors. Principal stakeholders are the people and institutions who hold shares in listed companies. Banks and investment companies may well have a direct interest that is represented in funds loaned to the company. Meanwhile, *The People* are principal stakeholders in public-sector organizations. Company shareholders should exercise their voting rights with due regard to the need to ensure there is ethical behavior and accountability from company officials.

Legal System. There are a multitude of federal and state laws that relate to the way private- and public-sector organizations are established, maintained, and extinguished. Many larger organizations have responded by setting up compliance functions to address the variety and magnitude of such legal provisions. Company directors and officials can face severe penalties where specific laws are breached.

Regulators. Most industries have an associated regulator that sets standards and represents the public in ensuring organizations behave properly. The SEC,

Exhibit 3.4.   Audit Model 3

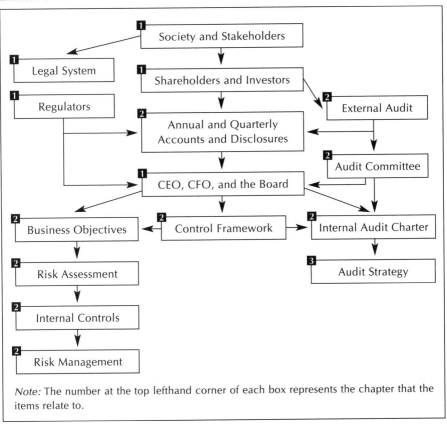

Note: The number at the top lefthand corner of each box represents the chapter that the items relate to.

American Stock Exchange, New York Stock Exchange, and NASDAQ regulations are some of the more well-known models.

CEO, CFO, and Board.   Shareholders appoint a CEO and board of directors to direct and oversee the organization on their behalf. These officers have a responsibility to discharge their duties in a professional manner and account for the results to the shareholders. A management team will be appointed in public sector bodies and have a similar responsibility to the government and general public. The board should adhere to the highest standards of ethics, and ensure they conduct their business in an acceptable and documented manner. Moreover, the board should have in place suitable mechanisms through which it may judge its own performance and conduct.

Annual Accounts and Disclosures.   The organization reports to its stakeholders through published financial and performance statements. These reports act as a window to the outside world, and business analysts spend a great deal of time examining the detailed facts and figures in company accounts on behalf of their clients. Listed companies, along with many other organizations, have to make various disclosures on an annual and quarterly basis, in particular resulting from the Sarbanes-Oxley Act. The published accounts should be reliable and now have to be personally certified by the principal executive and CFO.

External Audit.   The external auditors are appointed by the shareholders to make sure the board have provided a full and reliable account of the company's financial performance over the previous year. The financial statements will be checked by the external auditors before they are formally published. External auditors should ensure they are independent in their audit work and are able to exercise an appropriate degree of professional skepticism at all times. This part of the audit model is a major contribution to governance, as material published by the organization is independently verified.

Audit Committee.   A further layer of governance that is growing in importance is the audit committee. This forum, established by the board, comprises independent directors who provide an additional oversight role, focusing on the specialist areas of financial accounting, ethics, audit, accountability, risk management, and control. The audit committee is not there to undermine the board but provides advice and support regarding the specialist areas in question. Moreover, it should ask challenging questions of the board, on the premise that it is better that these tough questions come from an in-house audit committee than from external regulators.

Internal Audit Charter.   The internal auditor's role and position in the organization is set by the audit charter that is agreed to by the board and audit committee. To be of any real use, this charter should be set firmly within the governance, risk management, and control arena.

Business Objectives.   The next stage of the model relates to the setting of formal corporate objectives that document the mission of the organization and what there is to achieve.

Risk Assessment.   Anything that impacts the business objectives can be seen as a potential risk. These risks need to be understood, isolated, and weighed in terms of significance. Formal risk assessment gives an organization a head start in understanding where its vulnerabilities lie and where it has scope for advancement. The bottom line is that risks that affect the organization's ability to deliver and achieve its objectives have to be addressed for there to be any real chance of success. Control risk self-assessment and regular risk surveys are good ways of promoting risk assessment throughout the organization.

Internal Control.   Controls should be in place to address risks that have been assessed as significant. The current climate stresses the importance of controls over financial reporting and disclosures, as well as compliance with various standard regulations. The systems of internal control need to be maintained, updated, and made right as part of the way employees work.

Risk Management.   Controls fit into the wider remit of risk management, and managers and their teams need to build risk mitigation into their overall strategies. There are many different potential responses to risks, depending on the nature, significance, and cost of controls. The organization needs to weigh up the available measures on a regular basis and ensure the adopted response meets the expectations of the board and stakeholders. That is, the response to risk fits the risk tolerance levels that have been defined by the board in its risk and control policy.

Control Framework.   The entire risk management and control policy should be incorporated within the adopted control framework. Standard models such as COSO sit on a foundation of ethical values and propriety, which may be seen as the "tone at the top" that is set by the board and top executives.

Audit Strategy.   The audit model includes the response from internal audit to the corporate risk policy and approach that is used in the organization. Based on the audit charter, and driven by the corporate risk assessment that the board and management have developed, internal audit should construct a strategy that reflects the future direction of the organization and risks that arise in achieving this strategy.

——— SECTION 10 ———

SUMMARY: TOP TEN CONSIDERATIONS

A summary of the ten main points covered in the chapter follows:

1. The nature of internal audit work is to "assist the organization by identifying and evaluating significant exposures to risk and contributing to the improvement of risk management and control systems."

2. The risk-based systems approach to performing internal audit assurance work has the following key stages:

   - Plan the engagement.
   - Ascertain systems objective.
   - Identify inherent risks.
   - Assess risks for impact and likelihood.

- Evaluate current risk management and internal controls.
- Isolate areas where internal controls are crucial.
- Test for evidence of risk exposures due to control weakness.
- Discuss and agree to action on internal controls.
- Report results.
- Follow up.

3. While assurance work involves the auditor, responsible manager, and third parties (the board and audit committee), straightforward consulting engagements tend not to involve this third party. Many consulting engagements result from direct requests from clients, and a formal criteria should be established to judge whether such requests should be accepted. Consulting can cover the provision of "counsel, advice, facilitation, process design, and training." One approach to formal consulting engagements involves the following stages:

- Entry
- Terms of reference
- Contract
- Analysis
- Release

It is only after a careful assessment of costs and benefits that formal consulting projects should be resourced and carried out.

4. Compliance has always been an issue for the internal auditor. There are some audit shops that conduct compliance-based audits as the best way to add value to a highly regulated business environment. Meanwhile disclosure compliance has led to special teams being established outside internal audit to address the growing importance of accurate and timely external returns. Compliance testing will always be important to the auditor, as good risk management means that key controls should be examined to make sure they work as intended.

5. The internal audit role in fraud prevention, detection, and investigation is the subject of ongoing debate. The risk of fraud is something that auditors consider whenever performing audit work, although not necessarily as a primary consideration. Estimates put employee fraud in the States as running at $600 billion a year. Standards argue that "the internal auditor should have sufficient knowledge to identify the indicators of fraud but is not expected to have the expertise of a person whose primary responsibility is detecting and investigating fraud." Some organizations resource a specialist fraud investigations team, and others ask the internal audit shop to perform this role, with help from external specialists if

required. It is possible to define a staged approach to fraud investigations as follows:

- Allegation
- Background research
- Preliminary report
- Investigation plan
- Support
- Definition of barriers
- Strategy
- Full investigation
- Interim reports
- Witness statements
- Suspect interview
- Final report
- Action
- Review

6. Information systems (IS) auditing is a specialist branch of internal auditing, although all auditors should have a basic level of knowledge in reviewing IS as part of general audit work. An approach to auditing an information-based application may incorporate the following stages:

- Plan the engagement planning.
- Ascertain the systems objective.
- Identify inherent risks.
- Assess risks for impact and likelihood.
- Evaluate current risk management and internal controls.
- Isolate areas where internal controls are crucial.
- Test for evidence of risk exposures due to control weakness.
- Discuss and agree to action on internal controls.
- Report results.
- Follow up.

7. Control risk self-assessment (CRSA) is one development that can have a major impact on the audit role. It may involve getting work teams together and working through the following process:

- Design and introduce the CRSA concept.
- Identify team objectives.
- Discuss key issues and plans.

- Identify risks that impact objectives.
- Work out which risks need to be addressed.
- Consider current arrangements for addressing key risks.
- Determine what needs to be built into the risk management strategy.
- Consider the extent to which new measures give the team a better chance of achieving their objectives.
- Report the results and action plans in a meaningful manner.

8. There is official IIA advice on the audit role in respect of CRSA which argues that audit involvement ranges from:
   - No role
       to
   - Auditing the risk management process as part of the internal audit plan
       to
   - Active, continuous support and involvement in the risk management process
       to
   - Managing and coordinating the risk management process

9. It is possible to develop an blended approach to audit work taking on board all the available approaches and styles that have been mentioned. The idea is to assess the area under review and, depending on what is found, adopt the approaches and techniques that give most value to the client, board, and audit committee.

10. The audit model may be extended to include the key issue of audit strategy. That is the risk-based response from internal audit to the organization's own corporate risk assessment and overall strategic direction.

—— SECTION 11 ——

YOUR PERSONAL DEVELOPMENT EXERCISES

The centralized Human Resource Department (HRD) deals with all aspects of employment across the organization. HRD is responsible for:

1. Human resource planning to ensure that employment plans support the staffing strategies for each of the organization's business units.

2. Recruitment and selection, including the use of assessment centers for staff selection exercises.

3. Employment compliance in ensuring that all parts of the organization comply with federal and state employment laws and local regulations.

4. Employment records and staff databases.

5. Compensation and promotion policies.

6. Development and training programs.

7. Staff discipline and complaints regarding conduct and working practices.

The HRD is headed by the newly appointed Chief HR Officer, who reports to the Director of Support Services. It is structured into four teams:

1. **Team one** handles HR planning, staff recruitment, compensation, and promotion. This team consists of a manager, three team leaders, and nine staff members. It is a well-trained team, but they have never been involved in any wide-ranging change initiatives before.

2. **Team two** focuses on induction, training, and development, as well as business unit advice. The team consists of a team leader and two staff members. It is a good team, but they have had little to do in the past due to lack of training budget. They mainly handle induction training for new staff.

3. **Team three** oversees records, compliance, and discipline. The team consists of a team leader and three staff members. They are responsible for processing employee records but are disorganized, and there is a high error rate for the information that is placed on employee records.

4. **Team four** handles employee relations and staff complaints. The team is made up of a team leader and two staff members. This is a new team, who are working on setting up standards and procedures to ensure nondisciplinary staffing issues are resolved at an early stage.

The board has just approved a paper (Strategic HR Issues) from the Director of Support Services on key staffing matters, which contains the following key points:

- A recent takeover of a smaller company will mean some 2,000 staff will be added to the company payroll, and two HR staff from the newly acquired company will need to be assimilated into the HRD.

- The number of staff disciplinaries is on line for a 50 percent increase over the last year, and the company has been criticized in many cases as having poor and inconsistent documentation relating to staffing issues held at business-unit level and copied to the HRD.

- A similar company in a neighboring state has been the subject of a major scandal where staff promotion practices were investigated and found to be discriminating against ethnic minorities and women.

- The board has targeted the HRD as a pilot site for a CRSA program that has been recommended by the audit committee.

- Over the last few months, three employees in three different business units were found to have forged academic certificates after a health and safety check by external inspectors. Their qualifications were not verified by HRD, breaching what is supposed to be standard practice.

- The Staffing Handbook is out of date and has not been reviewed for more than three years.

- Staff training has been haphazard, and the board has recently approved a large investment for training and development that will be spent over the next two years.

- A new site will be opened later in the year, and this will involve a large recruitment drive to start in a few months' time.

- The HRD information system is currently being reviewed, and an interim report from the feasibility study suggests that the existing system will have to be scrapped and replaced within the next twelve months.

- There has been no internal audit work in HRD for some four years, and the last time an audit was undertaken, it led to a major dispute between the previous Chief Human Resource Officer and the lead auditor. This resulted from an audit report that criticized the state of the HR database, which was found to be unreliable, and breached data integrity rules for personal data. The audit approach adopted four years ago was described by HR staff as confrontational and unhelpful.

- An effective HRD service is seen as of strategic importance to the business and is listed as one of the current top ten board-level risks.

The audit committee has looked at the paper (Strategic HR Issues) and has asked the CAE to concentrate on HRD in the next quarter's audit plan and prepare a paper for the audit committee meeting scheduled for next week covering the audit approach that may be adopted for audit work in the HRD. Unfortunately, the Director of Support Services (DSS) and Chief HR Officer are both out of the country until the end of next week. Before going abroad, the DSS did e-mail the CAE and indicate that all key issues regarding HRD were documented in the strategic HR issues paper.

Your Task

Prepare a paper for the CAE setting out the various approaches that may be applied to each of the four separate HRD Teams, in response to the request from the audit committee (using the information listed above). Make any suggestions that seem sensible, and provide as much detail as possible. Make sure you list the pros and cons of the approach selected for each team, and discuss the use of the "blended approach" that is found in this chapter. Make sure the approach considers the work of the four teams in HRD and addresses the issues raised in the Strategic HR Issues paper.

4

QUALITY ASSURANCE AND COMPETENCE

SECTION 1
THE QUALITY CONCEPT

The challenges for the new-look internal auditing call for many things. They call for sound procedures in addition to a well-trained staff and a mechanism for managing the risk of poor standards—that is, a quality assurance mechanism. The internal audit shop is judged on its quality, performance and reputation. Moreover, Practice Advisory 2000-1 places this clear responsibility on the CAE by saying:

> *The chief audit executive is responsible for properly managing the internal audit activity so that:*
> - *Audit work fulfills the general purposes and responsibilities described in the charter, approved by senior management, and accepted by the board.*
> - *Resources of the internal audit activity are efficiently and effectively employed.*
> - *Audit work conforms to the Standards for the Professional Practice of Internal Auditing.*

The internal audit department issues assurances on corporate governance, risk management, and control, while at the same time it needs to consider how it can be assured of delivering a good service. The solution to this dilemma is found in Attribute Standard 1300, which states:

> *The CAE should develop and maintain a quality assurance and improvement program that covers all aspects of the internal audit activity and continuously monitors its effectiveness.*

Quality depends on good standards, well-trained and motivated staff, a clear sense of direction, a defined methodology (or blend of methodologies), good documentation, supervision, reviews, and a generally well-managed internal audit outfit. If there are gaps in any one of these components, there is a danger that the risk of poor performance will materialize and dent the credibility of the audit process. In one sense, internal auditing is all about credibility because the audit product is change: change in improving risk management and control; change in dealing with areas where assurances are not available; and change in response to advice from consulting engagements. Any shortfalls in the internal audit products will place a question mark over the changes suggested by the internal auditors and thus undermine the audit process. Quality assurance is primarily about answering the question, "Who audits the auditors?"

> ### For Further Discussion
> To what extent is quality built into the audit process, and in what way has quality improved over the years?

------ SECTION 2 ------

PROFESSIONAL INTERNAL AUDITING STANDARDS

The IIA standards mentioned throughout the text form a clear framework for the audit role, position, and performance. The attribute standards are mandatory and help construct the shape and form of the well-positioned audit shop. The performance standards are mandatory and describe the activities of a quality audit service. Implementation standards are set within this framework and deal with specific services relating to assurance, consulting, fraud, and information systems auditing. Practice advisories provide additional nonmandatory guidance that is cross-referenced to the relevant standards. As already mentioned, this orientation guide is based around IIA standards. Here, we note the main components of the attribute and performance standards and the code of ethics, which together guide the internal auditors' behavior.

Attribute Standards

1000—Purpose, Authority, and Responsibility

The purpose, authority, and responsibility of the internal audit activity should be formally defined in a charter, consistent with the Standards, and approved by the board.

1100—Independence and Objectivity

The internal audit activity should be independent, and internal auditors should be objective in performing their work.

1200—Proficiency and Due Professional Care

Engagements should be performed with proficiency and due professional care.

1300—Quality Assurance and Improvement Program

The CAE should develop and maintain a quality assurance and improvement program that covers all aspects of the internal audit activity and continuously monitors its effectiveness. The program should be designed to help the internal auditing activity add value and improve the organization's operations and to provide assurance that the internal audit activity is in conformity with the Standards and the Code of Ethics.

Performance Standards

2000—Managing the Internal Audit Activity

The CAE should effectively manage the internal audit activity to ensure it adds value to the organization.

2100—Nature of Work

The internal audit activity evaluates and contributes to the improvement of risk management and control and governance processes.

2200—Engagement Planning

Internal auditors should develop and record a plan for each engagement.

2300—Performing the Engagement

Internal auditors should identify, analyze, and record sufficient information to achieve the engagement's objectives.

2400—Communicating Results

Internal auditors should communicate the engagement results promptly.

2500—Monitoring Progress

The CAE should establish and maintain a system to monitor the disposition of results communicated to management.

2600—Management's Acceptance of Risks

When the CAE believes that senior management has accepted a level of residual risk that is unacceptable to the organization, the CAE should discuss the matter with senior management. If the decision regarding residual risk is not resolved, the CAE and senior management should report the matter to the board for resolution.

Code of Ethics

The purpose of The Code of Ethics of the IIA is to promote an ethical culture in the global profession of internal auditing. A code of ethics is necessary and appropriate for the profession of internal auditing, founded as it is on the trust placed in its objective assurance about risk, control, and governance. The Code of Ethics applies to both individuals and entities that provide internal audit services.

THE IIA CODE OF ETHICS

Principles: *Internal auditors are expected to apply and uphold the following principles:*

Integrity: *The integrity of internal auditors establishes trust and thus provides the basis for reliance on their judgment.*

Objectivity: *Internal auditors exhibit the highest level of professional objectivity in gathering, evaluating, and communicating information about the activity or process being examined. Internal auditors make a balanced assessment of all relevant circumstances and are not unduly influenced by their own interests or by others in forming judgments.*

Credibility: *Internal auditors respect the value and ownership of information they receive and do not disclose information without appropriate authority unless there is a legal or professional obligation to do so.*

Competency: *Internal auditors apply the knowledge, skills, and experience needed in the performance of internal auditing services.*

Rules of Conduct

1. **Integrity**

   Internal auditors:

   1.1 Shall perform their work with honesty, diligence, and responsibility.

   1.2 Shall observe the law and make disclosures expected by the law and the profession.

   1.3 Shall not knowingly be a part to any illegal activity, or engage in acts that are discreditable to the profession of internal auditing or to the organization.

   1.4 Shall respect and contribute to the legitimate and ethical objectives of the organization.

2. **Objectivity**

   Internal auditors:

   2.1 Shall not participate in any activity or relationship that may impair or be presumed to impair their unbiased assessment. This participation includes those activities or relationships that may be in conflict with the interests of the organization.

   2.2 Shall not accept anything that may impair or be presumed to impair their professional judgment.

   2.3 Shall disclose all material facts known to them that if not disclosed, may distort the reporting of activities under review.

3. **Confidentiality**

   Internal auditors:

   3.1 Shall be prudent in the use and protection of information acquired in the course of their duties.

3.2 Shall not use information for any personal gain or in any manner that would be contrary to the law or detrimental to the legitimate and ethical objectives of the organization.

4. *Competency*

Internal auditors:

4.1 Shall engage only in those services for which they have the necessary knowledge, skills and experience.

4.2 Shall perform internal auditing services in accordance with the Standards for the Professional Practice of Internal Auditing.

4.3 Shall continually improve their proficiency and the effectiveness and quality of their services.

The IIA's professional standards and code of ethics form important benchmarks that should be met by practicing internal auditors. Auditors should study, understand, and apply them when conducting audit work. One argument suggests these standards should be committed to memory by all current and would-be audit staff, and any problems regarding their interpretation and observation should be resolved as soon as possible. There is really no excuse for an auditor not to know the standards framework that has been set forth above. Likewise, there is no excuse for not complying with the requirements of these standards. Internal auditors are advised to study the detailed standards and guidance issued by the IIA, including the implementation standards, the draft additions that appear from time to time, the more detailed practice advisories, and the IIA's monthly journal that contains articles and updates. Recognized textbooks, such as Sawyer's *Internal Auditing,* are also a good source of information for the aspiring auditor.

> ### For Further Discussion
> *How easy is it to comply with IIA standards, and what aspects of these standards pose particular difficulties?*

—— SECTION 3 ——

DOCUMENTATION STANDARDS AND REVIEW

As is the case with regard to internal auditing, quality is largely dependent on good procedures, and Performance Standard 2040 makes it quite clear that:

The CAE should establish policies and procedures to guide the internal audit activity.

Meanwhile Practice Advisory 2040-1 sets out the importance of procedures:

> *The form and content of written policies and procedures should be appropriate to the size and structure of the internal audit activity and the complexity of its work. Formal administrative and technical audit manuals may not be needed by all internal auditing entities. A small internal audit activity may be managed informally. Its audit staff may be directed and controlled through daily, close supervision and written memoranda. In a large internal audit activity, more formal and comprehensive policies and procedures are essential to guide the audit staff in the consistent compliance with the internal audit activity's standards of performance.*

In other words, much depends on the size of the audit team and the degree to which audit staff are supervised. Most of the standards and procedures may be documented in an audit manual that is published or held on the computer, and this will provide a good source of guidance on the way audit work is planned, performed, and reported. The audit manual should aim to:

- Bring the professional standards to life in a way that fits the local context.
- Ensure a degree of consistency in the way internal audit is performed across the audit team.
- Form a source of guidance and reference material that can be used to direct the audit effort, or at least point to sources where relevant material may be obtained.
- Support the induction training for new staff and ensure they understand the jargon and approaches that are used by the team.
- Form a set of standards against which to measure compliance with procedure and the performance of individual auditors and the audit team.
- Act as a mechanism for updating audit methods and ensuring they reflect the rapid progress made by the profession.

The Audit Manual

It costs money to develop, set up, and maintain a good manual and the above benefits must be weighed against the inconvenience of preparing such a document. There is one view that suggests that professional staff will automatically adopt professional standards and that manuals are really not required. This view must be set against the fact that there are many different interpretations of the audit approach, and the manual is a good way of getting a clear focus and direction among the audit team. The manual distinguishes the important issues from the low-priority matters. In fact, it is best to develop the manual after having carried out a CSA exercise within the internal audit shop, so that the resulting procedures may focus on high-risk aspects of running the audit service. The manual could cover such areas as:

- Audit charter and aim of the service.
- Background to the development of the service.
- A note on independence, professional standards, and ethics.
- Relationships—reporting lines, audit committee, and role in corporate governance, risk management, and control, perhaps even setting out what the audit committee represents.
- Notes on control frameworks and an indication of sources of further information.
- Audit services—including assurance and consulting roles.
- Importance of good working relationships with clients and others.
- Note on external audit and other review functions.
- Risk-based audit planning and developing the audit strategy to address the audit universe.
- The audit process—covering engagement planning, fieldwork, reporting, and follow-up.
- Consulting projects, requests for assistance, and CSA services where appropriate.
- Investigatory work such as fraud and compliance checks, with links to the corporate fraud policy.
- Reporting processes with specimen reports and the annual audit report with links into board-level assurances on internal control and the attestation process.
- Standardized documentation with worked examples, along with security and file retention and privacy measures.
- Quality assurance arrangements and the importance of working to professional standards.
- Note on techniques such as interviewing, data interrogation, statistical sampling, flowcharting, analytical review, and so on.
- Sundry administration covering timesheets, time monitoring, travel and expenses claims, teleworking, performance management, staff discipline, use of contract staff, and so forth.
- Glossary of terms.

The audit manual may be used to set a bar for internal audit staff, the idea being that each staff member should be developed and equipped to reach and even surpass the levels set out in the manual.

Working Papers

It is one thing to set standards covering audit services, methods, and documentation, but it is also important to get down into some detail about the working papers that are applied to each individual audit. One way of assessing working papers is to work through the various IIA standards and advisories and consider what each one says about the subject:

- *Performance Standard 2330:* "Internal auditors should record relevant information to support the conclusions and engagement results." This sets the pace for audit documentation. Each assignment must be reflected in an audit file specially set up for the purpose. Audit evidence is essentially material that supports and gives credence to the findings from an audit. Where sufficient evidence has been obtained, the audit may be finalized and reported. Even where this evidence originates from a comment or observation, it must still be recorded and placed on file to meet best-practice standards. Relevant information means evidence that has an impact on the terms of reference for the audit and adds value to the audit product. Newly appointed auditors tend to gather everything that they come across during the audit and dump it into the audit file. Over the years, they become more discerning and select only those items that really add to the audit, and discard the rest. The key factor in any audit is time; time costs money, and time spent on one aspect of an audit takes away time from another part. The trend now is to define relevance in terms of the types of risks that exist in the area under review. The greater the risk, the more time and effort is spent by the auditor, and this is where more documentation would be prepared.

- *Performance Standard 2330.A1:* "The CAE should control access to engagement records. The CAE should obtain approval from senior management and/or legal counsel prior to releasing such records to external parties, as appropriate." Audit documentation belongs to the internal audit department, and ultimately the organization. It is confidential and must be kept so. Many auditors work with a portable PC and keep their files on the hard disk, with backup on CD or floppy disk or sent to the corporate audit network. The majority of information that supplies audit files comes from the client and is then entered onto manual or automated audit files. Notwithstanding this fact, the files must be considered to be under the jurisdiction of the CAE, and access will be restricted. Note that in some organizations there is a policy of exchanging files between the internal and external audit functions. Requests from external agencies and others need to be checked with legal counsel to assess whether there is a legal obligation to reveal such documentation. If a field auditor is asked to supply audit files, this request must be referred back to the CAE, who in turn may seek further advice. Practice Advisory 2330.A1-2 recommends the development of a formal policy on granting access covering issues such as:

1. *Process for resolving access issues;*
2. *Time period for retention of each type of work product;*
3. *Process for educating and reeducating the internal auditing staff concerning the risks and issues regarding access to their work products;*
4. *Requirement for periodically surveying the industry to determine who may want access to the work product in the future.*

The policy should also address practicalities such as providing copies of specific documents only and marking each item "confidential" and not for wider release and ensuring no documents are provided unless absolutely necessary. Documents that fall under attorney-client privilege will be subject to a separate procedure.

- *Performance Standard 2330.A2:* "The CAE should develop retention requirements for engagement records. These retention requirements should be consistent with the organization's guidelines and any pertinent regulatory or other requirements." This is a particularly straightforward requirement that means exactly what it says. The rules regarding record retention are becoming more of an issue with increased fines for improper destruction, concealment, or alteration. The increasingly high profile of internal audit may mean that in future, audit documentation that relates to important parts of the organization may be reviewed by, say, investigators, law enforcement agents, or SEC regulators. The Sarbanes-Oxley Act covers anyone who "knowingly alters, destroys, mutilates, conceals, covers up, falsifies, or makes a false entry in any record, document, or tangible object with the intent to impede, obstruct, or influence an investigation or proper administration of any matter within the jurisdiction of any department or agency of the United States or any case filed under the bankruptcy code, or in relation to or contemplation of any such matter or case. . . . [Such individuals] may be fined, imprisoned for not more than 20 years, or both."

- *Practice Advisory 2330-1:* "The CAE should establish working paper policies for the various types of engagements performed. Standardized engagement working papers such as questionnaire and audit programs may improve the efficiency of an engagement and facilitate the delegation of engagement work." The audit manual will need to contain a section on working papers that should set out the criteria that they have to meet to be acceptable. The advisory hints at standardization and the fact that certain documents may be set up in advance and used by the audit team. Different types of work will call for different types of documentation. This is particularly relevant for consulting work, where the documentation will be prepared to suit the engagement. One way of managing audit work is to get the audit manager to help set the terms of reference for the engagement, in conjunction with the client, and then define a time budget and the types of standardized documentation needed to support the audit. Armed with these ingredients, the audit team assigned to the work can proceed with its tasks and develop the audit file as each part is completed. It is the file that holds the results of each stage of the audit, and the standardized documentation can be reviewed by the audit manager as the audit is carried out. There is a further test that needs to be applied to documentation: it should help improve the efficiency of the audit. Any document that is not able to pass this test and is not legally required should be discarded.

Working papers serve a useful purpose, which is described in Practice Advisory 2330-1:

- *Provide the principal support for the engagement communications.*
- *Aid in the planning, performance, and review of engagements.*
- *Document whether the engagement objectives were achieved.*
- *Facilitate third-party reviews.*
- *Provide a basis for evaluating the internal audit activity's quality program.*
- *Provide support in circumstances such as insurance claims, fraud cases, and lawsuits.*
- *Aid in the professional development of the internal auditing staff.*
- *Demonstrate the internal audit activity's compliance with the Standards for the Professional Practice of Internal Auditing.*

It is possible to set out criteria for good working papers, and one such list appears below:

- *Useful.* If there is no real reason to prepare or copy a document to the audit file, it should not be retained. Always ask the question, "Do I really need this document? Or do I really need to record this information?" Do not hold something just because it exists; it has to make a defined difference. For example, a large procedures manual for the area being audited that is soon to be replaced need not be copied and held on file if there would be no real benefit gained.

- *Complete.* It is very annoying to review an audit file and find a link to another document or activity that either has not been carried out or cannot be traced through the file. If the terms of reference say that the information system will be examined to ensure the records have been properly stored, and there is no record of this test, this can become a source of much confusion. A record should note that this part of the work was not undertaken because of reasons abc, and agreed with the client. Or if the test was completed and the sample of records was found to be okay, a record of this test and conclusions drawn should be properly filed. An interview record that ends with a note to follow up the manager's concern about a file that was taken by an auditor and not returned should be cross-referenced to a separate note on what was done about this problem.

- *Practicable.* Information, evidence, and documents should all contribute to the audit product. And this should be reflected in the working papers for the audit file in question. The costs of maintaining a document should be outweighed by the value that is derived from the act. In some situations, it is just not feasible to prepare a working paper because of the inconvenience involved. For example, a client may inform the auditor that a note was sent to the team by a senior manager who left the organization last year, instructing staff to stop carrying out certain supervisory checks. If this point is confirmed by other staff, it will probably not be necessary to contact the ex-employee to seek written confirmation. It is just not worth the effort unless the work involves investigating fraud or irregularity. Working papers may be held in any suitable medium, but if wholly automated, they need to be kept secure, marked for version control, and properly backed up (off site).

- *Cross-referenced.* In the next chapter, we illustrate the flow of an audit and the way effective documentation can be used to capture this process. For this system to work, the audit paperwork must be cross-referenced so that each stage or aspect can be linked to the point that it is taken forward, to end up as an audit opinion and formal report. For example, an evaluation that suggests there may be weaknesses in controls over the employment of contract staff should be cross-referenced to any testing done on recent employment arrangements—which gives results that are cross-referenced to the part of the audit report that deals with this problem. An audit working paper file is not just a collection of assorted documents; it is a mechanism for capturing the flow of an audit from setting the objectives, to performing the work, to reviewing routines, and subsequently reporting the results.

- *Reviewed.* Quality assurance consists of mechanisms for ensuring the quality and impact of the audit product. One key aspect is supervision and review of all audit work. The manager assigns the work, the auditor performs the work and prepares a file of evidence. The in-charge manager needs to review the working paper file and draft report to ensure that the objective has been achieved and that audit standards and working practices have been employed properly by the field auditors. The working paper file should record the results of this review so that any later examination of the file will verify not only the documentation but also the fact that the work has been checked to some extent. This is a simple but quite important point of principle.

- *Headed.* Each document within the file or that supports the file should be headed in a way that makes it clear where it belongs and what it represents. This is standard practice in audit shops and saves a great deal of "fluffing around time" when flicking through an audit file.

- *Linked to audit objectives.* High-impact auditing tries to get from the audit objective straight to findings and report in the most direct way possible. One way of encouraging this principle is to link each document into the audit objectives, making clear what bearing that document has on the reason why the audit was performed in the first place. For example, if an engagement objective is to assess whether a key head office control is working at a local office, we may well pursue this matter during the audit by means of interviews and examination and working through the local office staff's understanding of the head office material. It is easy to get lost in the muddy waters of head office versus local autonomy politics and lose the plot. Linking efforts back to the objectives and constantly revisiting the validity of the original audit objectives is vital.

- *Linked to findings and report.* As with the above point, the audit effort and documentation should flow through to the audit report. It is helpful when the working papers follow this journey to the report in a clear and simple fashion. The link between papers and findings is described in Practice Advisory 2330-1, which suggests:

  Working papers that document the engagement should be prepared by the internal auditor and reviewed by management of the internal audit activity. The working papers should record the information obtained and the analyses made and should support the bases for the observations and recommendations to be reported.

- *Minimal.* Only record something if you really have to. Simple.

- *Checked.* A single error in the audit findings and report can cause embarrassment to the auditor. Two mistakes may raise a giggle from people whenever the CAE passes them on the corridor. Three or more errors will start to cast doubt on the veracity of the audit process and could lead to moves to outsource the entire service. There is not much scope for flexibility on reporting inaccurate, misleading, or inconsistent information. The only way around this problem is to check and double-check all key matters at various stages of the audit. If the client manager says in an interview that there was a $55,000 overspend on the entertaining budget last year, but the audit files record this as $155,000 and a separate budget monitoring report puts this down as $25,000, this matter will have to be carefully checked if this information needs to be placed in the audit report. If these three different figures come from three different methods for calculating the spend, there is no problem so long as the discrepancy and methods used are explained in the audit report. If there is a mistake somewhere in the quoted figures the auditor should find out which figure should be used, and perhaps mention the fact that there are different figures in existence. The audit staff should check their work, the lead auditor should also check, and the supervising audit manager should likewise ensure that important facts are sound. Last, the client should be asked to confirm key facts before the report is finalized.

- *Summarized.* It is quite helpful if the working paper contains summaries wherever possible. Long and detailed interview records need not be read by a reviewing audit manager where there is a summary box on the front sheet. Summaries also help focus the auditor's mind on key aspects of the document that have to be explained in plain English. A working paper that contains a heading, audit objective, and list of detailed calculations is unhelpful to anyone looking at the file. A summary—and, better still, conclusion—linked to the audit report gives a much better view for reviewers and anyone else who needs to access the file.

- *Identifying the auditor.* The working paper should identify the person completing the document along with others involved in the work and the party reviewing the record.

- *Consistent.* The working paper should hang together and tie up loose ends. If the audit team is listed by name but no records are produced by one member, this needs to be explained. It may be that a junior auditor did some testing work that was fed into an overall summary done by the lead auditor. Or an auditor may have fallen sick and been unable to work on the engagement. Whatever the reason, the various strands of the audit should not leave unanswered questions and gaps. If a testing schedule sets out all approved spending for the last six weeks but leaves out two weeks from the document without explanation, this causes a problem. It may be that a spending freeze was imposed for two weeks and nothing went through the system, but if this is not explained, then it will always appear odd.

- *User-friendly.* The files should be prepared in a way that helps the field auditor and reviewer. Many can be standardized, but such formats should not lead to a mechanistic audit approach that revolves around filling in forms rather than thinking through key risks and appropriate responses. There should be a careful consideration of standardization and flexibility in the audit fieldwork.

- *Logical.* Chapter 5 shows that an audit can be carried out to flow logically from start to finish. This flow can be represented in the documentation in a clear and sensible manner. Working papers should be dated, and the dates should demonstrate a logical and systematic process for performing the audit that involves planning, fieldwork, and reporting. Within the fieldwork, there will again be a logical flow of finding out what goes on, to analyzing risk and controls, testing findings, and then discussing and reporting these findings to the client.

Some audit departments categorize their files as permanent or current files. The current files relate to the actual audit engagement in hand and record the results of the audit. The stages involved in performing an audit will result in working papers for each part, and they should be held in a file that is prepared for the individual audit. Practice Advisory 2330-1 makes several suggestions about what should be documented for an audit:

- *Planning documents and engagement programs.*
- *Control questionnaires, flowcharts, checklists, and narratives.*
- *Notes and memoranda resulting from interviews.*
- *Organizational data, such as organization charts and job descriptions.*
- *Copies of important contracts and agreements.*
- *Information about operating and financial policies.*
- *Results of control evaluations.*
- *Letters of confirmation and representation.*
- *Analysis and tests of transactions, processes, and account balances.*
- *Results of analytical auditing procedures.*
- *The engagement's final communications and management's responses.*
- *Engagement correspondence if it documents engagement conclusions reached.*

The permanent file contains documents of continuing importance that relate to more that just the individual audit. Items, such as an information systems strategy, gathered for the engagement file may be copied to the permanent file if they have a wider impact. Documentation is an important aspect of audit work. Good and efficient documents and working papers help the audit task and allow the auditor to concentrate on important matters that confront the client and the organization generally rather than worry about how to record things and what goes in which file. It takes quite a while before the new auditor can automatically drop key material into an audit file in a sensible and professional manner, with the least amount of cost and time. It is best to start with the standards, then some practice, then the acquisition of sufficient expertise over time.

Superimposed over documentation standards is the process of engagement review. This process ensures that standards are being applied, that the documentation is complete and reliable, and that it supports the audit findings and report. Practice Advisory 2340-1 contains a wealth of advice on audit review, and some of the key points made are summarized below:

- The CAE is responsible for ensuring good supervision.
- Supervision should continue throughout the audit process.
- The review starts with assessing whether assigned auditors are able to perform the work.
- It involves giving instructions during planning and developing an audit program.
- Working papers and the draft report prepared by the auditors should be reviewed.
- The review process should be used to help develop the audit staff and input into the training process.
- During the review, the supervising auditor should watch for judgments made that are inconsistent with the direction set by the CAE.
- Questions to be addressed by the field auditor may be listed as part of the review process that may be kept or discarded (after being actioned), depending on the adopted policy.

Audit Automation

It is one thing to audit information systems and issue opinions on what is going well and where there is need for improvement. The internal audit shop also needs to make sure it is up with the best in terms of its own information and automation strategy. Audit automation is simply based on ensuring all appropriate tools are applied to the audit process to ensure a high degree of both efficiency and effectiveness. Rather than provide a general discussion about audit automation, we note the areas covered by an automation product called Audit Leverage. This is a database application that helps to automate many of the standard tasks that the internal auditing department is probably already performing using, say, disparate Excel spreadsheets, Word documents, Access databases, and hard copies, none of which talk to each other or are accessible by the entire audit staff. Using the audit process as a framework for assessing the types of task involved in the audit process, it is possible to list the application of Audit Leverage software, as follows:

Planning:

- Risk assessment and audit prioritization.
- Annual audit planning and budgeting.
- Audit universe tracking and analysis.
- Audit project management.
- Graphical staffing and scheduling of audits time.
- Time tracking and approvals.
- Time summary reporting and analysis.
- Budget-to-actual comparisons for the various phases of an audit or across multiple audits.
- Hours charged to particular areas of risk.
- Audit staff demographic data.
- Skills tracking, work experience, and audit assignments tracking.
- Audit staff performance evaluations.

Fieldwork documentation:

- Workpapers, online review notes (from manager to staff and back to the manager) and on-the-fly audit programs.
- Template library of standard audit programs and common audit issues.
- Electronic password-protected sign-off of workpapers and audit steps.
- Findings, recommendations, and custom audit report generation.

Reporting and follow-up:

- Management responses and follow-up tracking of management's action plans.
- Enterprisewide analysis of all audit issues that have come up during a given time period.
- Identification of problem areas and trends.
- Performance of root-cause analysis of audit findings.

The remote synchronization capability empowers traveling auditors to work at remote fieldwork sites while disconnected from the network. When they arrive at their hotel room, they can dial in to synchronize their automated work with the central copy of the database on the network. This enables managers back at headquarters (or at a third location) to identify problem areas in the workpapers, identify potential time budget overages, and suggest midstream corrections to the field team before they leave the site. This also cuts down on the need for managers to travel to the field.

The documentation module of Audit Leverage complements existing software tools rather than attempting to replace them. So, for example, users continue to use Excel, ACL, or IDEA for analysis and then attach those files to a particular audit in the automated process, just like attaching a file to an e-mail message. They can also continue to use Word for items like internal control narratives or walk-throughs. Workpaper attachments are most commonly Word or Excel files or ACL/IDEA files, but they can also be photographs, scanned documents, Internet links, pdf files, flowcharts (in Microsoft Visio, PowerPoint, or any other flowcharting program), or any other type of file that could normally be attached to an e-mail message. The net result of all this is that audit staff spend more time auditing and less time on internal audit department administration and documentation, while at the same time improving audit quality, their ability to monitor risks across the enterprise, and their reporting capability.

> ### *For Further Discussion*
>
> *How useful is the current audit manual, and in what ways could documentation standards be improved?*

──── SECTION 4 ────
INTERNAL AND EXTERNAL REVIEWS

It is one thing to set up solid standards and good documentation and employ sensible people to do the job. Proper supervision in the form of a clear direction from the CAE focusing on a risk-based strategy may well lead to a world-class internal audit process. Unfortunately, this is not enough. There needs to be a regular review commissioned by and reporting directly to the CAE to check that all is well. Attribute Standard 1310 requires:

> *The internal audit activity should adopt a process to monitor and assess the overall effectiveness of the quality program.*

Quality sits firmly at the door of the CAE. There are several options for promoting quality assurance within the audit shop. The CAE may assign this task to a senior auditor, who reports directly back to the CAE. Moreover, the task may be rotated between the senior audit staff so that different people get involved in the process. Internal reviews tend to revolve around compliance checks, based on assessing the extent to which the standards and practices that are agreed to and defined in the audit manual have been employed during each individual audit. The audits to be examined in, say, one particular quarter may be randomly selected, and the assigned senior auditor should not have been involved in any of the audit files that are being examined. A slightly better model involves getting someone from outside the audit shop—for example, an internal consultant, or ex-member of audit staff who now works in a different part of the organization—to perform the internal review. Basic compliance checks could be commissioned, although anything more than that may be difficult for a non-auditor to cover.

Supervision

Complementing formal internal reviews is supervision of the audit by the audit manager or lead auditor, as has already been mentioned. Supervision is about making sure the audit team assigned to the engagement is working properly and helping them deal with problems and concerns that may arise during the course of the work. Where there are junior staff assigned to audit work, close supervision is quite important. Where the policy is to use more experienced people, with perhaps a move away from the team approach, the audit manager supervision is more akin to a review process with a hotline to the audit manager where there is a particular issue that cannot be resolved. Supervision should be constructive and help the audit staff develop and mature into the job. If mistakes are being made, or progress is slow, the supervisor should try to work out how to provide better direction and format to the audit. Mistakes may mean the auditors have a training need, or that the procedures are unclear, or inconsistent advice has been given to them by different senior auditors. All these concerns suggest that strategic improvements may be considered over and above the individual audit in hand.

Internal Reviews

In terms of the formal internal review, the IIA's Practice Advisory 1311-1 contains many useful suggestions. Selected highlights include:

- Supervision is important to check that set processes are being applied in practice.
- Feedback from audit customers and stakeholders may be secured in the form of surveys and interviews.
- Performance metrics should be considered as should time budgets and completion targets.
- The review should result in a view on the quality of audit performance and identify appropriate measures for improving this quality.
- Internal reviews should be conducted periodically.

- Review can be based on self-assessment exercises.
- Benchmarking against best practice can be used to improve the audit service.
- The results should be reported directly to the CAE.
- The CAE will then decide whether to share these results with others—for example, the board, external audit, and audit committee.

External Reviews

The CAE can review the audit service but cannot really say that this is an objective review, just as a business unit can only be objectively assessed by outsiders, with no obvious vested interest in the results from the review. This is where external reviews come into play, and each audit shop should undergo such a review at least every five years. External reviews may be seen as auditing the auditors, where they are performed by independent professional personnel and are fully reported. It is important that the CAE can point to a format for verifying the internal audit process, to maintain the credibility that is fundamental to the audit product. An unreliable audit process is completely pointless. If audit clients have no faith in the work and sincerity of the internal auditors who cover their operations and programs, everything else falls over. The IIA Practice Advisory 1312-1 covers external assessments, and key points are summarized below:

- Compliance with professional standards is a cornerstone of the review.
- External reviews are required every five years.
- The results should be communicated to the board.
- External reviewers should be independent outsiders such as "IIA quality assurance reviewers, regulatory examiners, consultants, external auditors, other professional service providers, and internal auditors from outside the organization."
- Reviewers should hold no conflicts of interest or obligation to the organization.
- Peer reviews on a reciprocal basis are acceptable so long as this involves more than just two organizations.
- The reviewer should be a competent professional (e.g., CIA, CPA, CA, or CISA), have at least three years' recent internal audit management experience, and possess industry and IT expertise.

External reviews are much broader than the interview versions and go beyond basic compliance issues. The terms of reference may be set by the CAE in conjunction with the board and audit committee, and as such should be geared at various high-impact issues. If a CSA exercise has been completed, the results would have isolated priority risks to the internal audit service and key controls that should be in place to counter these risks. These matters would make useful terms of reference for any wide-ranging review of the service. In one sense, it is wrong to list the items that should fall within the external reviewer's scope of work because much depends on the considerations that have been mentioned above. Bearing this in mind, it is still possible to list some of the matters that might be addressed in an external review:

- Use of professional standards, guidelines, and codes that represent best practice.
- Whether the audit charter reflects the aims and scope of the audit service.
- The range of approaches and methods applied to audit work.
- The balance between assurance and consulting work.
- The extent to which audit has developed a value-add proposition and the suitability of the implementation of this idea.
- Whether risk-based auditing is happening and the extent to which this is successful.
- Internal audit's impact on improving corporate governance, risk management, and control.
- The role of internal audit in providing attestation statements to support the executives' annual disclosure and reporting obligations.
- Whether audit staff are equipped to perform to the required standards.
- The perceived value of internal auditing to client management, the board, and the audit committee, across the organization.
- The use of effective techniques such as data interrogation, statistical analysis, and automated procedures.
- The level of motivation and satisfaction expressed by internal audit staff.
- Training and personal development programs and their effectiveness.
- Whether there is innovation and forward thinking from auditors, and a good understanding of world-class practices.
- The use of benchmarking and results from techniques such as the IIA's GAIN program.

The results should go to the CAE, who should communicate these results to the board and audit committee. As is standard practice, the draft should be discussed with the CAE before the report is finalized. Internal audit needs to conduct its work in line with professional standards. If this is achieved, then generally the criteria mentioned above under considerations that may fall within an external review will probably be satisfied. As such, the external review will have as a bottom line this need to meet standards. IIA Attribute Standard 1330 explains what the term "conducted in accordance with the standards" means in practice:

> Internal auditors are encouraged to report that their activities are "conducted in accordance with the Standards for the Professional Practice of Internal Auditing." However, internal auditors may use the statement only if assessments of the quality improvement program demonstrate that the internal audit activity is in compliance with the Standards.

Any problems must be disclosed. Attribute Standard 1340 confirms this point by stating:

> Although the internal audit activity should achieve full compliance with the Standards and internal auditors with The Code of Ethics, there may be instances in which full compliance is not achieved. When noncompliance impacts the overall scope or operation of the internal audit activity, disclosure should be made to senior management and the board.

If there is anything that interferes with audit's ability to be truly professional, this fact cannot be hidden away. It must be disclosed. Formal disclosure creates a major pressure on each and every member of the internal audit outfit to perform and perform well. There are no hiding places for suspect practices and incompetent staff.

> ### For Further Discussion
> What aspects of the audit process have been covered in the most recent external review of the internal audit shop, and how useful were the recommendations from this review?

—— SECTION 5 ——

AUDIT COMPETENCE

So far, we have argued that the role of internal audit is now fundamental to the corporate governance equation. It could be said that the role of internal audit has the *potential* to be fundamental, but this depends on whether the audit department is up to the task. There really is a new-look internal audit, able to apply a sophisticated blend of audit approaches and techniques to add value to the business and to help the board and audit committee exercise their directing and oversight roles respectively. Much depends on whether the auditor is competent to do this job. As Practice Advisory 1210-1 states:

> Each internal auditor should possess certain knowledge, skills, and other competencies.

The Advisory goes on to argue that this means being proficient in:

- *Internal auditing standards, procedures, and techniques.*
- *Accounting principles and techniques.*
- *Management principles.*
- *Fundamentals of subjects such as accounting, economics, commercial law, taxation, finance, quantitative methods, and information technology.*
- *Dealing with people and communicating effectively.*

The above is seen as something that the audit shop should collectively possess, although not all staff will have expertise in all these areas. Proficiency is seen as being able to function without constant reference to material and assistance. This proficiency should be supported by suitable educational achievements and experience, which should be verified. We can continue our journey through competencies by referring to mandatory Attribute Standard 1200, which states:

> *Engagements should be performed with proficiency and due professional care.*

This means that suitable competencies should be in place individually and collectively. If these competencies are not in place, the audit function will have to seek assistance to ensure it can do a good job, which becomes particularly relevant for smaller audit shops. There are caveats, and we have already explained in Chapter 3 that the internal auditor need not be an IT expert or specialist fraud investigator to perform the audit role. Standard 1220 mentions that the auditor will only be reasonably prudent and competent and is not infallible. We have also said that internal auditors can perform consulting engagements where it would add value to the organization, but only if the auditor possesses the appropriate skills to carry out such work. In fact, Attribute Standard 1210.C1 makes it clear that such consulting projects should be declined if they cannot be carried out competently.

Competency Framework

Due professional care applies to all the work that is carried out by the audit shop but again this does not mean that all risks can always be identified through assurance procedures. The importance of defining and developing suitable audit competencies for the new-look internal auditor is crucial to the future of the profession. Most audit shops have achieved a heightened expectation from senior executives and board members, having explained their potential impact on the crucial risk and control architecture that all organizations need to construct. The task is now to deliver these solutions, endorsements, and advice on risk management and internal controls. The IIA has undertaken research into audit competencies, which resulted in a comprehensive publication from the

IIA Research Foundation called the Competency Framework for Internal Auditing (CFIA)–(Feb. 1999). This included a skills taxonomy, which is briefly noted below:

1. *Cognitive skills:*
   - Technical—communication (ideas, reports, presentations), numeracy, computer literacy, internal auditing technologies.
   - Analytical—research/reasoning, organizational analysis, systems design.
   - Appreciative—discrimination (e.g., knows when to ask questions), value orientation (appreciates training, quality, challenge, etc.), judgment.

2. *Behavioral skills:*
   - Personal—morality, directed personality, inquisitive, flexibility, ability to cope, intelligence.
   - Interpersonal—communication, people skills, team management.
   - Organizational—organizational awareness, functional management (for internal audit), organizational management.

The idea is to move internal auditors from a backward-looking, checking role performed on auditees, toward a forward-looking assurance and consulting service, carried out to add value to the organization (its stakeholders) and management. This concept underpins the new competencies set by CFIA. Competence is driven by the new context of internal auditing, which in turn responds to the new pressures placed on private- and public-sector organizations. These new pressures are derived from the heightened expectations from society for better corporate governance, as outlined earlier in the book. Competence is about being able to do the job and do it well. If the audit shop decides it will help set up and facilitate CSA workshops, this calls for a different skills-set than traditional audit work. The workshop success is heavily dependent on facilitators who understand the context, are able to energize the group, and are good at facilitating.

Competence and Performance

While most auditors understand the context of CSA and how it fits into the risk management and controls-reporting process, they are not necessarily good at energizing groups and facilitating progress. Having set these two elements as competencies for some members of the audit team, staff may be developed accordingly. If not, the extra skills will have to be brought in to assist the audit shop in supporting its plans regarding CSA events. The set competencies should also be aligned to the value-add proposition, so that the audit services, supported by newly acquired services, actually benefit the organization and do not just help the auditor get a better paying job. Better competence should mean a better job is done and therefore overall performance is enhanced. This is why competence should be linked to performance management and target setting. A failure to meet personal targets may mean defined competencies need to be further developed. On the other hand, the development of new competencies should mean targets are achieved, or it may be appropriate to stretch these targets for improved performance.

> ### *For Further Discussion*
> What new audit competencies have come to the fore in recent years, and why have these skills become important to the internal auditor?

—— SECTION 6 ——
INTERVIEWING

One of the most important skills that an auditor requires is the ability to ask and receive answers to relevant questions—that is, interviewing skills. The best way to find something out is to simply ask the person who would know. The first contact an auditor may have with a new client may be the opening interview that kicks off the audit. If this goes well, the rest of the audit will have a platform on which to build a good job. At the end of the audit, there will be an exit interview, again an important stage that will be followed by a draft audit report. Interviewing is a two-way process that benefits from feedback as the points in issue are discussed by both sides to the meeting, and it helps if the auditor can understand the perspective of the client. There is one view that people have a persona that represents their public face, but under this is the real person with fears, aspirations, and personal views. This is much like a system that is being audited: the official procedures, and then what staff really do at work. The challenge is to get below the surface and glimpse the reality, which starts with the interview process. There are several aims of an audit interview:

- Get to know the respondent.
- Introduce the audit objective.
- Secure information required for the audit.
- Promote the importance of risk management and internal controls.
- Enhance the reputation of the audit shop.

- Work out what to do next as a result of the information received.
- Ask about anything else that is seen as an important aspect of the interview.

There is a lot to be gained from the interview situation, and a good auditor will see this as a technique that should be mastered over the years. A typical interview will involve the following stages.

Pre-interview Preparation

There is a temptation to phone the client, say that you are starting the audit, make a date, and turn up ready to go. Although invigorating and fast, it is not recommended as the best way to behave. It is far better to take time, think through the audit objective, and prepare. Points to note include the following:

- First, determine the best way to make contact. It may be that an e-mail, phone call, correspondence with attached note of the audit, or a personal visit may be the best way to set up the meeting.
- Next, identify the person best to contact, and decide whether that should be alone or perhaps accompanied. By the same token, decide whether more than one auditor should attend the meeting. Some people are into videoconferencing and feel that personal contact should be reserved for special occasions.
- Before setting off to the meeting, do some background research and find out what information is published about the area in question. Find out what is already known about the business by looking at previous audit files and permanent audit files.
- Talk to the person who last had contact with the area to see if there is anything that should be taken on board.
- Make a list of areas that need to be covered during the interview, or even as some do, compile a list of key questions.
- Determine whether your audit shop has a policy of sending out the main questions in advance of the interview and a list of documents that the client could perhaps make available during the interview.
- On a wider front, ensure that you have adequate training to handle all types of interviews, even where there are difficulties and potential sensitivities.
- Review any policy the audit shop may have on audit protocols, which should really include a section on client interviews.
- Having done the preparations, set a date, time, and venue to suit the client and provide an agenda and background information if required.
- Before going into the interview, consider doing a self-check. Are you in the right frame of mind to have a positive impact on the client, and are

you ready to see the world from the client's eyes? People who go into interviews with a positive and helpful mindset will get more from the meeting and will be able to give more to the client.

- Think through the image you want and need to project. Dress codes are useful to consolidate the feeling of self-worth. It is said that the first few minutes of an initial contact set the scene for the rest of the interview. Caring about one's appearance is a good start.

Opening

The interview should start with a meeting of the minds. In other words, both parties should agree to meet on the playing field of audit, assurance, assistance, and consulting work. Both sides should see the benefit of working together and progressing the audit to its conclusion. This is what is known as establishing rapport. The opening stage is about introducing both parties, clarifying the objectives of the interview, and agreeing to get fully involved. Points to note are:

- It is helpful if the audit aim and process can be made clear early on and that the client see the audit as not only an obligation but also a worthwhile endeavor.
- Some feel that the auditor should match the client in terms of handshakes, first names, degree of formality, humor, and so on.
- There should be an explanation about where the interview fits into the audit process. It should be part of ongoing discussions where the client and staff should be encouraged to get fully involved in the audit. At some stage, the new-look auditor will have to be distinguished from the old-fashioned (police road block) attitude that was the order of the day years ago.
- It is important to make clear the difference between assurance and consulting roles, and that assurance work has a direct reporting line into the CEO, board, and audit committee. An interview is not just a process of asking questions; it is also a tool for setting an environment to encourage the full involvement of the client. This also means explaining practices that may discourage the client, such as note taking and verifying factual answers.
- A consideration of nonverbal communication (body language) helps assess negative reactions from a client and provides clues where further explanations may be offered by the auditor.
- At the opening part of the interview, make clear that the audit process involves analysis and examination and that it is not just about performing an interview and jumping to conclusions at this stage. Some clients ask for a "position" from the auditor as if the interview will result in an audit

conclusion and report. Correcting this possible misapprehension should be part of the opening phase of the interview.

- It may be an idea to have several strategies for dealing with various "problems." For example, quiet people may be encouraged to open up if you work to find out what makes them tick. Aggressive people may need to let off steam before entering into a constructive dialogue. When meeting people with a reputation for being "tricky," some basic facts should be obtained to help verify some of the information that you get from them. Excessively talkative individuals may have to be gently interrupted to get them back on track. Areas with known problems may benefit from the offer of consulting advice to help focus the conversation. And so on.

Main Part

This is the main questions-and-answers part of the interview. Armed with a list of areas to cover, the experienced interviewer may move between the listed items as the client responds to them, rather than sticking rigidly to the set order. This is why it is generally not a good idea to list entire questions and then read them off from the list. Flexibility and focus are complementary skills that help enhance the meeting. The following are some points to note:

- Listening skills are important. Positive listening involves being encouraging, testing one's understanding, taking an interest, and generally getting best value from the time and expense incurred.
- Take notes to record the information being given, and periodically reiterate the points made to confirm they make sense and reflect what has been said.
- Make a list of outstanding documents, points, and follow-up items. Check these at the end of the interview and make sure each outstanding item will be concluded.
- Avoid judgmental subjects such as whether the interviewee is more capable than his or her line manager.
- Use a mix of appropriate types of questions. Closed questions require a yes/no response and can be used for basic factual confirmations such as "have I got your job title right?" Open questions such as "tell me how you manage risk in your team?" encourage open responses. There are many variations on this theme, but the aim is to achieve a good balance between encouraging the free flow of information and retaining the focus on the objective of the interview, and not wasting time.
- Do not agree with anything that is disagreeable or that should be further discussed. While it is great to get along with the client and enjoy a positive

and easy relationship, it is too easy to cut corners and agree with everything that is said. Difficult issues need to be probed and improper practices noted but not condoned. A core competency for the auditor is to "keep it real" and not fold over under pressure.

- Watch for single-point generalizations by the client. This is where one isolated occurrence is seen as signifying a wide-ranging change of policy.
- Adopt an awareness stance if requested by the client. For example, most operational issues can be associated with the risk management and control system, and the auditor may explain some of the concepts behind this thinking. But only provide these insights if this is what the client has asked for.
- Be efficient. Busy managers cannot afford to take time off to "shoot the breeze." An interview is not a chance to sit around and chew things over—it is a focused series of questions and answers that helps move the audit along.

Closing

It is to be hoped that the opening stage of the interview will have set up a positive and mutually beneficial platform for the process of asking for and receiving relevant information. The questions-and-answers stage should have been an opportunity for the client to set out key risks and any concerns over associated key controls, again doing so in a positive mode. The final part is to close the interview properly:

- Go through a brief summary of important issues and understandings.
- List outstanding items and confirm the action required, by whom, and by when.
- Discuss what happens next and the link to the rest of the audit process.
- Work out how the client will be kept up to date with progress on the audit and findings that may arise along the way.
- Thank the client for the time and help and ask for any outstanding questions.
- Leave an open door so that short interviews can be convened thereafter if necessary.

Post-interview

It is a good idea to work through the interview notes for sense and completeness:

- Typing them up is a good way of doing this.
- A front sheet may be used to summarize the main points arising from the interview.

- Make sure the record is cross-referenced to any other documentation that is referred to during the interview.

Common Ground Congruity

Observing the above standards, practices, and protocols normally leads to a good interview, which is particularly important for the opening meeting with the client and the wrap-up meeting to discuss the main audit findings. However, there are many interviews that go badly wrong, and end in acrimony on both sides, despite all the preparation and planning carried out. At times, this can be confusing to the new auditor, although such problems may possibly be explained through a model we can call the common ground congruity approach. This approach is based on three interfacing factors, as shown in Exhibit 4.1 and described below.

1. *Auditor Agenda.* The auditor's agenda may cover several perspectives and a success assessment criteria that includes the need to:
   - Look good.
   - Get cooperation.
   - Spread risk and control messages.
   - Prepare assurances on adequacy of controls.
   - Get to the truth.
   - Help the client improve things.

Exhibit 4.1.   Common Ground Congruity (CGC)

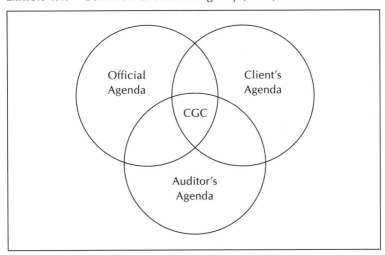

2. *Client Agenda.* Meanwhile, the client may be more concerned with the need to:

- Look good.
- Decide whether to cooperate.
- Avoid a "bad" report.
- Ensure staff and work teams do not get inconvenienced/stressed.
- Get rid of the auditor as soon as possible.
- Listen to and "hear" any hidden messages.
- Check whether the audit will help the business at all.

3. *Official Agenda.* The third aspect is the official agenda—that is, the reason for the interview—that revolves more around the need to:

- Establish contact between the two parties.
- Agree about the work to be done and the timing.
- Set terms of reference.
- Deal with any foreseeable problems.
- Improve the risk management and control system.
- Adhere to interviewing protocols.

The key is to recognize these different agendas and the importance they hold for all three perspectives of the interview. Some strategies to achieve common ground congruity include:

- *Accepting different agendas.* Being aware of the concerns and unspoken views from both the audit side and also the client side is a good starting place. It is also good to focus on the aim of the interview—such as the official agenda—and ensure that this is not lost sight of.

- *Probing unspoken areas of concern.* Being aware of unspoken issues does not mean they are just ignored. If there are signs that the conversation is touching on a hidden agenda, this could be probed. The auditor should appreciate that a reluctance from the interviewee does not necessarily mean this person does not wish to cooperate and has something to hide. It may just be that one of the "outside" issues has been touched on and needs to be explored further. If the client has been receiving complaints from members of staff, this may interfere with their wish to be forthcoming with the auditor about work practices. It may be necessary to give the manager time to explain how staffing issues affect the way work is organized and also confirm that the audit is not about reviewing the manager's performance and certainly is not related to any complaints that are going through the official procedure.

- *Being honest about expectations.* At times, the auditor can reveal some of the audit agenda issues such as increasing an awareness of internal controls as an add-on to the main audit. In terms of the assurance role, it may also be best to make it clear that an official opinion on the state of internal control must be provided as a result of the audit report. Providing a background to this assurance-reporting requirement may help clarify this role.

- *Respecting private areas on both sides.* The auditor may be aware of issues that may be on the mind of the manager. If so, the auditor should try to get these perceived by the manager in terms of risks to the achievement of business objectives. That way, the problems will then feature in the risk management strategy. But there may be private areas of the client's agenda that must be left unspoken, simply through basic mutual respect. If the manager is working extremely long hours and this is something that a staff counselor from Personnel is tackling, it may be that the subject is both personal and confidential, and the auditor may need to respect that viewpoint.

- *Watching out for fog.* Fog spoils the view. It gets in the way of good communications and makes it difficult to give and receive information during an interview. A manager who has a poor view of internal audit may cause a degree of fog that puts negative connotations on most of what the auditor says. Being aware of this fog helps the auditor think through ways of overcoming aspects of perception that make it hard to progress the audit.

- *Being human.* Having a sense of humor and understanding of problems facing a busy management and hard-working staff promotes better communications. Training schemes that cover interviewing skills are very useful but should not seek to restrict some of the natural affiliations and interests that an auditor may have by insisting that there is one style of interview. So long as the objective of the interview is met and the client's and auditor's agendas are understood and managed, the style that is adopted will be one that most suits the auditor.

- *Above all, widening the overlap to achieve common ground congruity.* The common ground congruity model is based on developing the area where the three forces overlap. Any reasonable ways to increase this congruity should be applied to gain as much space and common ground between the auditor and client.

It takes time to internalize these strategies and make them a natural part of the way that interviews and meetings are set up and managed. The payoff is the better impact that can be achieved when the strategy is applied successfully. The interview is an important method for getting to the bottom of things in the quickest way possible. It is good to remember that there is nearly always a dense fog that interferes with the ability of two people to communicate with each other. This fog is made up of differing expectations, some misunderstanding, and the past experiences of each party, and it represents a challenge that needs to be over-come. The good interviewer should either get rid of the fog, learn to work in a foggy climate, or get so close to the other party that the fog doesn't really matter.

> ### For Further Discussion
> *What audit interviews have gone terribly wrong in recent years, and what strategies were used to save the day?*

——— SECTION 7 ———
THE AUDIT MODEL

Professionalism is now added to the audit model, as shown in Exhibit 4.2. Pro-fessionalism is about being able to deliver the requirements of the set risk-based audit strategy.

Society and Stakeholders. The audit model is driven primarily by the needs and interests of society, that is, the need for good company performance that contributes to the economy, and both fair and transparent business practices. Stakeholders include all those who have a direct or indirect interest in the way business, commerce, and public services are conducted.

Shareholders and Investors. Principal stakeholders are the people and insti-tutions who hold shares in listed companies. Banks and investment companies may well have a direct interest that is represented in funds loaned to the com-pany. Meanwhile, *The People* are principal stakeholders in public-sector organi-zations. Company shareholders should exercise their voting rights with due regard to the need to ensure there is ethical behavior and accountability from company officials.

Legal System. There are a multitude of federal and state laws that relate to the way private- and public-sector organizations are established, maintained, and extinguished. Many larger organizations have responded by setting up compli-ance functions to address the variety and magnitude of such legal provisions. Company directors and officials can face severe penalties when specific laws are breached.

Regulators. Most industries have an associated regulator that sets standards and represents the public in ensuring organizations behave properly. The SEC, American Stock Exchange, New York Stock Exchange, and NASDAQ regula-tions are some of the more well-known models.

Exhibit 4.2.   Audit Model 4

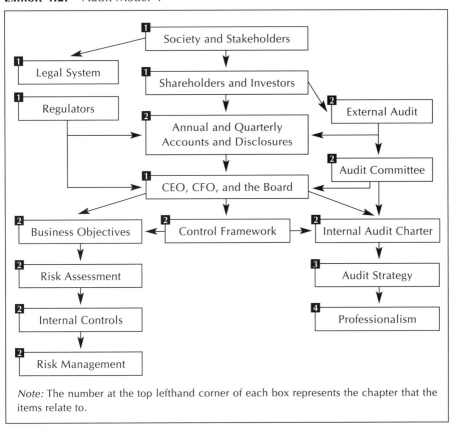

Note: The number at the top lefthand corner of each box represents the chapter that the items relate to.

CEO, CFO, and the Board.   Shareholders appoint a CEO and board of directors to direct and oversee the organization on their behalf. These officers have a responsibility to discharge their duties in a professional manner and account for the results to the shareholders. A management team will be appointed in public-sector bodies and have a similar responsibility to the government and general public. The board should adhere to the highest standards of ethics and ensure they conduct their business in an acceptable and documented manner. Moreover, the board should have in place suitable mechanisms through which it may judge its own performance and conduct.

Annual Accounts and Disclosures.   The organization reports to its stakeholders through published financial and performance statements. These reports act as a window to the outside world, and business analysts spend a great deal of time examining the detailed facts and figures in company accounts on behalf of their clients. Listed companies along with many other organizations have to make various disclosures on an annual and quarterly basis, in particular resulting from the Sarbanes-Oxley Act. The published accounts should be reliable and now have to be personally certified by the principal executive and CFO.

External Audit.   The external auditors are appointed by the shareholders to make sure the board has provided a full and reliable account of the company's financial performance over the previous year. The financial statements will be checked by the external auditors before they are formally published. External auditors should ensure they are independent in their audit work and are able to exercise an appropriate degree of professional skepticism at all times. This part of the audit model is a major contribution to governance as material published by the organization is independently verified.

Audit Committee.   A further layer of governance that is growing in importance is the audit committee. This forum, established by the board, comprises independent directors who provide an additional oversight role, focusing on the specialist areas of financial accounting, ethics, audit, accountability, risk management, and control. The audit committee is not there to undermine the board but rather provides advice and support regarding the specialist areas in question. Moreover, it should ask challenging questions of the board, on the premise that it is better that these tough questions come from an in-house audit committee than from external regulators.

Internal Audit Charter.   The internal auditor's role and position in the organization is set by the audit charter that is agreed upon by the board and audit committee. To be of any real use, this charter should be set firmly within the governance, risk management, and control arena.

Business Objectives.   The next stage of the model relates to the setting of formal corporate objectives that document the mission of the organization and what it is there to achieve.

Risk Assessment.   Anything that impacts the business objectives can be seen as a potential risk. These risks need to be understood, isolated, and weighed in terms of significance. Formal risk assessment gives an organization a head start in understanding where its vulnerabilities lie and where it has scope for advancement. The bottom line is that risks that affect the organization's ability to deliver and achieve its objectives have to be addressed for there to be any real chance of success. Control risk self-assessment and regular risk surveys are good ways of promoting risk assessment throughout the organization.

Internal Control.   Controls should be in place to address risks that have been assessed as significant. The current climate stresses the importance of controls over financial reporting and disclosures, as well as compliance with various standard regulations. The systems of internal control need to be maintained, updated, and made right as part of the way employees work.

Risk Management.   Controls fit into the wider remit of risk management and managers, and their teams need to build risk mitigation into their overall strategies. There are many different potential responses to risks, depending on the nature, significance, and cost of controls. The organization needs to weigh up the available measures on a regular basis and ensure the adopted response meets the expectations of the board and stakeholders. In other words, the response to risk needs to fit the risk tolerance levels that have been defined by the board in its risk and control policy.

Control Framework.   The entire risk management and control policy should be incorporated within the adopted control framework. Standard models such as COSO sit on a foundation of ethical values and propriety, which may be seen as the "tone at the top" that is set by the board and top executives.

Audit Strategy.   The audit model includes the response from internal audit to the corporate risk policy and approach that is used in the organization. Based on the audit charter and driven by the corporate risk assessment that the board and management have developed, internal audit should construct a strategy that reflects the future direction of the organization and risks that arise in achieving this strategy.

Professionalism.   Having designed a high-impact audit strategy, there needs to be a high-impact audit department in place to deliver set goals. This is, the next part of the audit model, where professionalism is an essential component of the audit model. Professionalism is based on several key factors, including:

- Independence
- Competent and motivated audit staff
- Good procedures and documentation
- Quality assurance mechanisms, such as supervision and internal and external reviews

----- SECTION 8 -----

SUMMARY: TOP TEN CONSIDERATIONS

A summary of the ten main points covered in the chapter follows:

1. A quality internal audit service is fundamental to ensuring a successful role in corporate governance, and official standards require that "the CAE should develop and maintain a quality assurance and improvement

program that covers all aspects of the internal audit activity and continuously monitors its effectiveness." Quality depends on:

- Good standards
- Well-trained and motivated staff
- A clear sense of direction
- A defined methodology (or blend of methodologies)
- Good documentation, supervision, and reviews
- A well-managed internal audit outfit

2. One cornerstone of quality is the adoption of professional auditing standards. The IIA standards cover attributes and performance standards, implementation standards, a code of ethics, and various practice advisories. The attribute standards cover:

1000—Purpose, Authority, and Responsibility

1100—Independence and Objectivity

1200—Proficiency and Due Professional Care

1300—Quality Assurance and Improvement Program

3. The performance standards cover:

2000—Managing the Internal Audit Activity

2100—Nature of Work

2200—Engagement Planning

2300—Performing the Engagement

2400—Communicating Results

2500—Monitoring Progress

2600—Management's Acceptance of Risks

4. The IIA Code of Ethics contains the following key principles:

- Integrity
- Objectivity
- Credibility
- Competency

5. Good documentation is also important in ensuring quality. The IIA standards require that "the CAE should establish policies and procedures to guide the internal audit activity." The audit manual is a device for capturing documentation standards and should be kept up to date. Documentation standards should ensure professionalism and security and should cover rules on access and retention. Working papers should be prepared in line with several considerations, including that they be:

- Useful
- Complete

- Practicable
- Cross-referenced
- Reviewed
- Headed
- Linked to audit objectives
- Linked to findings and report
- Minimal
- Checked
- Summarized
- Identify the auditor
- Consistent
- User friendly
- Logical

6. Supervision, internal reviews, and external reviews are all important in checking that the audit staff and the audit shop itself are professional and up to date. The standards require that "the internal audit activity should adopt a process to monitor and assess the overall effectiveness of the quality program." External reviews may be quite wide ranging and may address considerations such as:
   - Use of professional standards
   - Audit charter
   - Range of approaches and methods in use
   - Balance between assurance and consulting work
   - Value-add proposition
   - Risk-based auditing
   - Impact on corporate governance, risk management, and control
   - Whether world-class practices are applied

7. Competent auditors are able to work in line with professional standards and standards require that "each internal auditor should possess certain knowledge, skills, and other competencies." The IIA's Competency Framework (CFIA) recognizes several key aspects of competence:
   - Cognitive skills—technical, analytical, appreciative, value oriented, and able to make judgments
   - Behavioral skills—personal, interpersonal, and organizational

8. Good interviewing skills are essential to the effective internal auditor. One model of the stages for high-impact interviews may appear as follows:
   - Preinterview preparation
   - Opening

- Main part
- Closing
- Postinterview

9. Common ground congruity is a model that tries to explain the perceptions behind three different agendas:

- Auditor agenda
- Client agenda
- Official agenda

The idea is to seek as much common ground between these three overlapping agendas and make progress in all interviews and contact between the client and auditor by:

- Probing unspoken areas of concern
- Being honest about expectations
- Respecting private areas on both sides
- Watching out for fog
- Being human

10. The audit model for Chapter 4 includes the new component of professionalism. This is based on many of the factors already mentioned, including:

- Independence
- Competent and motivated audit staff
- Good procedures and documentation
- Quality assurance mechanisms, including supervision and internal and external reviews

——— SECTION 9 ———

YOUR PERSONAL DEVELOPMENT EXERCISES

We have defined the standards to which staff will be working in discharging the audit role. We have also defined the types of competencies that underpin this ability to perform to the required standards. For the newly recruited internal auditor, there is a journey ahead to achieving full professionalism. A college diploma or university business degree is a start, but the new graduate is still a long way from being a professional internal auditor. There are a number of things that the new auditor may do as part of this development, including the following:

1. *Study the introductory text.* This book provides a basic introduction to internal auditing. It is a short text that should be assimilated by the

newly appointed employee. By working through the chapters, you are obtaining what may be seen as a minimum amount of knowledge that is needed to make a start at a new career. There is nothing in the book that should prove difficult for the new starter, and the material is roughly consistent with the standards set by the IIA, as a benchmark for best practice.

2. **Do the development exercises.** At the end of each chapter, there are various exercises that should be tackled relating to the material covered in the relevant chapter. These exercises are designed to help turn the theoretical coverage into practical elements of performing the job. Moreover, the exercises help you assess the extent to which you have assimilated the text. To act as a challenge, the exercises may be used by your new employer to help you work through the text and demonstrate that all key learning points have been understood.

3. **Look at the audit manual published by your new employer or prospective employer.** Internal audit can be somewhat jargonized, and there are certain terms, methods, and protocols that are familiar to experienced staff but that appear strange to newcomers. Each employer will have a guide published on the Internet, CD, laptop, or network, or in a manual that sets out their interpretation of the audit role and process. It is a good idea to get hold of the relevant material and work through its contents. The ideas and terms will form a useful basis for any discussions with new colleagues, particularly around points that need to be further explained or topics that have not been covered in this introductory text.

4. **Check www.theiia.org.** The Institute of Internal Auditors is the only professional body that specializes in internal auditing. It is based in the United States, but many countries have their own equivalent or a chapter that together form a global body, with an international representation. The IIA has a Web site that contains a wealth of information on audit standards, guidelines, specific topics and research, as well as training, development, books, and other resources that underpin the profession. Nonmembers will find some interesting material, and members will have access to much more information through IIA's password-controlled facility. A great deal of benefit may be gained from searching the Web site and accessing material relating to both the profession and the wider corporate governance, risk management, and control arenas.

5. **Check the Internet generally.** Many internal audit shops around the world have their own Web sites and material dedicated to the way they perform the internal audit role. Many useful hours may be spent looking through the windows of various audit outfits and learning about the variety of audit styles, approaches, and viewpoints.

6. *Read the business press.* We have mentioned the corporate governance, risk management, and control debate, and this is derived from an ongoing battle to ensure corporate excellence is matched with corporate responsibilities to stakeholders and others. This is against the background of fraud, abuse, and blurred ethical lines that makes it hard to distinguish between acceptable business practices and outright abuse. The business press, including Web site–based material, has much to say about audit committees, external audit, independent directors, disclosure requirements, SEC regulations, corporate accountability, ethical standards, internal control, risk management, corporate liability, fraud, corruption, and many other issues that relate loosely to the governance debate. Nothing stands still, and the development of initiatives, scandals, and calls for better solutions can be viewed through the business press as each new story unfolds. Keeping an eye on these ongoing developments will be a crucial element of your personal career development.

7. *Get a copy of the core audit competencies.* People tend to respond positively to an employer who makes clear what is expected from each member of the staff. As a short cut to this process, it is a good idea to obtain a copy of the agreed competencies for the internal audit staff. If these competencies are not published, then just ask a senior figure, What makes for a good internal auditor? The answer to this question will provide a benchmark against which you can plot your personal development. It is simple. Get hold of the competencies and assess which ones you already possess, which are being developed, and which need much more work. Then set out a plan that means you can move closer to the targets that have been set. For example, if auditors are expected to be skilled at performing presentations to groups (say, client managers or the audit committee), this skill may be developed and practiced. Some of the exercises at the end of each chapter may be turned into papers that can be presented at the next audit manager's meeting, as a means of practicing and getting feedback on this skill. If this is not possible, you may volunteer to do a presentation to the next meeting of a local community group that you belong to, again to get experience and help develop confidence in presentation skills.

8. *Think about training and development.* Training is a great way of developing the knowledge and understanding that underpin professional audit work. Getting into suitable training courses creates a good opportunity for progress, so long as what has been learned can be put to use back at the workplace. The events need not be audit-specific, as developing good report-writing skills can be learned from an open program that covers report writing generally. On-line or CD-based training may

also be used as a convenient way of working at your own pace, in your own time and convenience. Training related to the set competencies is much more effective than courses that do not have this link.

9. *What about certification?* A good way of consolidating the learning process is to enroll in the IIA certification program. This involves formal study, then preparation, followed by an multiple-choice exam whereby the knowledge gained through these studies can be demonstrated to the examiner. Professional auditing standards encourage full qualification as do many employers. Having gained the qualification, this is only the start, and there is a requirement to obtain further development. In fact, Attribute Standard 1230 argues that "internal auditors should enhance their knowledge, skills, and other competencies through continuing professional development."

10. *Check your interpersonal skills.* The new-look auditor is able to review businesses' areas and programs and is able to help and advise busy managers. Much depends on being able to focus in on key issues and help move things forward in the right direction. A lot of audit work involves close analysis and formal examination, but an equal amount of audit work involves understanding the client and being able to relate to their experiences. In other words, much depends on good interpersonal skills. Do a self-check and find out how good you are at understanding people and communicating well with them. Armed with this knowledge, the results may be used in your personal development plan. If you find that you have poor listening skills and are easily bored and distracted, it is possible to practice this skill by taking more of an interest in listening carefully to those people you meet. It is possible to buy a short text on listening skills and work on some of the exercises that are suggested to improve your technique.

11. *Talk to other auditors.* You cannot develop in a vacuum. Therefore, a good technique is to talk to colleagues about their experiences as part of the learning process. We have said many times that there is a new-look auditor who has moved on from the traditional checking-based approach. Some newly appointed auditors misread this point and assume that most experienced auditors are old-fashioned and not worth talking to. This is wrong. What is happening is that the analytical and formal skills honed by the auditor over the years have been added to forward-looking consulting skills that complement the existing skills database. The experienced staff can provide a wealth of advice and tips to the new starter and are a source of great help if asked. Where the audit shop tends not to use audit teams but assigns projects to individuals, it can get a little lonely. Social events and office lunches and even coaching meetings are

great ways to keep in touch and swap notes. Conferences and IIA society affairs are good ways of broadening your horizons and meeting auditors from different companies and sectors. The Discussion Points included at the end of each section in this book can be used as a basis for formal audit networking.

12. *Commit to the profession.* The final point to note is that there are many people who see internal auditing as a wonderful profession. They are committed to a career in the profession and keep themselves energized and alert over many years. Most audit work involves a lot of traveling and meeting new people as well as working to tight deadlines, reviewing what is, in effect, a series of new operations or systems. Assurance work is much the same as consulting work in this respect, although assurance work has the added complication of resulting in a widely published report, thus adding more tension to the project and relationship with the client. Some argue that it takes a certain type of person to thrive in this environment, while others say it is just a matter of training, experience, and development. If it all comes together and you enjoy the work and achieve good results, there is no reason why you should not commit to a career in internal audit.

In the past, many staff members spent a spell in internal auditing as part of their management development program and went on to become senior managers. The insights into how the business works and the discipline from performing professional audit work to set standards would contribute to well-rounded managers with good potential once they have moved out of audit. Nowadays, there are a great number of auditors who remain in the profession and develop into top people doing first-class jobs, again within the internal audit world. Whatever the format, there is much that can be gained from time spent in the field, and the twelve steps outlined above should be part of this process of continual personal development.

5

THE AUDIT PROCESS

THE AUDIT PROCESS

In one sense, there is no audit process as such. The audit process will depend on the approach that is adopted. We have described several different approaches to audit work in Chapter 3. It is important to set a context for audit work so that the actual fieldwork can be related to the bigger corporate picture. Most organizations now have to report on their internal controls, and although this is primarily based around the financial reporting system, there is a view that the broader control dimension needs to be considered to give a complete picture to shareholders and other stakeholders. Keeping it general so as to include listed companies, the rest of the private sector, and also public-sector organizations, it may be argued that each business manager (and work team) needs to implement something along the lines of the following ten-step process across all aspects of the business:

1. Get clear business and team objectives.
2. Ensure staff have a good understanding of the corporate risk management and internal controls policy and control framework in use.
3. Identify the risks that impact the achievement of these objectives, including the risk of failing to comply with formal disclosure regulations.
4. Work out which risks are most significant in terms of materiality and likelihood.
5. Clarify which controls (key controls) are most important in mitigating these high-impact risks.
6. Fit the control design into the wider risk management strategy for addressing risk.
7. Isolate any gaps in the risk management strategy that mean there is not a reasonable expectation that objectives will be achieved.
8. Ensure key controls are working in a way that guards against significant risks.

9. Provide formal quarterly statements on the state of internal controls with a view on whether this system provides a reasonable expectation of keeping risks to the business to an acceptable level.

10. Keep the controls under review, and update the assessment whenever there are changes that impact the risk profile and control infrastructure.

The internal auditor should try to fit audit work into the above process on two levels:

1. *Assurance.* By providing a separate objective review of the adopted arrangements to determine whether the process is sound and falls in line with corporate policy on risk management and control as well as whether the process addresses all key aspects of the ten-stage process above.

2. *Consulting.* To offer help, advice, and support to promote the design and implementation of a suitable risk management and control process, which may include facilitating the development of a system based on the ten stages above.

The new-look internal auditing will involve more than checking compliance with set standards and procedures. It involves understanding the way the organization promotes a system akin to the ten stages above; or where little progress has been made, it involves helping management set up the necessary arrangements. This starts with a suitable audit strategy and then fieldwork based around the ten key stages of business risk management.

For Further Discussion

What challenges are brought to bear when the internal auditor seeks to perform large consulting engagements?

—— SECTION 2 ——

RISK-BASED STRATEGIES

The audit process starts with a clear and well-thought-out strategy. Many internal audit staff have grown up with an audit risk model that assigns risk scores to each "audit unit" across the organization. So areas that were large, not recently audited, and financially based, and where there had been problems in the past, would probably end up in the annual audit plan. Audit tended to see risk in terms of the potential for fraud or abuse and noncompliance with financial regulations. This was defined as "audit risk," and each planned audit would be conducted from the viewpoint of what was important to auditors rather than to executives and stakeholders. Risk-based audit strategies turn this idea on its head and start with a value proposition that asks, "How can we best service the organization in promoting robust and transparent arrangements for governance, risk management, and control?" The audit process starts with the corporate risk assessment, which is then fed into the audit strategy. The first point of principle is that internal audit must formulate long-term plans. Performance Standard 2010 dictates:

> *The CAE should establish risk-based plans to determine the priorities of the internal audit activity, consistent with the organization's goals.*

It is not possible to adopt a purist consulting approach where the audit team sits back with no discernible plans in place and wait for requests from management. Audit must formally plan how to apply its resource. There is help at hand in the form of Practice Advisory 2010-2, which provides guidance on the planning front with the following key position:

> *The internal audit activity's audit plan should be designed based on an assessment of risk and exposures that may affect the organization. Ultimately, the audit objective is to provide management with information to mitigate the negative consequences associated with accomplishing the organization's objectives. The degree or materiality of exposure can be viewed as risk mitigated by establishing control activities.*

Advisory 2010-2 has provided a road map of sorts that guides the task of developing risk-based plans, with selected extracts noted in bold below:

- **"The audit universe can include components from the organization's strategic plan. By incorporating components of the organization's strategic plan, the audit universe will consider and reflect the overall business plan objectives."**

  Auditors used to split up the organization into segments that constituted the audit universe. This universe might end up with various financial applications, such as payroll, budgeting, income, banking, treasury management, and payments. There may be other information-based processes, such as performance measuring, financial reporting, ordering, and business planning. Added to this may be various business units, operations, projects, and support services. Each audit unit could then be assigned a risk factor to determine whether it entered into the current annual audit plan. This audit concept tended to involve reviews of past data and results, much like the annual external audit of last year's accounts when they have been closed. Internal audit thought-leaders involved in the CFIA research (see Chapter 4) considered the trend toward forward-looking audits where the "review role" was being replaced by a much more progressive "pre-view role." In other words, the audit shop is driven by the organization's set strategy, with a focus on future success and credibility rather than investigations into past performance. The CAE then derives audit plans from corporate objectives and views the audit universe from the standpoint of the board's forward-looking strategies. This is a crucial shift from days of old.

- *"Strategic plans are also likely to reflect the organization's attitude toward risk and the degree of difficulty to achieving planned objectives."*

  Risk perspectives from internal auditors have also shifted from the concept of "audit risk" to the more relevant "corporate risk." What concerns the board, executives, and senior management can be summed up in terms of risk, and this is built into the organization's strategy for progress. Taking these strategic plans as a starting place for developing the audit strategy makes good sense. There is just one caveat to this formula: When the board has not obtained a firm grasp of risk concepts and risk management, and has developed a business strategy without taking on board any assessment of risk, the CAE may offer to provide an educational role to the board or suggest that a suitable party be employed to perform this role, and ensure that strategic plans are robust and recognize significant risks. With any luck, this will result in a revised strategic plan that is risk-focused, which can then form the basis of the audit strategy.

- *"It is advisable to assess the audit universe on at least an annual basis to reflect the most current strategies and direction of the organization. The audit universe can be influenced by the results of the risk management process."*

  The audit universe becomes less like a fixed set of auditable units and more akin to a dynamic interpretation of the changing dimensions that come together to form "the organization." This changing dimension will adopt varying forms and structures as it evolves in response to market conditions in terms of E-business, mergers, demergers, and major restructuring exercises. As the organization flexes and adapts to its environment, the audit universe also flexes in conjunction with these changes. The audit universe should be restated at least annually, and it is possible to employ a policy whereby it changes more often and most certainly whenever there are new programs, business reprofiling, and anything else that impacts the strategic plans and associated resource alignment.

- *"When developing audit plans the outcomes of the risk management process should be considered."*

  The ten-stage process that was mentioned in Section 1 of this chapter is in fact the business risk management process. Audit plans should be based on and linked into the organization's risk management process. The questions we have asked are, "What do we need to provide assurances on? And in what way can we be useful in promoting risk management?" These questions cannot be asked in a vacuum but must instead be derived from a review of what is happening in the various business lines, support teams, and programs. The audit strategy is firmed up through an analysis of the state of risk management across the organization. Different parts and sections will have made different degrees of progress. Meanwhile, the organization itself will be in a state of continual grouping and regrouping that presents fresh challenges in the way risk is managed in newly formed business outfits. A great deal of information for shaping the audit strategy will come from talking to executives about changes that are happening or are going to happen in their areas of responsibility. Assurance services and consulting input may be planned into the audit schedules, since the adopted approach will depend on whether the organization has been able to establish a suitable system of risk management and control reporting.

- *"Audit work schedules should be based on, among other factors, an assessment of risk priority and exposure. Prioritizing is needed to make decisions for applying relative resources based on the significance of risk and exposure."*

This is a continuation of the previous point made. Risk management is essentially about how to assign resources and where decisions need to be focused. Audit planning follows suit and is essentially about assigning resources in line with risk priorities. Once the corporate body has decided where to focus its priorities, internal audit may likewise develop its plans, based around the same prioritization, so long as the corporate body knows what it is doing.

- *"A variety of risk models exist to assist the chief audit executive in prioritizing potential audit subject areas. Most risk models utilize risk factors to establish the priority of engagements such as: dollar materiality; asset liquidity; management competence; quality of internal controls; degree of change or stability; time of last audit engagement; complexity; employee and government relations; etc."*

Having worked out the corporate risk profile, the internal audit shop will have to decide how to assign its resources. The factors mentioned above can help guide this decision. Some auditors argue against using a set criteria and feel that the audit effort should be based on the corporate interpretation of risk and not a set of factors designed by the internal auditors. It may be that the audit committee has a view on fraud, impropriety, financial misstatement, and regulatory noncompliance and wants these factored into the way audit develops its plans.

Another approach is to prepare awareness seminars to get business managers and finance staff to appreciate the importance of regulator compliance and encourage them to build these into their own business risk assessments. In this way, the managers and executives will be speaking the same language as the audit committee and auditors, both external and internal. Where the audit team has a compliance approach and has to visit hundreds of local sites that should be employing clear operational standards and financial procedures, it is possible to assign compliance-based factors to each site and assess relative risk. In less rigid environments, risk assessment would need to be developed at a local level, by those most involved in the operation or program. One further approach is to set out a number of high-level strategic reviews in the audit plans to cover the organization's governance process, overall risk management arrangements, and the control framework in use (e.g., COSO).

- *"Changes in management direction, objectives, emphasis, and focus should be reflected in updates to the audit universe and related audit plan."*

Internal audit plans need to be fluid. Many audit shops have moved on from five-year plans updated each year and now adopt response-based strategies, which reflect the current or planned situation. As the organization changes, so do the audit strategy, plans, and even approach.

- *"The chief audit executive should, at least annually, prepare a statement of the adequacy of internal controls to mitigate risks. This statement should also comment on the significance of unmitigated risk and management's acceptance of such risk."*

We have already mentioned that the new corporate era requires the senior executive and CFO to prepare a published statement on internal control, primarily to support the financial reporting and regulatory compliance requirements. The Sarbanes-Oxley Act and resulting NYSE rules mean that all listed companies now require an internal audit function. Where the internal auditor is able to provide an objective view on the state of internal controls, this gives the executives and board a head start in the reporting stakes. The annual audit plan provides a snapshot to the board and audit committee on what will be audited during the year and what consulting work will also be provided. When formulating the audit plan, one eye should be kept on the annual audit report that will be prepared at the end of the year. If the audit plan covers areas that are uppermost on the list of "top board-level risks," the audit report will have much more impact than one that covers a great deal of low-level detail. Meaningful reporting starts with meaningful planning, and this starts with understanding what risks and associated controls affect the business most.

From the above, it is clear that the auditor must reach outside the audit office to formulate meaningful plans. This point is made clear in Performance Standard 2010.A1:

> *The internal audit activity's plan of engagements should be based on a risk assessment, undertaken a least annually. The input of senior management and the board should be considered in this process.*

The audit plan will also include consulting projects that have been agreed to. The following criteria are used in Performance Standard 2010.C1 to assess whether a requested project should be included in the plans, depending on whether there is potential for the work to:

- *Improve management of risks.*
- *Add value.*
- *Or improve the organization's operations.*

Having prepared the annual audit plan in conjunction with the matters discussed above, it will need to be properly resourced. This is an important point covered by Performance Standard 2030, which states:

> *The CAE should ensure that internal audit resources are appropriate, sufficient, and effectively deployed to achieve the approved plan.*

The resourced audit plan will then need to be formally adopted by the board and audit committee, and any limitations in terms of audit resources will need to be identified. There are two basic approaches to annual audit planning:

1. Determine the level of audit coverage by reference to the state of risk management and control in the organization and the level of assurance activity required by the board and audit committee, and the level of consulting input requested from senior management. Then secure resources to support the plan from the internal audit staff, and seek an appropriate budget to meet any shortfall.

2. Determine the level of audit staff available within the audit team and budget that has been assigned. Then assign these to the coverage by reference to the state of risk management and control in the organization, the level of assurance activity required by the board and audit committee, and the level of consulting input requested from senior management. Then notify the board of any shortfall in audit coverage due to resource limitations.

A risk-based audit strategy and meaningful plans that are properly resourced are key to a successful audit service. The CAE may wish to employ a planning process that fits the way the organization plans and enables the smooth transition between financial years. For organizations with a March 31 year-end, it is possible to plan in the manner shown in Exhibit 5.1. This timetable will be operated in a stable environment. Any upheaval and urgent change programs, such as a large company takeover or product diversification, may shift the planning horizons. Much also depends on the balance between assurance and consulting work. As with the external audit profession, the trend now is toward more assurance- and attestation-based work, with consulting services taking a back seat. This balance, however, may change over the years. In terms of the overall audit planning process, the general stages may be as set out in Exhibit 5.2 and described below:

1. ***Board/audit committee agenda.*** The start of everything will be the corporate governance, risk management, and control agenda set by the board and overseen by the audit committee. This is based on a CAE presence with the board and the internal audit process's being viewed as a linchpin for ensuring that performance, conformance, and accountability meet stakeholders' needs. If this stage is missing, the rest of the planning stages will be less effective.

2. ***Audit charter.*** The charter will set out the terms of reference, role, and responsibilities of the audit shop. Planning needs to be framed by a formal definition of roles, and it is only the matters that fall within the remit described in the audit charter that should be addressed in the plans. For example, if the audit team does not get involved in fraud

Exhibit 5.1. Audit Planning Cycle

October–November:	Announce the planning process and provide FAQs.
November–December:	Secure information on risk assessment throughout the organization through interviews and/or questionnaires. Talk to the audit committee on audit coverage and reporting formats.
December–February:	Analyze information received and send out draft plans for comment. Also make clear the criteria for accepting consulting projects and request proposals.
February–March:	Compile comments from client and put together annual audit plan; send to audit committee for approval. Hold discussions with audit team and consider outline plans.
March–April:	Implement new year plan and establish review mechanism to ensure regular updates.

Exhibit 5.2. Planning Stages

1. Board/audit committee agenda (*governance, risk management, and control*)
2. Audit charter
3. Audit strategy
4. Annual audit plan
5. Quarterly audit plan
6. Work program
7. Preliminary survey
8. Assignment plan
9. Audit fieldwork
10. Report
11. Follow-up

investigations and there is an in-house forensic team that assumes this role, it will impact the audit plans. In other words, there may be less need to provide large contingency allowances that might otherwise be required for resourcing any fraud investigations.

3. *Audit strategy.* The next stage is to develop a formal strategy to deliver the audit objective. It is best to start with the organization's own corporate objectives, to reinforce the view that audits do not work to their own mysterious devices. Ideally, the audit strategy will be risk based and reflect the growing importance of risk management and control within all organizations.

4. *Annual audit plan.* This document will form a type of "contract" or understanding between the audit shop and the audit committee. It will list the audits that should be completed during the year and indicate whether they are large, medium, or small projects as well as indicate the quarter that each audit relates to. The planned hours should be matched with the audit hours available from staff. Moreover, a contingency allowance should be provided consisting of unallocated hours, for ad hoc consulting work and urgent projects. Note that most audit committees have a remit to commission special investigations by the internal auditor or external party, if required. The annual plan will be formally adopted by the audit committee. One version, among many, appears in Exhibit 5.3.

5. *Quarterly audit plan.* The annual audit plan should be broken down into four quarters, and each defined audit should be tentatively assigned

Exhibit 5.3.   Annual Audit Plan

Ref	Audit	Risk Score	Source	Type	Special Factors	Qtr 1	Qtr 2	Qtr 3	Qtr 4
1.2	Contract A	27	Request	Assure	abc . . . 15 days	X			
1.5	KPIs	30	Risk plans	Assure	abc . . . 10 days		X		
2.7	Payroll	28	Risk plans	Assure	abc . . . 15 days	X			
3.6	Claims	33	Risk plans	Assure	abc . . . 5 days				X
3.2	Projects	26	Request	Consult	abc . . . 5 days			X	
Etc.									

to a quarter: April–June; July–September; October–December; and January–March. In practice, the thirteen-week, quarterly planning period is extremely important in the current business environment. It now has more meaning than the annual plan because organizations move so quickly that three monthly reviews can better capture emerging risks than an annual event can. Meanwhile, Sarbanes-Oxley recognizes the role of quarterly reviews in the way internal control disclosures are being requested. For listed companies, the quarterly planning review provides an opportunity to restrike the annual plan and respond to the new concerns that invariably arise in most business and government sectors. Plans that have fallen behind from reality have no real use to anyone. Plans based on an annual risk process may likewise become a standing joke. As risks change, as risk responses change, and as control profiles weaken or gain vigor across the organization, so the response from internal audit needs to change to reflect this fact. Quarterly planning is a useful way of capturing these developments and is increasingly becoming a key decision-making time frame.

6. ***Work program.*** It is possible to take the quarterly audit plan and assign work to individual audit staff in outline. A further control is to develop monthly or six weekly work programs that can be planned in some detail. In terms of short-term work programs for audit staff and teams, it is possible to determine:

 • Vacation leave.

 • Planned absence for medical attention.

- Nonavailability of staff on long-term sick leave.
- Training needs that involve assignment to different types of audit work.
- Rotation of audit responsibilities if this policy is employed.
- Work balance between audit managers and audit teams.
- Absences due to conferences, seminars, examinations, and other reasons.
- Short-term assignment of staff to other locations.
- Vacancies and recruitment drives.

It is then possible to brief each audit team and hand out monthly work programs that are pretty well finalized. It is also possible to establish a close monitoring system that provides monthly reports on the progress of the planned work, which allows quick action where there are obvious problems.

7. *Preliminary survey.* Having received an audit engagement from the work program, there is still some way to go before the detailed field-work is carried out. The background work is called the preliminary survey, and this allows appropriate terms of reference to be firmed up and agreed.

8. *Assignment plan.* This is about taking the set terms of reference and working through how to best deliver the audit objective. Much of this stage in the planning process involves practicalities and preparing the ground for the fieldwork.

9. *Audit fieldwork.* This is about performing the actual audit and compiling evidence on the adequacy of risk management and controls.

10. *Report.* Findings, an opinion, and report should be formally communicated at the end of the audit fieldwork. These matters should also be discussed with the client during the course of the audit as the picture is developed through the analysis and evaluation carried out by the auditor, ideally with help from the client and operational staff.

11. *Follow-up.* This stage simply asks whether agreed actions and decisions have been fully implemented and whether the adopted risk management strategy is working well.

There is a natural link between planning, performing, and reporting. The distinct stages flow together to form a whole—that is, a good and valuable audit. Excellent planning occurs where the planner starts to think about the report and works backward to consider what needs to be done to get to this report, and the positive action that should result. Each and every audit that is carried out by audit staff should in some way relate back to the big-picture strategic planning that begins with the boardroom's aims for successful performance and the audit committee's wish to ensure that pertinent accountability and transparency is also achieved and disclosed.

For Further Discussion

What exactly is risk-based auditing, and is it any different from the basic approach to long-term planning that has been employed by internal auditors for many years?

SECTION 3

PRELIMINARY SURVEYS

This very useful technique links the monthly work schedules/program to the assignment plan. The approved annual audit plan sets out which audits need to be done for the year, split into four quarters. The lead auditor is given the job through the work plan and needs to launch into the fieldwork and complete the audit within the budget hours. The audit itself will be driven by the terms of reference that have been set and agreed upon by the auditor and client. Each engagement must have a clear objective. The term *objective* is defined as:

> *Broad statements developed by internal auditors that define intended engagement accomplishments.*

The preliminary survey was traditionally about doing a little background work, say on the previous audit files so that an assignment plan can be established. Performance Standard 2201 makes clear the need to focus on risk and control issues by saying:

> *In planning the engagement, internal auditors should consider:*
>
> - *The objectives of the activity being reviewed and the means by which the activity controls its performance.*
> - *The significant risks to the activity, its objectives, resources and operations and the means by which the potential impact of risk is kept to an acceptable level.*
> - *The adequacy and effectiveness of the activities risk management and control systems compared to the relevant control framework or model.*
> - *The opportunity for making significant improvements to the activity's risk management and control systems.*

This Standard hints at the vast scope for flexibility and the use of a blended audit approach that was discussed earlier, while Performance Standard 2200 states:

> *Internal auditors should develop and record a plan for each engagement.*

Note that an engagement is seen as:

> *A specific internal audit assignment, task, or review activity, such as an internal audit, Control Self-Assessment review, fraud examination, or consultancy. An engagement may include multiple tasks or activities designed to accomplish a specific set of related objectives.*

The approach will fit the type of engagement in question. The preliminary survey is viewed by Practice Advisory 2210.A1-1 as being:

> *A process for gathering information, without detailed verification, on the activity being examined . . . to:*
>
> - *Understand the activity under review.*
> - *Identify significant areas warranting special emphasis.*
> - *Obtain information for use in performing the engagement.*
> - *Determine whether further auditing is necessary.*

More recently, the preliminary survey has developed a crucial role in the audit process, and to appreciate its importance we need to revisit the ten-stage business risk management process that should be happening in all significant organizations:

1. Set clear business and team objectives.
2. Ensure staff have a good understanding of the corporate risk management and internal controls policy.
3. Identify the risks that impact the achievement of these objectives, including the risk of failing to comply with formal disclosure regulations.
4. Work out which risks are most significant in terms of materiality and likelihood.
5. Clarify which controls (key controls) are most important in mitigating these high-impact risks.
6. Fit the control design into the wider risk management strategy for addressing risk.
7. Isolate gaps in the risk management strategy that mean there is not a reasonable expectation that objectives will be achieved.
8. Ensure key controls are working in a way that guards against significant risks.

9. Provide formal quarterly statements on the state of internal controls with a view on whether this system provides a reasonable expectation of keeping risks to the business to an acceptable level.

10. Keep the controls under review and update the assessment whenever there are changes that impact the risk profile and control infrastructure.

We have already mentioned one version of internal auditing argues that the auditor needs to consider where the audit area stands in terms of developing effective systems of risk management. This ten-stage model can also be used to work out which audit approach would add most value to the business. This can be done during the preliminary survey stage by considering the following:

- If a business area has progressed well along the ten stages, the audit terms of reference and approach may be based on verifying the self-assessment procedures and perhaps examining some of the key controls that are relied on to drive the risk management strategy.

- Where the ten stages appear to have been completed but the results are superficial, it may be necessary to focus on whether a box-ticking approach is being employed that highlights a poor control culture that needs to be further developed.

- In these two examples, the auditor is concerned with giving assurances that risk management is in place and controls are working. If, on the other hand, the ten stages are not at all developed, the auditor may provide better value-add by helping the client team get started along the lines of a consulting project. Assurances in this instance involve commenting on the client's developmental plans and then describing some of the steps being taken to achieve an embedded risk management process.

- Where the client is failing to implement the corporate risk policy despite much assistance and advice, the auditor may consider an investigation into blockages and why there is this problem. In this case, the focus is different, and the engagement may need to report back at a higher level because of possible sensitivities that may arise.

- The auditor and client may devise an integrated approach where the auditor helps the work team brainstorm risks and then the results are used to set the terms of reference for the ensuing audit.

- In extreme cases, the auditor may need to stand back entirely from assurance audit work and hold control awareness seminars because there is a general lack of appreciation of controls, compliance, and financial reporting issues that needs to be addressed before even starting to talk about risk management practices.

- If, for example, the survey reveals that a major new information-based performance system has just been approved that will change the way staff work, this may become the biggest risk facing the client. Internal audit may again need to step back from the audit role and offer to help the client in the task of assessing risk and controls over the new information system.

- The auditor should also look out for questionable practices when performing the preliminary survey. In addition to the assurance and consulting aspects of audit work, there is also a need to watch out for red flags, which may suggest not all is well. Performance Standard 2210.A2 places a responsibility on the auditor to be on guard for such problems by stating: *"The internal auditor should consider the probability of significant errors, irregularities, noncompliance, and other exposures when developing the engagement objectives."* This is the great challenge for the auditor: to tell senior management that everything is okay or to help clients make things okay but also to make inquiries when the client or certain staff are culpable and/or negligent in causing noncompliance.

- The preliminary survey should involve close discussion with the client manager and selected team members and a visit to the work area. The documentation and plans in respect of risk management efforts, including control self-assessment events, should also be considered. The auditor will need to check to be sure that the client manager has a good understanding of corporate policies on risk management, regulatory disclosure requirements, and internal control design.

It is crucial to work closely with the client at the preliminary survey stage and make a professional judgment about ways forward. If there is conflict between using an assurance approach or adopting a consulting role, the assurance role will rule supreme. Assurance works well when there is a risk management system in place to consider or the client is not really cooperating properly. Consulting works best where the client has a desire to promote corporate policies and either needs help to set up good risk management arrangements or needs to address any gaps in the current arrangements. A good preliminary survey will determine the form and direction of the audit so that a suitable assignment plan may then be prepared. Some audit teams carry out an assessment of the control environment along the COSO lines before deciding on the most appropriate approach to adopt. There has always been a need to carry out risk assessment during the planning stage of an audit. Practice Advisory 2210.A1-1 recommends that background information be gathered as part of this attempt to isolate key risks, including a consideration of:

- *Objectives and goals.*
- *Policies, plans, procedures, laws, regulations, and contracts which could have a significant impact on operations and reports.*

- *Organizational information—for example, number and names of employees, key employees, job descriptions, and details about recent changes in the organization, including major system changes.*
- *Budget information, operating results, and financial data of the activity to be reviewed.*
- *Prior engagement working papers.*

The Advisory goes on to encourage the auditor to make physical contact with the site to be audited and talk to key personnel as part of the survey, and also meet users of the outputs from the operation. Reports, plans, and any studies relating to the area should also be considered. The preliminary survey should result in a formal report to the CAE that will recommend that the audit be conducted, deferred, or canceled and help determine the shape and form of the audit so that an assignment plan may then be prepared.

Preliminary Survey: A Worked Example

Audit Engagement: The Corporate Antifraud Policy

The audit example provided here is based on one version of the risk-based systems approach to assurance audits and is not used as an example of any particular best practice. It is provided simply to illustrate some of the points made about the audit process. The example is broken down into stages. The first part appears here (preliminary surveys), and the remaining parts of the worked example are noted at the end of the respective sections in this chapter covering assignment planning, ascertaining, evaluating, testing, developing findings, and audit reporting.

The annual audit plan includes an audit of the corporate fraud policy. This was requested by the audit committee as an important feature of the internal control framework that has been adopted by the board. The audit committee wanted assurances from internal audit that the fraud policy and response plan represented an effective control over the risk of employee fraud and abuse. The audit manager assigned the work to a lead auditor, who carried out the following tasks:

- Contacted the financial controller (there is no compliance officer in post), who is the process owner for the fraud policy, and arranged a meeting for the following week. This person would have known about the pending audit from the quarterly audit plan that is circulated to senior management.
- Lead auditor and audit manager met with the chair of the audit committee to discuss the audit in question. The chair had no particular concerns over and above the need to ensure there is an effective fraud policy in place.

- Reviewed the audit files to establish what past work had touched on the fraud policy and also compiled a list of fraud detection work and any fraud investigations that had been carried out over recent years.

- Searched the Internet for any material from respected Web sites such as the IIA and ACFE to secure some basic background on the design and implementation of antifraud policies and programs.

- Met with the company attorney to discuss any issues that should be taken on board when reviewing the current fraud policy.

- Met with the financial controller and discussed the current head office arrangements for managing the risk of fraud, and together developed an outline terms of reference for the audit that made clear the scope and direction of the engagement. The agreed terms of reference are reproduced below:

   1. *To review the existing arrangements for ensuring that:*

      (a) staff understand the corporate antifraud policy and their roles and responsibilities in respect of fraud prevention, detection, and response.

      (b) there are suitable measures for reporting suspicions of fraud and irregularity.

      (c) there is a capacity to investigate fraud and irregularity to professional standards.

   2. *To issue a formal audit report to the audit committee, CFO, and financial controller in respect of findings and recommendations arising from the audit.*

   3. *The audit will not involve any special tests that seek to detect fraud and irregularity but will focus on the controls in place that ensure the corporate fraud policy addresses the risk of fraud within the organization. To this end the policy and other relevant documentation will be examined and appropriate staff will be interviewed.*

   4. *The audit will be conducted by Fred Fedricks and start on xx 200x.*

As a result of this, the lead auditor prepared a preliminary survey audit report. This report was reviewed by the audit manager and signed off by the

---

For Further Discussion

What sources of information are recommended to help auditors obtain some background material before starting the audit proper?

CAE, and contained the work carried out, the draft terms of reference, and a recommendation to start the audit as soon as practicable. It was presented to the audit committee for comment and then finalized.

——— SECTION 4 ———
DEVELOPING ASSIGNMENT PLANS

Having gone through the detailed preliminary survey to work out just where internal audit fits into the risk management jigsaw, we can turn to more practical aspects of planning the engagement. There is no real cut-off between the preliminary survey and assignment planning stages as these will tend to flow into each other as the audit scope is firmed up. Performance Standard 2210 makes clear the need to link objectives of the audit into the risk management process by saying:

> The engagement's objectives should address the risk, controls and governance processes associated with the activities under review.

Consideration of risk, controls, and governance applies to both assurance and consulting work as made clear in Performance Standard 2210.A1:

> When planning the engagement, the internal auditor should identify and assess risks relevant to the activity under review. The engagement objectives should reflect the results of the risk assessment.

The consulting equivalent, 2210.C1, runs:

> Consulting engagement objectives should address risks, controls and governance processes to the extent agreed upon with the client.

We have discussed risk-based auditing as an extension of the corporate assessment of risk that each organization should be developing. For the individual engagement, there is a further assessment of risk to determine how best to employ the assigned audit budget for that audit. Before we can get involved in releasing an assignment plan, we will need to think through the way the audit will be performed. Practice Advisory 2010-1 helps with this task and indicates what should be covered when putting together a work schedule for each engagement. This should at least incorporate the following concerns:

- *What activities are to be performed.*
- *When they will be performed.*
- *The estimated time required.*
- *The dates and results of the last engagement.*
- *Updated assessments of risks and effectiveness of risk management and control processes.*

- *Requests by senior management, audit committee, and governing body.*
- *Current issues relating to organizational governance.*
- *Major changes in enterprise's business, operations, programs, systems, and controls.*
- *Opportunities to achieve operating benefits.*
- *Changes to and capabilities of the audit staff.*

Not only is there a lot to take on board, there is also a need to respond to changes and events as they arise during an audit, which might alter its direction. There are several standards that deal with engagement planning as follows:

Performance Standard 2220: *"The established scope should be sufficient to satisfy the objectives of the engagement."* We start with the objectives set through the preliminary survey, and the next stage is to determine width and breadth. For an assurance audit that is set, for example, "to consider the adequacy and effectiveness of internal controls over system xyz" for the system in question, we will want to determine:

- **Where this system starts.** A system tends to involve inputs, process, and outputs. Information, requests, transactions, and so on will arrive in the system and then generate a response. A marketing team may get a request from a business manager to help launch a changed product and this proposal may become the input to the system. The proposal may be reviewed and then a specialist team from marketing assigned to the launch project. Proposal response may be included in the scope of an audit of marketing, and we will need to work out where the marketing system starts. The auditor may see the system as starting with the proposal, or it may include the guidelines issued by marketing to business and program managers, and here, the system starts with the way proposals are prepared before they get to the marketing team.

- **Where it stops.** Returning to the input, process, output model, we will need to draw a line where the system stops, for audit purposes. If there is a large transport outfit attached to a retail company and the audit terms of reference include a review of "the adequacy of controls and compliance with procedures in the fleet management system for store deliveries," we will need to define the system in question. The delivery system may end when goods are sent to the stores, or it may end when the inventories are updated and accounted for. Alternatively, the auditor may consider returns that are sent back to the warehouse, or the system may also include the truck returning back to the depot and being readied for the next journey.

- **Timing issues.** Assurance audits tend to revolve around what has happened and what is happening in one part of the business. Consulting engagements tend to be more concerned with what is being planned. This is a moot point. It is difficult for an assurance auditor to report that the existing system was ignored because the client is thinking about adopting improved working practices in line with an overall change strategy. Likewise, a consulting audit that concentrates on past events may have little relevance to the client. As discussed earlier, it is possible to provide a blended approach where the assurance work focuses on the design and roll-out of an approved strategy and whether there has been adequate consideration of risks and controls built into the implementation strategy. Whatever the format, there needs to be a clear view on the extent to which the audit will consider past, current, and future arrangements. If, for example, we need to test whether staff are complying with a procedure involving head office returns, we will need to decide how far to go back in terms of reviewing documentation that provides evidence of compliance (or noncompliance).

There is a view that auditors should try to keep the review as up to date as possible and concentrate on recent rather than the previous year's transactions. Fraud and other special investigations are different, and these will focus on specific past periods. Also, the past can gives clues to the future; so if we are concerned about the way large revenue contracts are managed in one business line, the way they have been managed in the past will provide some insight into how they may be managed in future.

- *Compliance and fraud aspects.* Some non-auditors believe the audit role focuses primarily on fraud and compliance, and this used to be the case in the past. When setting the scope of the audit, the extent to which these items are considered as part of the audit should be clearly defined. For example, the scope may include reviewing management's arrangements for ensuring compliance, or whether there are adequate measures to detect irregularity built into the controls established by management. Where the auditor is particularly concerned with compliance, then this should be included within the scope of the audit and mention made of direct compliance testing.

- *Information implications.* The integrity of information systems employed to support the area being audited may or may not be included in the scope. Again, it is necessary to make clear the audit input and whether the information systems will be directly examined as part of the audit coverage, or whether the audit will focus on the way management ensures information is reliable and complete. An audit of the budgeting system may focus on the way each business unit builds up its spending lines and monitors actuals against planned spend, using tailor-made spreadsheets. Auditing the integrity of spreadsheets is a specialist skill that IS auditors may possess, and a decision will have to be made early on as to whether this task will form part of the audit or whether the focus should be on the way budget holders manage their spending, with passing reference only to the information system adopted for this task.

- ***Response to client requests.*** Chapter 4 addresses interviewing, which includes the opening meeting with the client when agreeing on the objectives of the audit. This meeting may go on for some time, and the client may list some of the issues and problems in the area under review. At the end of the discussions, the auditor will be thinking about the audit objective for the work that is being planned. A great deal of confusion can arise where the client assumes the problems that he or she mentioned are automatically included in the scope of the audit. Specific requests are straightforward, in that the auditor may respond by including these within the scope or place the request to one side for a future audit (perhaps a consulting engagement).

  It is the matters that were mentioned in passing that need to be properly defined and clarified. They should be clearly placed in the scope of the audit or mention made of the fact that it will not be covered. For example, in one audit, the client made great play of a dispute within his section where some newer members of the team were lodging an official complaint that they had not received a bonus that was recently paid to longer serving members of the team. The client manager expressed concerns about this complaint to the auditor, and many team members spoke to the auditor about the complaints and asked whether internal audit supported the new members' stance or not. The auditor had not made it clear in the documented scope of the work that the coverage did not include a consideration of the complaint, and this misunderstanding caused some difficulties during the audit.

- ***Broad brush or narrow detail.*** Many audits deal with parts of the business that have corporate procedures, senior managers, supervisors, teams, and front-line staff who administer the service. The scope of the audit should make clear whether the coverage is high-level strategic, in terms of covering the top end of the operation—for example, strategy, management, and use of corporate policies—or whether it focuses on the front-line operation (e.g., team working, customer contact, and operational procedures). There is a middle ground where strategic direction is traced down to what the teams are doing on the ground, and the way objectives cascade downward. Much depends on the time that is assigned to the job and the objectives of the audit.

Performance Standard 2220.A1: *"The scope of the engagement should include consideration of relevant systems, records, personnel, and physical properties, including those under the control of third parties."* This Standard is useful in that it encourages the auditor to build on what was established through the preliminary survey. There is a temptation for some auditors to adopt a consulting style to their work, where much play is made of the interviews with senior management, who essentially disclose what they believe is happening in their section and where improvements are needed. The temptation is to focus on what is being said and start to write the report based mainly around representations made by managers, staff, and people who have come into contact with the area in question.

Standard 2220.A1 relates to assurance work and argues that the scope should include coverage of "hard" aspects of the operation as well as disclosures that are made to the auditor. The auditor needs to be concerned with the documentation made and held in the operation, the actual location and resources employed in the systems. Where parts of the operation are outsourced or provided by associates, this does not mean they necessarily fall outside the scope of the audit. Management for the area in question is responsible for all aspects of the operation, including anything that is contracted out. If auditors stood back from any externalized services and simply assumed they were okay, the audit process could become pretty superficial.

The Standard means the auditor will go outside the organization and consider services that are provided by external parties. It is good practice to build in audit access whenever services are provided by outsiders and to make clear the need for audit to get behind the returns made by this party to verify and examine matters of detail, when required. Standard 2220.A1 also means the auditors need to come into contact with personnel who are involved in the area under review. That is, the audit cannot be performed from a desk in the audit offices, or even in the client's work area. The audit plans need to reflect this fact and ensure that contact with relevant staff from the client's side is part of the agreed scope of work.

Performance Standard 2220.C1: *"In performing consulting engagements internal auditors should ensure that the scope of the engagement is sufficient to address the agreed-upon objectives. If internal auditors develop reservations about the scope during the engagement, these reservations should be discussed with the client to determine whether to continue with the engagement."* Consulting work is different from assurance-based work. Where the client has asked that audit get involved in a particular engagement, there are generally no problems. If the work fits the governance, risk, and control agenda and the audit staff is equipped to perform the engagement, or if the work adds value to the business and again fits in with auditors' competencies, then it is likely to go ahead.

But where there are concerns about the scope of the work, in terms of what should be looked at and what falls outside the remit of the auditor, this has to be considered very carefully. For example, the client may be developing a local procurement capacity for a new business unit and want help from audit to establish this initiative. If aspects of the project regarding compliance with the organization's corporate procurement policy are kept away from the auditor and are classified as confidential, this may set alarm bells ringing. In this instance, the auditor may decline to get involved as it may compromise his or her position in the organization, with this restriction in place.

Performance Standard 2230: *"Internal auditors should determine appropriate resources to achieve engagement objectives. Staffing should be based on an evaluation of the nature and complexity of each engagement, time constraints, and available resources."* This is pretty straightforward. The preliminary survey will result in clear objectives and terms of reference, including the scope of the work involved. At this stage, the appropriate resources will have to be formally assigned. We would hope that some staff would have already been marked out for the engagement and be on standby in this respect. While staffing will revolve around who is available, it would be helpful if it also involves a consideration of who should best perform the work, based on the complexity and special factors in question. In practice, it is hard to wait around for the right auditors to become free, and the new-look auditor will tend to be able to work on many different types of projects and be suitably flexible. In addition to the skills, knowledge, and any constraints on audit resources, Practice Advisory 2230-1 also encourages a consideration of specific training and development needs of audit staff. Where staffing cannot be achieved from in-house resources, the Practice Advisory suggests that external resources may be considered.

Performance Standard 2240.A1: *"Work programs should establish the procedures for identifying, analyzing, evaluating, and recording information during the engagement. The work program should be approved prior to the commencement of work, and any adjustments approved promptly."* We have used the term *work program* when referring to a schedule of audits assigned to various audit staff over, say, the next four to six weeks. This term may also be applied to programs established through the assignment planning stage of an individual engagement, to guide and direct the audit team. The term *engagement work program* is defined as *"a document that lists the procedures to be followed during an engagement, designed to achieve the engagement plan."* This need for direction on an audit is reinforced through Standard 2240.A1, which provides the level of detail required to perform the audit. This is a useful technique in that the audit manager may, through the preliminary survey, determine the program that is needed to complete the audit in question and then assign tasks to members of the audit team. The program could be designed to record details of assigned auditors, start date, completion date and reviewing auditor as well as reference to documentation that is prepared for each task in the program. It is good practice to follow up on any outstanding matters from the previous audit carried out in the area in question, unless the past audit work is old or has been superseded by events.

Performance Standard 2240.C1: *"Work programs for consulting engagements may vary in form and content depending upon the nature of the engagement."* This Standard makes clear the need to flex the working papers to fit the type of work being performed. An assurance audit may involve ascertaining the system in question, isolating risks to the operation, evaluating the controls that are in place, and then forming an opinion on these controls, linked to the resulting audit report. The audit file may contain documentation that relates to each of these stages of the audit to promote the smooth flow of work as the auditor works toward a conclusion and recommendation.

Consulting engagements depend entirely on what is needed to discharge the requirements from the set terms of reference—that is, the objectives and scope of the engagement. The work program in this sense will set a flow of tasks that is derived from the planning stage, and this will probably be different from the standard flow in an assurance engagement. Standard 2240.C1 promotes this flexibility to avoid the problems from excessive standardization. In fact, consulting work is simply based around what is agreed between the auditor and client. This agreement is crucial to the success of consulting work, and Performance Standard 2201.C1 sets out the need to verify and record this agreement by saying:

> Internal auditors should establish an understanding with consulting engagement clients about objectives, scope, respective responsibilities, and other client expectations. For significant engagements, this understanding should be documented.

There is a lot to take on board when developing a formal assignment plan because once the work is under way, any flaws in the direction, resources, and support will result in a flawed audit. Practice Advisory 2200-1 suggests that a full meeting be held between audit and the client, and representatives for the area under review to go through the planned audit terms of reference. Practical matters may be highlighted including timing of the audit fieldwork, reporting lines and information on how audit operates, and any key sensitivities and issues that need to be taken on board during the work. On bigger engagements, it is an idea to encourage the client to assign a contact person whom the auditor can use for any problems, or assistance that may arise during the audit. There will also be many practical matters that will need to be considered by the audit shop.

Some of the points regarding the way the engagement planning stage may be addressed are noted below:

- Brief the audit team and make it clear who is doing what and when. The audit program and work schedules will document what is agreed upon.
- Appoint a lead auditor for the fieldwork stage, and ensure this person is the key point of continuity throughout the audit in question.
- Make clear what matters need to go to the audit manager, who may have several audits on the go at the same time, and what should be managed at lead auditor level. Some of the points may relate to changing the time budget assigned to the job, shifting audit staff, and calling in specialist auditors such as the information systems auditor.
- In terms of audit manager and lead auditor split, agree to the review arrangements and also review the staged work, working paper files, interim reports, and time-monitoring information for audit hours that are charged each week.
- Energize the audit team and make sure they have a clear focus and motivation.
- Ensure the team is supported (e.g., by an audit administration officer) who will organize hotels, allowances, travel, car hire, and any matters to do with getting the team settled into the job.
- Check the use of standardized documentation to be applied to the job; if this is automated, make sure backup file arrangements are clear. Check security arrangements for files and papers that are removed or copied to audit files.
- Ensure the audit manager makes clear how he or she will keep in touch with the team and when visits will be made. It is generally a good idea to adopt a policy that involves the audit manager turning up unannounced during the audit.
- Prepare contingency arrangements for use where there are staffing absences or any change in the direction in the audit. Make sure any firm checkpoint dates, say, for an interim audit report, that have been given to the client are kept to. Or provide an allowance for these dates to ensure they can be met in the event of any problems.

Control Objectives

There is some discussion among auditors as to whether control objectives should be compiled as part of the planning stage of the audit. The control objective is a statement derived from the objectives of the client's system that drills down into performance, compliance, accountability, and disclosure issues to ensure the scope of the audit covers all aspects of governance. We need to return to the nature of internal audit work to progress our discussion of control objectives. Practice Advisory 2100-1 includes the following statement:

> *Specifically, the primary objectives of the overall management process are to achieve:*
>
> * *Relevant, reliable, and credible financial and operating information.*
> * *Effective and efficient use of the organization's resources.*
> * *Safeguarding of the organization's assets.*
> * *Compliance with laws, regulations, ethical and business norms, and contracts.*

Where an assurance audit deals with management processes, it should consider the above aspects and determine whether these broad criteria have been met. An operation may be achieving the set performance targets but needs also to make reliable returns, be efficient, protect company resources, and comply with all relevant laws and so on. These issues are often not uppermost on the minds of business unit managers, who may be driven by one-dimensional performance targets. In extreme cases people have been known to simply fabricate the figures to ensure targets are met. Control objectives may help drive the audit along the performance, conformance, and accountability lines and ensure that managers' activities are tempered by corporate and personal integrity. A customer complaints information system may have the following objective:

> *To ensure all concerns that customers may have about the company are brought to the attention of the appropriate management and action taken to address these concerns in a timely manner.*

Control objectives may be added to this overall system objective to bring out any additional considerations that need to be managed to ensure the system works and is both efficient and accountable. Management may set these control objectives for the audit in question, and audit may help them in this task. Control objectives for the customer complaints system will reflect what needs to be covered during the audit to ensure a good focus and may include, for example:

* *To ensure the information produced by the system is reliable and complete.*
* *To ensure the procedures comply with best practice, local regulations and the overall corporate complaints policy.*
* *To ensure the complaints are addressed closest to the point of origination.*
* *To ensure that employee irregularity may be detected from complaints where appropriate.*

This list could go on and on. Some auditors use control objectives that revolve around the three key criteria of time, cost, and quality to isolate which aspects of the criteria have the most bearing on the system in hand. As part of the planning process, the control objectives may be discussed and agreed upon with the client, if this approach is being used. Some auditors feel that control objectives are hard to explain to clients as they put an "audit spin" on the work, which may cause some reluctance from the client and staff.

Walk-through Tests

One further matter that should be considered in the planning stage of the audit is the use of walk-through tests. Testing is discussed later when we deal with the actual audit fieldwork. This more involved consideration of testing will consist of material on compliance and substantive testing. At this stage, we need only briefly mention walk-through tests, which is a technique for checking that the system that has been described by the client and personnel has been properly understood by the auditor. The walk-through test introduces the concept of audit independence to the client because it tends to involve the auditor's asking the client to use a specimen transaction to explain what happens in the operation, so that the auditor properly understands the way the operation works. For example, when talking to the Human Resources Manager about how the performance appraisal is operated for operational personnel, an employee's personnel file may be examined to consider the way the system works and how plans, targets, and reports are compiled and recorded in the personnel file that has been selected. The independence concept comes to the fore as the client can observe the way actual documentation is used by the auditor to assess how a system works, in a hands-on manner.

A management consultant may simply take everything that is said by the client for granted, but the auditor will want to "get dirty" and have a look at work files, procedures, and information used by staff who operate the system. Walk-through tests also give the auditor an initial feel for the way things are operated at the front line. It may also involve observing staff at work. As a procedure is being explained by the business manager, the auditor may ask to see the workforce in action, again to get a feel for how the operation really works. The final point to note is that walk-through tests are not about catching people out but are simply ways of ensuring the system, risks, and controls are understood in outline before the main part of the audit is started.

Planning and Control

Audit plans should enable good control over each engagement that is performed. That is, planning and control are two related concepts that underpin

Exhibit 5.4.   Planning and Control

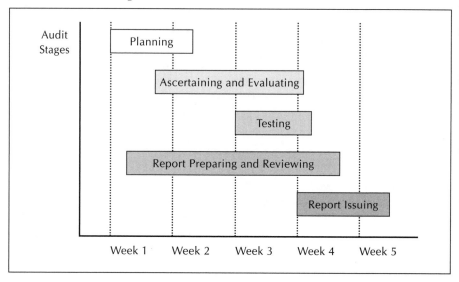

the management of each individual audit. For larger audits, a form of Gantt chart may be developed where the auditor's time charged to each stage of the audit can be plotted against the hours that were originally assigned. A simple example of one such five-week Gantt chart is shown in Exhibit 5.4. The shading represents the well-known notion that as the audit progresses, the knowledge about the area under review becomes more complete, and each stage box becomes increasingly darker.

Assignment Planning: A Worked Example

Audit Engagement: The Corporate Antifraud Policy (continued)

Having set the form and direction of the audit and agreed that it should go ahead, the next stage is to plan the work involved. This involved taking the set terms of reference and carrying out the following tasks:

- Audit job coded and set up on the time management system as a live audit engagement, coded as Assurance Audit: Special Requests from Audit Committee.
- Lead auditor officially assigned to the job.
- Audit team of two junior audit staff also assigned to the job.
- Lead auditor and audit manager completed the assignment planning document, which contained the details shown in Exhibit 5.5.

Exhibit 5.5. Assignment Plans

Audit: Corporate Antifraud Policy
Code: A (Assurance)
Type: 3 (AC Request)

Prelim Survey Report Ref: 223

1. To review the existing arrangements for ensuring that
   (a) Staff understand the corporate antifraud policy and their roles and responsibilities in respect of fraud prevention, detection, and response.
   (b) There are suitable measures for reporting suspicions of fraud and irregularity.
   (c) There is a capacity to investigate fraud and irregularity to professional standards.
2. To issue a formal audit report to the audit committee, CFO, and financial controller in respect of findings and recommendations arising from the audit.
3. The audit will not involve any special tests that seek to detect fraud and irregularity but will focus on the controls in place that ensure the corporate fraud policy addresses the risk of fraud within the organization. To this end, the policy and other relevant documentation will be examined and appropriate staff will be interviewed.
4. The audit will be conducted by Fred Fedricks and start on xx 20xx.

Planned Dates	Budget Days		
Start: June 1, 20xx	Audit manager:	AH 5 days	5
Fieldwork complete: June 15, 20xx	Lead auditor:	FF 25 days	25
Draft report released: June 20, 20xx	Audit Staff:	TR 5 days	
		RS 5 days	10
		Total	40
Steven Obley	*Paula Derish*		
Signed: Audit Manager	Signed: CAE		

The audit team was then briefed by the audit manager and told:

- The lead auditor will manage the job in the field and update the client contact (financial controller) on a regular basis.
- The audit manager will visit the location from time to time to review progress and be available to discuss any concerns that arise during the course of the audit.
- The two audit staff will spend a week each on tasks assigned by the lead auditor.
- The audit administration officer will organize hotel and travel arrangements.

- The work will focus on the fraud policy and whether this is properly disseminated across the organization.

A further meeting was held between the financial controller and the lead auditor to discuss systems objectives. It was agreed that the fraud policy was designed:

- To encourage an awareness and understanding of the risk of fraud and define roles and responsibilities across the organization for fraud prevention, detection and response.
- To ensure that all concerns and suspicions are brought to the attention of the appropriate party in a timely manner.
- To make clear the firm line taken by the organization in respect of bringing criminal charges and taking disciplinary action against anyone involved in, or culpable in, fraud or irregularity.

It was also agreed that the audit should be guided by the use of three control objectives, defined as:

1. To ensure that all employees understand corporate standards on fraud risk management.
2. To ensure that all suspicions of fraud and irregularity are reported and properly investigated.
3. To ensure that appropriate action is taken after an investigation has been completed.

> ### For Further Discussion
> What are the views surrounding the pros and cons of using control objectives to help focus the audit?

—— SECTION 5 ——
AUDIT FIELDWORK

The fieldwork stage of the audit depends entirely on the objectives and type of audit that has been planned during the preliminary survey and assignment-planning process. Chapter 3 describes outline approaches for:

- Control self-assessment workshops
- Compliance reviews
- Information systems audits
- Fraud investigations
- Consulting engagements

The detailed fieldwork would then follow the defined stages for the approach that has been adopted by the auditor. This is particularly relevant for consulting engagements that address the specific aims set by the client and agreed to by the auditor. Assurance work could follow the lines set by risk-based systems auditing (RBSA), which is also described in Chapter 3. A useful model for setting a frame for assurance work may be derived from Performance Standard 2120.A1, which states:

> *Based on the results of the risk assessment, the internal audit activity should evaluate the adequacy and effectiveness of controls encompassing the organization's governance, operations, and information systems. This should include:*
>
> * *Reliability and integrity of financial and operational information.*
> * *Effectiveness and efficiency of operations.*
> * *Safeguarding of assets.*
> * *Compliance with laws, regulations, and contracts.*

This was mentioned earlier when we discussed the use of control objectives. Taking the terms of reference that have been set for the audit, the fieldwork is essentially about securing information, which Performance Standard 2300 has described by saying:

> *Internal auditors should identify, analyze, evaluate and record sufficient information to achieve the engagement's objectives.*

The auditor should adopt the best method available for achieving this aim but also perform this task in a systematic manner. The RBSA suggests that there are three clear stages that may be applied to the audit process in the field:

1. Ascertainment
2. Evaluation
3. Testing

All these stages are driven by an assessment of risks to achieving objectives and determination whether the controls that are in place work and make sense. RBSA focuses on risk and falls in line with Practice Advisory 2010-2, which develops this theme by suggesting:

> *In conducting audit engagements, methods and techniques for testing and validating exposures should be reflective of the risk materiality and likelihood of occurrence.*

We can turn to the three stages of ascertainment, evaluation, and testing to consider the performance of audit fieldwork in assurance engagements.

Ascertainment

The description of the preliminary survey and assignment-planning stages earlier provide an initial understanding of the risks and types of control framework that are being applied to these risks. Ideally, the overall control environment will have been established by the auditor. What needs to happen now involves a more detailed consideration of the operation that is being reviewed. A great deal of information about an operational system may be obtained from interviewing the system managers and their staff and work teams. The ascertainment stage of the audit means finding out about:

- *The detailed operational objectives of the system in question.* This will consist of the formal published objectives, the way these objectives are interpreted by the work team and the relationship between system objectives and the personal targets applied to the work team and individuals. It may be an idea to capture soft objectives in the way the team develops a reputation as well as the formal hard ones that relate to performance and outputs. The published objective for a head office sales support team may be "to provide support and administration for sales staff who travel overseas," and we could review the system employed by this team to deliver this objective. In reality, the team's objective may be rewritten to read "to provide support, administration, and advice on safety and cultural adaptation for sales staff who travel overseas," because this is actually what the team does in practice. A further soft objective may to be encourage sales representatives to use the support team because they are well respected, and not go it alone.
- *Strategies and programs.* Overall objectives are achieved by implementing suitable strategies for their delivery. We need to find out about the programs in place in the area under review to satisfy Performance Standard 2120.A3, which states:

    Internal auditors should review operations and programs to ascertain the extent to which results are consistent with established goals and objectives to determine whether operations and programs are being implemented or performed as intended.

    For example, a new program to deliver the sales support team's objectives may be to employ local agents to promote the smooth progress of sales teams who are sent out to countries where the company has identified developing markets and new market potential. We will need to find out about this program in line with the preview assurance role where value-add auditing considers future strategies as well as existing systems. Whatever the approach, we will be concerned if the operation is not aligned with the views of executive management. Performance Standard 2120.A2 argues:

> *Internal auditors should ascertain the extent to which operating and program goals and objectives have been established and conform to those of the organization.*

- **Control objectives associated with the operational goals.** Discussed earlier, this may or may not be used by the auditor to give a balance of performance and conformance to the audit. If control objectives are adopted, this must be done with care and agreed to with the client as these objectives will drive and focus the rest of the audit. Examples of control objectives for the sales support team will need to be discussed. This may end up including items such as "to ensure that corporate policy on overseas sales initiatives comply with local and international laws and regulations," "to ensure all overseas sales staff utilize the support facilities and guidance," and "to ensure information on overseas locations is reliable and sufficient to support international travel and working policies."

- **The key risks inherent in the system.** Information on key risks may come from many sources. Previous audit work and even audit consulting engagements may feed information on outstanding risks in the system in question. This cross-over between consulting and assurance work is recognized in Performance Standard 2110.C2, which makes clear:

> *Internal auditors should incorporate knowledge of risks gained from consulting engagements into the process of identifying and evaluating significant risk exposures of the organization.*

The client may have already carried out a risk assessment that could be used to isolate significant risk. Where this assessment has not been carried out before, the blended audit approach that was described in Chapter 3, Section 8, may be applied to get the client's teams together in brainstorming their risks and then establishing which should be prioritized. For example, a recent review of the sales support team may have isolated key issues impacting the service such as volatile regions of the world, communication breakdown between the head office team and overseas sales personnel, and so on. These risks may be reexamined by the auditor, or if little work has been done on risk assessment, the auditor may need to work with the client in defining key challenges to the set objectives. This latter approach is more likely if control objectives have been set earlier because new thinking will be applied to these new perspectives on the system, inspired by the control objectives.

- *How the system works in terms of input, process, and output routines.* Risk-based auditing starts with objectives and risks and then considers the types of control standards, practices, information, and routines in place to mitigate excessive risk. For the sales support team audit, it may be a question of finding out how the team operates and what information they receive, use, and then disseminate. Inputs may come in the form of travel plans from a sales team (via the current international sales and marketing strategy). This information may be processed to assess what kind of support the sales team will need and a support plan developed for each sales personnel, for travel, accommodation, contacts, and local practices.

- *Procedures and working practices.* The auditor will want to look at the procedures applied in the system in question and also document the way work is organized and performed. The sales support team may be responsible for a protocols standard maintained on the company intranet and may also have a guidance manual that sets out how they work and what forms are applied to the process. Procedures manuals should be handled with care as they may be out of date or simply not used by staff. It is probably best to interview team members and to cross-reference any working practices to their issued procedures.

- *How the system fits into the organization.* Internal audit has a responsibility to provide assurances to the board and audit committee and should adopt "big picture thinking." This means that whenever an audit is being performed, auditors need to keep one eye on the way findings may be reported upward regarding the overall system of internal control and financial reporting. Each individual audit engagement should fit into the organization in a way that contributes to the success of the business and helps drive it forward. This principle is reinforced through Performance Standard 2130.A1, which argues:

  > *Internal auditors should review operations and programs to ensure consistency with organizational values.*

  For example, the work of the sales support team must fit into the overall push for international markets, but in a way that is acceptable and efficient and that fits the value base of the enterprise. If corporate values promote respect for different cultures, this view must feed through the activities of overseas operations, and the sales support team will need to reflect these values in the policies and procedures that are applied. If the sales support team provide orientation seminars for newly appointed sales staff, we would expect to see a session on corporate values and practical issues regarding respect, exploitation, and observance of local regulations and laws as well as adherence to the domestic position on overseas bribes from the Foreign Corrupt Practices Act. For all audits performed by internal audit, whatever the format, regard should be had to corporate governance as outlined by Performance Standard 2130, which asks:

> *The internal audit activity should contribute to the organization's governance process by evaluating and improving the process through which (1) values and goals are established and communicated, (2) the accomplishment of goals is monitored, (3) accountability is ensured, and (4) values are preserved.*

- *Important change issues, strategies, and concerns that impact the performance and integrity of the system.* The context of the audit that moves it from a review of past activities to work that enhances the way risks to the business may be managed comes from researching significant change issues. The ascertainment stage of the audit should include an account of future strategic changes. In our example, the sales support team may be working on a contingency planning project to support staff who travel to emerging economies that have unstable governments. Audit needs to find out about this project and ensure they understand the objectives, where it fits into the overall sales operation and the types of risks that arrive from sales drives to less stable parts of the world. These are all important considerations for the future of the support team and sales program and success of the company generally.

- *Ascertainment should result in a suitable record of the system being audited.* We have said that interviews with management will provide an outline of the system and information and documentation flows involved. Talks with staff and an examination of a few documents and working practices will further clarify the situation. At some stage, it will be possible to get a good understanding of the system that is being examined. This understanding may be "written up" in the audit files. This "write-up" may be in varying forms:

  - It could be noted in narrative form so that we arrive at short-numbered statements that run along the following lines: (1) travel request arrives from sales office; (2) support form supplied by support team; (3) form filled in by sales team leader; (4) travel and contacts plan prepared and agreed to; (5) travel and other forms processed, bookings made, and so on.

  - The audit documentation may simply be taken from the client, who may have an up-to-date model that describes the procedure in sufficient detail. The client may even be prepared to construct a suitable model documenting the systems employed by staff, if this would be the best way to record the system.

o The auditor could prepare a diagram that illustrates the system in outline. This may involve simple block diagrams with boxes showing each aspect of the process and how each relates to the other, such as the example in Exhibit 5.6.

Documentation may involve a detailed flowchart, which is useful for parts of the system that involve the flow of information and documentation. Many software packages produce flowcharts revolving around documentation and operations, using a simple code to indicate flows, movements, and relationships. There are many and varied types of flowcharts and protocols. It does not really matter which one is used by the audit shop so long as it is defined and understood by the audit staff. One simple example has the symbols shown in Exhibit 5.7.

A simple example may be prepared to illustrate the use of this flowchart to document the way internal audit handles requests it receives for special audits, as shown in Exhibit 5.8. Note that this flowchart starts with the request and ends with the draft report. It may be linked into other flowcharts that cover, for example, the detailed conduct of the engagement, broken down into fraud and nonfraud work.

Exhibit 5.6.   Simple Block Diagram

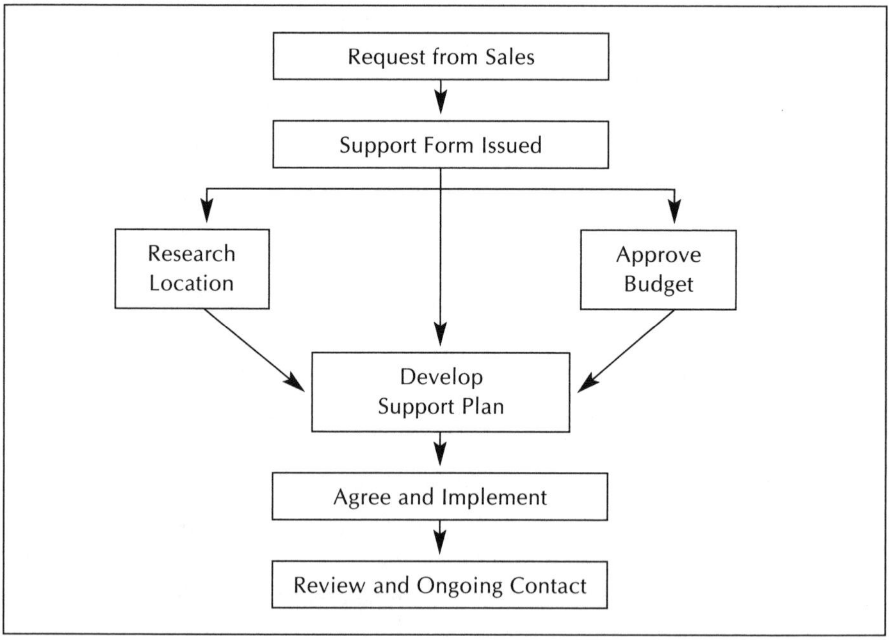

Exhibit 5.7. Basic Flowcharting Symbols

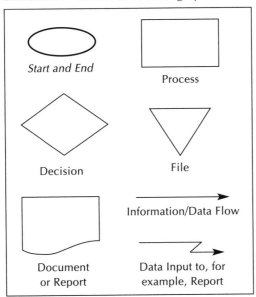

Ascertainment: A Worked Example

Audit Engagement: The Corporate Antifraud Policy (continued)

The lead auditor established the following:

1. Fraud policy—a copy of the latest version was obtained and examined. It was found to cover:
   - Definition of fraud
   - Roles and responsibilities
   - Links to code of ethics
   - Links to staff discipline
   - Fraud detection and red flags
   - Fraud prevention
   - Fraud detection
   - Where to go for advice
   - Whistleblowing procedure
   - Fraud response plan—what to do if presented with an allegation
2. Fraud response plan—this was found to contain details of:
   1. Who receives reports of any suspicions of fraud or irregularity
   2. How fraud should be investigated (e.g., special team, designated staff, audit)

Exhibit 5.8. Special Requests for Audit Cover

Conducting Requested Engagements

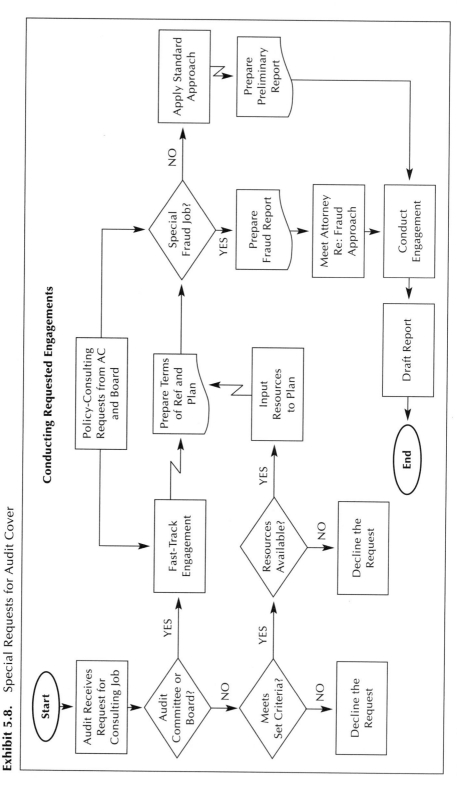

3. How to secure evidence in legally admissible form

4. When and how to contact the police

5. How to initiate recovery/restitution action

6. Who else to contact for advice

3. The formulation of the policy and updating procedure was described by the financial controller and documented by the auditor, as illustrated in Exhibit 5.9.

4. Fraud response procedures were documented, as shown in Exhibit 5.10.

The auditor met with most of the directors to discuss their input into the update of the fraud policy (which takes place every two years) and the inclusion of the latest fraud policy in the staff handbook that is issued to all new staff on appointment. As part of a walk-through test, the auditor was shown the last update file by the Financial Controller and viewed e-mail comments received from various company directors.

Evaluation

Having obtained a good idea of how the system works and the types of risks that could interfere with the ability to deliver, the next stage is to weigh the current

Exhibit 5.9.   Fraud Policy Formulation

Exhibit 5.10. Fraud Investigation Procedure

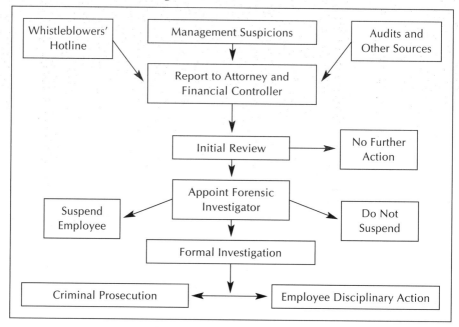

arrangements that are put in place by the client. Chapter 2, Section 7, dealt with the concept of internal controls. Evaluation is about comparing the controls that are in place with what is needed to provide a reasonable expectation of success. Some say the internal audit is about comparing what is with what should be, and then working out what needs to be done as a result of this judgment. There are eight key points that need to be considered when dealing with the evaluation stage of an assurance audit:

1. It is about supporting continuous improvement in controls. Performance Standard 2120 makes the following point:

   The internal audit activity should assist the organization in main-taining effective controls by evaluating their effectiveness and efficiency and by promoting continuous improvement.

   As the market changes, so do organizations as they respond with suitable strategic initiatives. These initiatives result in a strategic realignment of operational and support systems, that in turn change the risk profiles facing company executives. As these change, new systems bring in new risks, and control measures need to be adapted to address these future challenges. The key is to ensure controls respond to new positions and are kept up to date and improved so that they are robust, reliable, and flexible. Senior management may adopt a new strategy, reposition opera-tions, and tell their managers to get on and implement these changes. Meanwhile, front-line staff, who may be far removed from the strategic dimension, simply continue to do their job as usual. The change program may not have reached the front line, and controls may not flex to fill gaps created by removing a tier of management, or moving teams over to proj-ect work, or empowering business units to make decisions at a local level with little head office input. Evaluation is about checking the movement in control arrangements and the overall risk management practices to ensure they continue to do the job. For example, during an audit of the company payroll, it was found that due to a shortage of payroll staff, the service was to be externalized over the next few months. This then moves the key control focus away from payroll operations to data security, con-tract management, and obtaining attestation arrangements from the external service provider.

2. Control evaluation depends on criteria to assess existing and proposed controls. This task sits at the foot of management, as provided by Perfor-mance Standard 2120.A4, which states:

> *Adequate criteria are needed to evaluate controls. Internal audi-tors should ascertain the extent to which management has estab-lished adequate criteria to determine whether objectives and goals have been accomplished. If adequate, internal auditors should use such criteria in their evaluation. If inadequate, internal auditors should work with management to develop appropriate evaluation criteria.*

The auditor's evaluation will not only assess the control routines in place but also consider the criteria through which management estab-lishes controls. This may be based on the COSO model, control risk self-assessment, or other forms of ensuring all control issues are addressed. If, for example, during the payroll audit the contracting-out decision was deferred by a year, a new payroll operational procedures manual would, therefore, need to be prepared to cover the way the section performs its function. The control criteria employed by the company may be based around a policy on internal controls that requires all staff to have a good understanding of risk management and controls, and be retrained in the use of operational payroll procedures whenever these procedures are revised. Control evaluation in this context may focus on the way staff are developing competencies in control awareness and the importance of understanding and employing new procedures to guide the payroll staff.

3. Internal control questionnaires (ICQ) are used by some audit shops to assess controls. There are some standard systems whereby the auditor

may devise a list of questions designed to assess whether controls that may be expected to be in place are in fact present. The answers are set in a yes-no format where "no" suggests that there may be a problem that needs to be explored further. A standard control over payroll systems may be that no payroll staff are able to process their own employee payroll account, to guard against the risk of abuse. An Internal Control Questionnaire question may appear as, "Are there formal procedures in place covering the need to ensure payroll staff are not able to process their own accounts?" A no answer would suggest that this possible risk should be further examined. An extract from an ICQ is shown in Exhibit 5.11.

Standardized approaches to audit evaluation save time and ensure consistency but may be less appropriate for risk-based auditing where the risks change and standard responses may be less useful. Moreover, ICQs may promote a box-ticking approach that may not be appropriate when dealing with high-risk areas and continually adapting systems. ICQs can be useful when set assessment criteria are available and can be applied to reviewing the adequacy of the control environment of parts of the organization, in line with the COSO model of control.

4. Evaluation may in part be based on defining expectations and reviewing the extent to which these are being met by operational staff in the area being audited. "Hard" evaluations may be undertaken by considering the budgets, outputs, and returns from the operation and analyzing them to identify potential differences or inconsistencies. Practice Advisory

Exhibit 5.11. Internal Control Questionnaire (Payroll)

Risk 1: Staff Incompetence and Poor Performance				
Risk Ref	**Question**	**Yes**	**No**	**Comment and Further Work**
1.1	Are payroll staff vetted on joining the company?	Yes		1.1 Check small sample of new starters for vetting applied, per set procedure.
1.2	Are all staff formally trained in the use of the payroll operations handbook?		No	1.2 Check error rate of staff compared to industry standards.
1.3	Are personal development targets set for all payroll staff? And so on . . .	Yes		1.3 Examine small sample of personal development records.

2320-1 discusses analysis and evaluation and makes the point that its use may uncover:

- *Differences that are not expected.*
- *The absence of differences when they are expected.*
- *Potential errors.*
- *Potential irregularities or illegal acts.*
- *Other unusual or nonrecurring transactions or events.*

5. Analytical auditing may be used in an audit of payroll to assess the way the payroll costs relate to movements in staffing numbers across the organization. If staff on the payroll are decreasing while the overall wage bill for the company is increasing, it may indicate a move by business unit managers to employ people outside the official payroll arrangements and pay them through the purchasing system. A central control policy that says all staff should go through head office payroll may not be properly understood by management in some of the local offices, which may lead to inconsistent employment practices and compensation schemes. The analysis may point to areas that need to be further examined, where apparently sound control policies are not reaching all relevant parts of the organization.

6. Evaluation is also about considering soft controls—that is, the aspect of controls that relates to the way people communicate and work together as well as their overall perspective on compliance and propriety. There are those who argue that while controls represent the agreed response to defined risks, the overall concept of control is really dependent on the control environment that is in place. Furthermore, they argue that this control environment is about the way people see their role in the organization and how they relate to each other. Underpinning this are attributes such as integrity, respect, and fairness, which promote the value of control and lead to the design and use of good controls. Ignoring the people factors will mean the auditor may never really appreciate the way controls are applied in a particular part of the organization. Some auditors take this further and insist on a survey of staff in the operational area, based on the COSO model (control environment) that seeks to measure the adequacy of the values-platform upon which control design and maintenance rest.

7. Control evaluation should be designed to highlight aspects of the system that are at risk. That is, the evaluation needs to include an assessment of what should be in place to tackle inherent risks. Where there are insufficient measures in place, this indicates a weakness in controls that may lead to problems in the short and long run. Control gaps, deficiencies, or weaknesses should drive the direction of the audit testing stage that comes

next. Key controls that are being relied on by line management will like-wise feature in the testing plans developed by the auditor. One risk to a payroll function is that employees who leave the organization may remain on the payroll and continue to receive monthly bank transfers. This risk should really be countered by suitable procedures for staff terminations that ensure the payroll section is notified about those leaving and the date for final compensation, and that no further payments should be generated thereafter. This procedure may be in place but unable to respond to instant dismissals when compensation should stop immediately. The gap in con-trols may be compounded by a failure by the system to notify the team dealing with the final payment that overpayments to the staff member have been made for several months. The auditor's control evaluation in this instance should be able to isolate gaps in control and ensure any such problem is explored further (i.e., tested) in the next stage of the audit.

8. The auditor should also consider what's called compensating controls: unofficial measures that have developed to cover a known gap in official controls. Returning to our payroll example, it may be that one astute member of the payroll staff checks the latest terminations file issued to update the company employee e-mail list, to make sure payroll has a complete list of this week's terminations. In this case, the auditor will want to make sure official controls work properly or that effective com-pensating controls are turned into official procedure.

Evaluation: A Worked Example

Audit Engagement: The Corporate Antifraud Policy (continued)

Having established the process for preparing, updating, and disseminating the fraud policy, the auditor was then in a position to evaluate the existing arrange-ments for adequacy and effectiveness. This was performed through the use of Internal Control Evaluation Schedules, which in essence reflect the entire audit process, as shown in Exhibit 5.12. The control evaluation is based around:

- Key risks that have been rated high in terms of impact and likelihood, before controls are applied (Key Risks and Ratings column).
- Controls that are in place to mitigate the key risks that drive the evalua-tion (Key Controls column).
- The auditor's initial evaluation of these control measures (Initial Evalua-tion column).
- Which tests should be applied to assess the reliability of these controls and the impact of noncompliance and general weaknesses through poor controls (Test Plan column).

Exhibit 5.12. Internal Control Evaluation Schedule

Audit: Corporate Fraud Policy

Control Objective (1): To ensure that all employees understand corporate standards on fraud risk management.

Key Risks and Rating	Key Controls	Initial Evaluation	Test Plan	Opinion and Recommendations
1.1 Failure to formulate a fraud policy (rated 21).	1.1 Board requirement that fraud standard be prepared.	Not followed up by the board.	1.1 Examine board position and check that the reviewed fraud policy is discussed.	
1.2 Failure to disseminate fraud policy (rated 19).	1.2 Policy of providing policy to new staff.	Okay for new staff.	1.2 Check that new staff receive the policy.	
1.3 Policy does not address key issues adequately (rated 15).	1.3 Update each two years.	Time period may be sufficient.	1.3 Assess current policy against best-practice guidelines.	
1.4 Staff not aware of their roles and responsibilities (rated 20).	1.4 Fraud policy mentioned in staff handbook.	Okay.	1.4 Survey staff to assess the level of understanding among employees.	

(continues)

Exhibit 5.12. Internal Control Evaluation Schedule (*Continued*)

Audit: Corporate Fraud Policy

Control Objective (2): To ensure that all suspicions of fraud and irregularity are reported and properly investigated.

Key Risks and Rating	Key Controls	Initial Evaluation	Test Plan	Opinion and Recommendations
2.1 Staff unsure of what action to take if they come across suspicions of wrongdoing (rated 18).	2.1 Response plan within policy contains advice.	Insufficient detail and advice on this matter.	2.1(a) Assess fraud policy for adequate detail on roles. 2.1(b) Include relevant question in staff survey.	
2.2 Responsibility for receiving allegations unclear (rated 15).	2.2 Financial controller is nominated officer.	May be inappropriate.	2.2 Check competencies for this role and whether covered by Financial Controller's job profile.	
2.3 Culture of nonreporting in place impairs procedure (rated 19).	2.3 No specific controls.	Apparent weakness.	2.3(a) Test views in the survey and carry out interviews. 2.3(b) Review past frauds and assess whether they could have been reported earlier.	
2.4 Evidence damaged due to inappropriate response to allegation (rated 20).	2.4 Fraud policy states that staff should not conduct investigations.	Okay.	2.4 Review recent frauds and assess whether evidence treated properly at the outset.	

Exhibit 5.12. Internal Control Evaluation Schedule (*Continued*)

Audit: Corporate Fraud Policy

Control Objective (3): To ensure that appropriate action is taken after the investigation has been completed.

Key Risks and Rating	Key Controls	Initial Evaluation	Test Plan	Opinion and Recommendations
3.1 Staff disciplinaries not conducted to terminate staff involved in fraud (rated 23).	3.1 Disciplinary code calls for dismissal for fraud.	Okay.	3.1 Review recent frauds and assess disciplinary action taken.	
3.2 Criminal charges not brought against internal and external fraudsters (rated 25).	3.2 No policy of prosecutions as each case is considered on its merits.	Apparent weakness.	3.2 Review recent frauds and assess charges brought.	
3.3 Lost funds that could be subject to restitution not recovered (rated 20).	3.3 No specific mention in fraud policy.	Apparent weakness.	3.3 Review recent frauds and assess whether restitution was managed well.	
3.4 Lessons not learned from frauds in terms of improved controls (rated 22).	3.4 No specific mention in fraud policy.	Apparent weakness.	3.4(a) Review recent internal and external frauds and allegations, assess whether controls have been improved. 3.4(b) Assess whether general fraud intelligence from the business sector is used to improve controls.	

The testing column represents the test strategy. Test schedules will be prepared and performed and the reslts summarized and entered back onto the internal control evaluation schedule. After this, the ICE will then contain the audit opinion and recommendations (which will then feed into the management action plan).

Testing

The move toward risk-based auditing contrasts with the focus on testing that was the stamp of traditional internal audits. Many auditors were brought up over the years primarily as "testers." In other words, they spent most of their time working through a list of detailed tests that were designed to find out whether there were any errors or irregularities in the system in question. In an old-style audit of, say, the budgetary control system, the auditor might well have carried out the following tasks:

- Check all budget lines that were assigned.
- Calculate whether they add up to budgets for each business line in the company.
- Double-check that all budgets are assigned to a business manager or approved budget-holder.
- Check that a sample of payments are all coded to the right cost center.
- Make sure all overspends are approved at the appropriate level.
- Examine whether all data that should be held on the budgeting information system is correct, complete, and up to date.

This list might have taken many weeks to analyze and assess, resulting in a list of inconsistent or inaccurate transactions for each budget holder to examine and correct.

The new-look auditor is more concerned about the way risks are managed in the system in question. The auditor's views on the adequacy of risk management should be derived from a judgment made at the evaluation stage of the audit, accompanied by hard evidence to meet Performance Standard 2330:

> *Internal auditors should record relevant information to support the conclusions and engagement results.*

Testing still has a key role in RBSA but has to be used to fit the context. That is, testing is used to support the auditor's view on the adequacy of controls that guard against specific risks and whether these controls actually work. The newly appointed internal auditor will probably carry out extensive testing during the early years of an audit career and gradually become more and more discerning and focused in the use of this technique. There are seven key points that need to be made regarding this stage of the audit:

1. There are two main types of testing: *Compliance tests* check that controls that are being relied on to manage key risks are actually working in practice; *substantive tests* examine the implications of gaps in the design of internal controls. For an audit of budgeting, a key risk may be that budget holders within the organization spend more than the allotted limits set by the board-approved budget. A key control is periodic budget reports that warn the senior business manager where managers are nearing their limits and that provide urgent notification where an order would mean a budget overspend in the area in question. The business manager would then intervene to find out why there is a potential overspend and would be required to specifically authorize excess spending. To test this key control, the auditor may select a sample of spend items and consider whether any excessive amounts were properly authorized by the business unit manager. The auditor may also review overspends and analyze whether reports on potential overspends were seen and actioned by the business manager. If, on the other hand, there are no clear procedures for ensuring budget holders stay within their limits, this means a suitable control is not in place and the risk of significant unnecessary overspends could well materialize. To substantiate this contention, the auditor may well select a sample of spending and examine the extent of any overspending.

2. Everything that the auditor comes across during the course of planning and performing the audit is potentially evidence that supports the audit opinion. Evidence consists of all those matters that tend to support a point or position that is assumed by the auditor and that are sufficiently reliable. Much of this evidence comes from direct testing routines applied by the auditor that explore the tentative findings from the evaluation stage. There are no shortcuts here, as Practice Advisory 2310-1 sets four important attributes that need to be carefully considered by the auditor when performing an audit test, by saying:

   Information should be collected on all matters related to the engagement objectives and scope of work. Information should be sufficient, competent, relevant, and useful to provide a sound basis for engagement observations and recommendations:

   - ***Sufficient information*** *is factual, adequate, and convincing so that a prudent, informed person would reach the same conclusions as the auditor.*
   - ***Competent information*** *is reliable and the best attainable through the use of appropriate engagement techniques.*

- *Relevant information* supports engagement observations and recommendations and is consistent with the objectives for the engagement.
- *Useful information* helps the organization meet its goals.

3. Testing should be used sparingly because it costs time and money to plan and perform the necessary routines. Where there are compliance issues with staff failing to observe important standards and procedures, this point may be discussed with the manager for the area in question. Extensive compliance testing on, say, procedures for setting budgets in conjunction with departmental plans may give a precise figure on the extent of noncompliance, where, say, 25 percent of all budgets have not been set in line with corporate standards that act as a main control over this process. But if the client accepts that there is a major problem with noncompliance, due to the complexity of the budget-setting mechanism, it may be more appropriate to perform only a limited amount of compliance testing to support this view, and avoid extensive research into the scale of the problem. For substantive testing, the problem may be that there is no procedure for verifying the budget codes applied to spend items, meaning the risk of misinformation, which undermines the budgeting system, may materialize. The extent of substantive testing applied by the auditor to a sample of spending to assess the extent to which the budget codes are wrong would depend on whether the client accepts that there is a problem. If there is a clear need for a verification routine for coding payments, audit may simply note the problem and ask management to probe the extent of errors and clean up the database, while a solution is jointly explored by audit and management. Information on the extent of the problem may be requested by the chief finance officer, and audit would only perform this task if there is no one else that can be trusted to prepare these figures. There is really no point performing extensive audit tests where the conclusions are already supported and accepted by all key players.

4. Many auditors use sampling when performing their testing routines. Sampling is based on the idea that a small selection of items from a larger group can give an indication of the properties of the larger group. If we wanted to know the extent to which budget reports are examined by the company's financial controllers, which is seen as a key control over the system, we may select a time frame of the last month and then extract 5 percent of all budget reports issued in the month and find out if the financial controller has reviewed them at all. If this 5 percent selection equates to some twenty budget reports, we may find that fifteen were examined by the financial controller's staff but that five were ignored

because the controllers were too busy to review them. The tentative conclusion may be that 25 percent of reports examined were not reviewed, and this could add up to 100 reports each month or 1,200 a year. For substantive testing, we may wish to consider that poor controls over budgeting in one team of a large support section have led to regular overspends in that section. If there are no separate budget reports for this team, we may need to select a sample of 5 percent of the standard programs operated by the team in question over the year and examine the extent of overspending. This may result in ten programs being selected that when examined show that $50,000 is overspent, with an average of $5,000 each and potentially a $100,000 overspend for the same team over the year. Sampling saves time and means a relatively small number of items may be reviewed to give a ballpark figure for the entire population.

5. The above example is rather crude. Although some audit shops use 5 percent, 10 percent, or 15 percent guidelines for sampling plans, the results are not statistically significant. That is, they have no scientific relevance and are only useful if audit and management accept that rough estimates are okay to use on audit tests. Statistical sampling is simply the use of set parameters that mean the random sample selected is representative of the population it comes from within defined limits. Where the population is known, this prediction is supported by scientific validity, much as we know that a coin will fall on its head roughly 50 times if it is tossed 100 times. Most audit teams have access to statistical sampling software, and if the data is automated, most interrogation software has an in-built routine that can be used to determine statistically relevant sample sizes.

Each audit shop will have a policy in place that points to the use of nonstatistical and statistical sampling for deciding on the relevant sample size for larger databases and files. Randomness is based on each number's having an equal chance of being selected. If, for example, we wanted to select a sample of 75 employees for random audit testing from an employee database of some 10,000 employee records, the sampling interval would be as follows:

$$\frac{10,000}{75} = 133$$

Having selected the first record at random from 1 to 133, we would go on to select every 133rd item until we had our 75 records for the audit purpose. When dealing with sensitive items such as employee records, it is important that we can show that they were selected at random with no personal bias introduced. A random number generator will give much the same result. If the employee population contains different types of

employees—for example, associates who work on one- to two-year contracts and staff who are permanently employed—we may need to stratify
the population and draw two separate samples for audit testing. In other
words, we would divide the database into the two types of employees and
then use sampling.

Note that the larger the sample, the greater the chances are that the
sample will follow the properties of the entire population. If we are very
concerned about associates and wish to test that they have a signed contract of employment to a greater extent than permanent staff, we may wish
to use a proportionately larger sample. Sample size will be affected by
the degree of confidence we need from the sample, that is, what percent-
age of our sample will tend to coincide with the population. This may be
set at 95 percent for associates where 95 times out of 100, the sample will
reflect the population. For permanent staff, this may be set at, say, 90 percent and a relatively smaller sample used by the auditor. Precision is
another criteria that relates to the extent to which the results are reliable within plus or minus limits. So the error we find in the associate's
contracts may fall between 7.7 percent and 12.5 percent of the records
examined, that is, 10 percent plus or minus 2.5 percent. Attribute sampling is useful in measuring the number of times a control is not complied with, while variable sampling measures the extent of loss or other
variable and is useful when performing substantive testing and wishing
to measure the implications of poor controls.

The final criteria to set is the error rate. This is the level of error that
is expected from the population being tested. For example, error may be
seen as for example the number of contracts that are incomplete. This is
normally set at 5 percent, and most statistical sampling tables are based
on this figure. If the actual error rate is different, the quoted risk parameters need to be revised. The rate is determined by the auditor and is based
on pilot studies, discussions with management, and the results of previous audits. Armed with these three dimensions—confidence, precision,
and error rates—statistical tables (or software) may be used to obtain
sample sizes that are statistically reliable. In other words, the results may
be extrapolated with confidence to the entire population. Or more rightly,
the confidence gained from the sample may be defined and quoted when
performing such extrapolations.

6. Interrogation software has a link into testing. Where the auditor is examining a large automated database, the database (or parts of it) may be
downloaded to the auditor's PC and manipulated. Packages such as ACL
and IDEA may be used to extract a sample for testing, using a statistically valid sample size. The package may be used to examine the data

and look for errors, incomplete fields, duplications, inconsistencies and other matters that impact on the state of internal controls. It is important to set a test objective that relates back to either the state of compliance with a key control or the effect of poor controls in a part of the overall system that is being audited. In our budgeting system, we could run an interrogation against budgets set for a particular operation or program and look for inconsistencies that may suggest lapses in control. Budget lines where the spend code does not match the payment type may be extracted for further review and suggest that the budgeting procedures for codes that are set up are not working well. The list of budget holders may be run against a separate list of approved spending personnel to isolate inconsistencies in the way budget responsibilities are designated across the organization. When reviewing data in the budgeting system, we may care to use data interrogation to conduct various tests. One procedure may be noted as follows:

a. Set the audit objective and whether checking controls or just extracting data.

b. Ensure the right audit expertise is available for any complicated routines.

c. Check that the budget data is available and is not just about to undergo a data-cleansing routine.

d. Make sure the timing of tests makes sense in terms of the database being examined and any changes being planned by management.

e. Determine the procedure to be applied (e.g., to extract all budget lines that have increased by more than 5 percent or all spend items that are over a set limit).

f. Consider the file structure—fields, type (alpha, numeric or mixed), length of record in characters, and start position.

g. Consider security and confidentiality arrangements for the data in question.

h. Get hold of the data and download the sample onto the audit PC.

i. Check basic integrity and completeness of data.

j. Run the interrogation using IDEA, ACL, Excel, or whatever package is most suitable.

k. Make sure the audit evidence obtained is reliable and is held in audit files.

l. Decide what to do about data security, ownership, and retention issues.

     m. Determine the impact of interrogation on the audit objective set out in the first bulleted item above.

     n. Work out the next steps, particularly relating to unusual items revealed through the interrogations.

7. Documentation standards are important for testing information. Test results tend to constitute firm evidence that something is happening or that nothing of note needs to be reported. This evidence supports the audit opinion and is a fundamental aspect of the internal audit reporting role on internal controls. In the event of a dispute, the evidence audit used to verify a point made or a decision to take no further action can become very important. In sensitive areas, it may be crucial to determine why audit recommended a particular course of action, and the evidence secured to support this position must be readily available. The audit files should show clearly:

- The test objective.
- Whether it is a compliance or substantive test.
- The scope of the test and whether sampling was applied, and if so on what basis.
- The strategy for completing the test, including what was reviewed, for what periods, and to what extent.
- Who did what in terms of audit staff assigned to the audit and testing routines.
- The results of the testing procedures and conclusions that can be drawn from these results, having reference to the original test objective.
- Where any schedules or source material is held (e.g., a downloaded database).
- Cross-referencing to the control evaluation (prepared before the tests) and draft audit report (prepared after the tests).

Testing enables the auditor to acquire important information on whether tentative findings from control evaluation can be verified by hard evidence. If the audit of the budgeting system evaluated controls as poor because there were ambiguities in the definition of persons who are authorized to spend against various budget heads, audit may conclude that this system is at risk for abuse, error, and poor financial management in general. An audit report that goes on and on about the need for tighter controls over budget management may be well received by management, and they may implement all the changes suggested by internal audit.

However, controls cost money, and changes to control regimes must be either based on a regulatory requirement or made as a response to a key risk.

Improved control through a major review of budget management procedures must be seen to be worthwhile. Furthermore, an audit recommendation is more persuasive if it points to the dollar extent of regular budget overspend, the estimated number of unauthorized commitments made each year, and the results of a survey that indicated staff have a confused understanding of budget responsibilities, which is why many corporate strategies have major spend overruns. These facts should inspire an enthusiastic response from the client. Testing techniques can involve the use of a wide range of sources of information, and the ways that relevant information can be secured are limited only by the imagination of the auditor. Some of the sources include:

- *Interviews:* If the auditors need to know whether a control gap is causing a problem, at times people being interviewed will simply let it be known during an interview. Representations that are made at random may need to be explored unless the matter in question is obvious. For example, a budget officer may admit that the budgeting system is complicated and that this has led to many errors in setting up budgets. This may suggest that the system is poor and is an admission that may be reported as one comment from one person but not necessarily as a generally held view.

- *Analytical review:* This was mentioned earlier and can involve considering different sets of data or data over different time frames. Budgets that are set for sales expenses across different sales offices may be analyzed in conjunction with the size of sales teams at each office. To apply analytical review to this audit, the auditor could carry out the following ten steps:

  1. Define the objective—for example, assess whether there is a logical application of expenditure budgets in conjunction with the level of activity.
  2. Decide how the review will be carried out, what data will be used, and how it will be used.
  3. Formulate a selection criteria, looking at revenue budgets assigned per section across the organization for the new year.
  4. Work out a baseline to assess results, looking for increases on last year's budgets set in line with increases in planned activity levels.
  5. Define what would be an unusual trend, a limit over which the increase in allocated budget as compared to the level of increased activity should be further examined.
  6. Select the sample, and perform the procedure.
  7. Note the unusual items, ones that exceed the limit set in item 5 above.
  8. Examine these items further, looking for reasonable explanations for any unusual items.

   9. Draw a conclusion.

   10. Link the conclusion to the rest of the audit.

The results may support a view that the process for approving budgets is flawed because it is not based on a logical and systematic analysis of spending requirements across all sections. The technique is very useful in external audit where ratios, trends, time series analysis, and basic comparisons may be used to focus the audit on areas that appear to involve significant fluctuations. Error, miscoding, and the all-important financial misstatement may be uncovered by the use of this technique, particularly where a new (and controversial) accounting treatment has been recently adopted. If during the audit we wanted to consider the staffing budget for a government organization with four cash offices, we may find the profiles shown in Exhibit 5.13.

   The ratio analysis of number of transactions dealt with by staff reveals that office 4 may be an area for further consideration, in terms of the staffing budget that has been allocated across cash offices. There may well be suitable explanations, or the review may confirm that budgets are not being set in a systematic manner, which means the risk of inefficiency is increased.

- **Surveys:** This consists of asking people for their views and for set information in a structured and formal manner. A survey of selected budget holders may be used to find out whether they had confidence in the budgeting system and to help isolate some of the problems that were being experienced.

- **External confirmation:** Evidence that is gleaned from within an organization has the potential to be distorted by practices that have been adopted to suit the employees in question and not the organization overall. Spending against budget may be regularly miscoded to ensure it is applied to a different time frame than the period it should have been charged to, so as to enhance a performance bonus for certain managers. An audit test that involves seeking independent confirmation from the vendor regarding the

Exhibit 5.13.   Analytical Review

Cash Office	Number Cashiers	Ave. Volume of Monthly Transactions in 1,000	Volume/ No. Cashiers
1	10	1,100	110
2	5	585	117
3	15	1,490	99
4	7	330	47

date that the item (or service) was provided may be used to obtain reliable information on which dates should have been applied and so indicate non-compliance (or worse) with standard accounting practices.

- *Examination:* This is a general concept that means scrutinizing, checking, inquiring, and essentially having a look at something. In our budgeting example, the audit testing stage would naturally involve examining selected budgets and the way they are set, managed and reviewed. In other words, auditing involves more than just talking to people and then preparing a report from what has been said.

- *Verification:* This technique involves finding out if something exists and determining its status. It tends to involve viewing a physical object or contract or structure, rather than accepting at face value that something exists. If all budget holders are said to hold a personal and up-to-date copy of the budget manual, any such persons who are interviewed by audit may be asked to produce their copy to confirm this point.

- *Reconciliation:* In accounting systems and processes linked to an accounting routine, it is standard practice to record data in two sets of account, on the "debits equal credits" basis. It is also good practice to check figures that move from one account to another and to ensure physical items correspond to the amount that sits in the associated record. The risk of loss or error may be mitigated through reconciling the two amounts. The auditor may perform a similar reconciliation to judge whether two items that should correspond actually do match up in practice. If set budgets are transferred to another part of the organization whenever a program is reassigned as part of a strategic initiative, the auditor may assess the integrity of the adopted transfer arrangements by reconciling the old and new budgets. The arrangements will be designed to manage the risk of loss, irregularity, or error, and the audit test will confirm whether this risk is being adequately addressed by management.

- *Observation:* Some controls are implicit in the way people behave. One way to test the reliability of such controls may be to see them in action. This technique must be used with care. It does not mean to spy on people, and it should not get confused with covert surveillance, which is a technique used in fraud and similar investigations. A high-level budget committee may meet each month to approve large program spending, and this may be key to controlling high-risk ventures. Sitting as an observer in such a meeting may be one way to assess whether the criteria set for approving large budgets is applied in the way that fits the documented process.

- *Inspection:* This differs from observation in that it is carried out by people who have formal expertise in the matter being inspected. It tends to relate to technical matters that require a third-party opinion that is objective and necessary, because of the importance of the matter at hand. For example, items marked "High-tech design projects" may be given an unrestricted budget to reflect the complicated nature of the work. The auditor may feel these classifications may be used to abuse the budgeting system and may commission a review of these projects by an expert who can confirm whether selected projects really do fall under the assigned classification.

- **Reperformance:** Many controls are inherent in the way something is done, and the auditor can assess whether a routine works by redoing the task, weighing the auditor's results, and determining whether they fit what the client has reported. For example, budget holders may make a rough estimate of recent expenditures that have not yet hit the accounts as budget actuals, before spending further in an attempt to manage their allocation. The auditor may reperform this calculation to assess whether this is a reasonable way to manage the risk of financial exposure.

- **Vouching:** This means checking one record against another record that should correspond with the first. The budgeting audit may involve checking a small sample of orders placed against budget entries for the item in question to ensure such orders can be related to a particular budget line.

- **Anything else that makes sense:** The addition of this final item is designed to inspire some creative thinking from the auditor. If a supposition needs to be explored and "grounded in reality," the auditor must sit back and think how this might be done to lend credibility to the audit report, over and above pure supposition. If the auditor needs to know whether managers start spending just before the end of the budget period to reserve their budget intact next year, this may be a well-kept secret. If this practice leads to unwarranted risks, the auditor must sit back and work out how this suspicion may be confirmed, without excessive inconvenience and cost. This is quite a challenge.

Compliance and Substantive Tests

The two main types of testing may be illustrated by referring back to the example of an internal control questionnaire for payroll that was mentioned when we discussed evaluation earlier (see Exhibit 5.11):

1.1 Check small sample of new starters for vetting applied, per set procedure.

1.2 Check error rate of staff compared to industry standards.

1.3 Examine small sample of personal development records.

The test 1.1 is a compliance test to examine the vetting applied to new starters. The test 1.2 is a substantive test examining the implications of a lack of training for payroll staff. The test 1.3 is a compliance test that examined the use of personal development targets for payroll staff.

Testing still has a role in internal auditing as it sets the auditor apart from those review teams that make little use of formal evidence. There are those who feel that testing is a small component in the bigger picture of understanding control frameworks and whether they make sense. They feel the dark ages of extensive checking led to a negative reputation for internal audit as the in-house hit-squad. There are others who feel that testing and evidence should drive the audit process as stakeholders become more and more skeptical about the validity of information and representations provided by executives, managers, and employees generally. But then again, variety is the spice of life.

Testing: A Worked Example

Audit Engagement: The Corporate Antifraud Policy (continued)

This stage of the audit is based on implementing the testing strategy that was derived from the Internal Control Evaluation (ICE) mentioned earlier. The ICE detailed plans to perform the following sets of tests:

1.1 Examine board position and check the review fraud policy.

1.2 Check that new staff receive the policy.

1.3 Assess current policy against best practice guidelines.

1.4 Survey staff to assess the level of understanding among employees.

2.1(a) Assess fraud policy for adequate detail on roles.

2.1(b) Include relevant question in staff survey.

2.2 Check competencies for this role and whether covered by Financial Controller.

2.3(a) Test views in the survey and carry out interviews.

2.3(b) Review past frauds and assess whether they could have been reported earlier.

2.4 Review recent frauds and assess whether evidence treated properly at the outset.

3.1 Review recent frauds and assess disciplinary action taken.

3.2 Review recent frauds and assess charges brought.

3.3 Review recent frauds and assess whether restitution was managed well.

3.4(a) Review recent internal and external frauds and allegations assess whether controls have been improved.

3.4(b) Assess whether general fraud intelligence from the business sector is used to improve controls.

Each of these tasks should be carried out in the most efficient and effective way. In fact, the audit involved setting a precise test objective for each of the tasks in question. Not all these tests are documented here, as extracts only will provide an idea of how this stage of the audit was carried out. Using the test plans for Control Objective 2: "To ensure that all suspicions of fraud and irregularity are reported and properly investigated," a test schedule was prepared, which is shown in Exhibit 5.14. Organizational corporate HR database consisted of some 10,500 employees, and the following tasks were carried out:

- Database downloaded to audit PC and sorted into two groups:
    1. Group one for employees in post less than six months (500 staff).
    2. Group two, employees in post for six months or more (10,000).
- Two short questionnaires were designed, one for the first group of new staff and the other questionnaire for the second group of employees (staff in post for six months or more) and the following tasks carried out:
    ○ Sample extracted for each group and supplied with the relevant questionnaire that was sent via e-mail.
    ○ Late returns chased through follow-up telephone calls to persons in question.
    ○ Results analyzed by the auditor.
  Extracts from the questionnaire for group one are shown in Exhibit 5.15.

Exhibit 5.14. Test Schedules; Fraud Policy Audit

Test Plan	ICE Ref	Detailed Test Description	Results
2.1(a) Assess fraud policy for adequate detail on roles.		Compare current policy with best-practice guidance from the IIA and ACFE; extract aspects of the current policy that are weak on role definition.	Role of respective parties in the organization well defined with sufficient levels of detail. (working paper (WP) 7.12)
2.1(b) Include relevant question in staff survey.		Question for staff survey: Have your role and responsibilities in respect of fraud detection, prevention, and response to allegations been made clear? And if so, how was this achieved?	Staff has a poor understanding of their roles, and only 10% of employees in post more than six months could remember the policy or had a copy readily available; 25% of new employees (in post less than six months) looked

Exhibit 5.14. Test Schedules; Fraud Policy Audit *(Continued)*

Test Plan	ICE Ref	Detailed Test Description	Results
			at the fraud policy in their staff handbook. (WP 7.05)
2.2 Check competencies for this role and whether covered by Financial Controller.		Examine job detail of financial controller (FC) and assess whether it provides adequate coverage of competencies required to be the main representative on fraud issues; obtain FC's views on this point.	No mention of responsibility for managing the corporate fraud policy. (WP 7.21) FC has no interest in retaining this role. (WP 7.27)
2.3(a) Test views in the survey and carry out interviews.		Question for staff survey: Has your responsibility for reporting suspicions of fraud and abuse been made clear? And if so, how was this achieved?	80% of staff surveyed had been given no information on the whistleblowing procedures. (WP 7.05)
2.3(b) Review past frauds and assess whether they could have been reported earlier.		Examine the files of last three fraud allegations that have been recorded and assess whether the reporting system has operated effectively.	One of the three frauds examined was not reported earlier because the staff in question did not realize such a facility existed. (WP 7.08)
2.4 Review recent frauds and assess whether evidence treated properly at the outset.		Examine the files of the last three frauds and assess whether the response was managed so as to protect the available evidence.	No evidence of poor management of evidence at early stage during the investigation. (WP 7.14)

The final point to note about testing strategies and schedules is that a further level of documentation may be prepared to assist the process. The test plan came from the ICE and response to the key risks that were identified at this stage. The test plans were then recorded in the Test Schedules that provided more details of the test and then recorded a summary of the test results. An additional level of documentation can be prepared for each separate test, the Test Objective form that is attached to the test working papers. Tests 2.1(b) and 2.3(a)

Exhibit 5.15.   Fraud Audit Policy

Staff Survey

Dear ————————— ,

You have been chosen at random to take part in a survey being carried out by internal audit, concerning the extent to which staff are aware of the corporate fraud policy.

This information will be held by internal audit and will be kept confidential. Note that this is not part of the whistleblowing procedures that are available to report suspicions or information concerning wrongdoing by employees and others.

We appreciate your assistance and would ask you to return the survey by xx 20xx. For further information about this survey and its use in the audit, please do not hesitate to contact Fred Fredricks on xxx.

Extracts from the Survey:

Q.1. Have you seen the fraud policy issued by the company?   Yes   No

Q.2. Are you aware of the contents of this policy?   Yes   No

Q.3. Have your role and responsibilities regarding fraud   Yes   No
     prevention and detection been made clear to you?

Q.4. Please describe your understanding of your role in fraud
     prevention and detection.

     _____

Q.5. Are you aware of the company's whistleblowing policy   Yes   No
     on reporting wrongdoings?

Q.6. What action would you take if you felt that a colleague
     was involved in defrauding the company?

     _____

Q.7. Do you feel you would benefit from awareness training
     regarding the antifraud policy?   Yes   No

Q.8. Etc.

Questions for staff in post less than six months:

Q.1. Were you given a copy of the fraud policy when you   Yes   No
     started work?

Q.2. Have you read this policy?   Yes   No

Q.3. Has anyone explained the contents of the fraud policy?   Yes   No

Q.4. In what ways were the contents made clear to you?

     _____

Q.5. Etc.

from the test schedules were based on questions for the staff survey that has already been described. The survey will result in a stack of questionnaires completed and returned to the auditor, which will be held on the auditor's working paper files, either manually or automated. The Test Objective form is a covering document that is attached to the test papers (in this case, the returns and analysis of these returns) and may appear along the lines shown in Exhibit 5.16.

In this way the audit files recount the entire history of the audit testing procedures so that we do not have the usual problem of stacks of testing papers

Exhibit 5.16. Test Objective Form

Audit: Corporate Antifraud Policy
Test Objective Form: Ref 56

Objective: To assess staff awareness of the published Fraud Policy

Approach:	Sample:
Download employee database and extract two random samples of employees in post less than six months (DB 1) and those in post six months and over (DB 2).	Judgment based on small number to avoid excessive time. Database 1—10,000 employees: judgment sample of 100 employees selected by a random number generator and names (phone and e-mail contacts) selected for survey. Database 2—500 employees: judgment used to select sample of 20 new staff.

Results (extracts):

2.1(b) Staff have a poor understanding of their roles, and only 10% of employees in post more than six months could remember the policy or had a copy readily available; 25% of new employees (in post less than six months) looked at the fraud policy in their staff handbook
(Working Paper (WP) 7.05).

2.3(a) Eighty percent of staff surveyed had been given no information on the whistleblowing procedures.
(WP 7.05)

Etc.

Signed: Lead Auditor	Reviewed: Audit Manager
Date:	Date:

sitting on the auditor's files with no clear reference back to the audit opinion and report. The next part of this worked example appears when we discuss developing the audit findings.

For Further Discussion

Compliance testing is important because it uncovers problems with poor adherence to control standards. In contrast, is extensive substantive testing still appropriate to support internal audit findings?

—— SECTION 6 ——
DEVELOPING FINDINGS

We have found out about the system and its objectives, and considered whether the controls in place appear to address the risks that impact the system objectives. And we have looked for evidence of actual risks materializing so as to support or refute any concerns we may have about the state of internal controls. This is the detailed work that underpins a good risk-based systems audit. Having completed all the hard work, we can now start to put the jigsaw together and form an accurate picture of areas in the system that need to be tightened up. Before we get to the audit report we will need to develop the findings and bring together all the information that has been gathered.

The key to developing findings is twofold: it is to perform professional audit work, and it is to keep the client in touch with the findings that arise from this work, on an ongoing basis. Close working with the system owner and staff throughout the audit makes for a good result all round. Moreover, any control improvement plan that is designed should ideally be done through close working relations between the auditor and the manager in question, even when the audit focuses on assurance rather than consulting work. The audit result is the natural progression of the ascertainment, evaluation, and testing stages of the audit and in a sense happens during and throughout these stages, as the real picture comes together. The results are based on analysis and evaluation, even where these are derived from soft as well as hard issues. Performance Standard 2320 is firm in requiring:

> Internal auditors should base conclusions and engagement results on appropriate analysis and evaluations.

There is no shortcut to this equation. There is help in arriving at audit conclusions in the form of Practice Advisory 2410-1, which defines this concept as follows:

Conclusions (opinions) are the internal auditor's evaluations of the effects of the observations and recommendations on the activities reviewed. They usually put the observations and recommendations in perspective based upon their overall implications. Engagement conclusions, if included in the engagement report, should be clearly identified as such. Conclusions may encompass the entire scope of an engagement or specific aspects. They may cover, but are not limited to, whether operating or program objectives and goals conform with those of the organization, whether the organization's objectives and goals are being met, and whether the activity under review is functioning as intended.

All this information comes from the audit process, including the compliance tests and where applicable, any substantive tests that are performed. It is a requirement of the job that a professional internal auditor is obliged to form an opinion on the matters set out in the original terms of reference for the audit. There is no hiding place. Some audit shops have standards that have been agreed upon with the board and audit committee regarding the official audit opinion. They mark each audit with adjectives such as "satisfactory," "adequate," "inadequate," or "poor" in terms of the system of internal control and compliance with set standards. Having formed an opinion on what has been found during the audit, the auditor can turn toward forming recommendations. All suggested changes must be worthwhile, and the benefits of these changes, or actions in terms of improving the management of risk, must exceed the costs and inconvenience associated with making these changes. Moreover, the auditor should formulate recommendations in a way that delivers best value for the organization—that is, the board, audit committee, and client, or just the client if a pure consulting engagement. The findings and recommendations made by audit should meet professional standards, and these are established as attributes in Practice Advisory 2410-1, which suggests:

Observations and recommendations should be based on the following attributes:

- ***Criteria:*** *The standards, measures, or expectations used in making an evaluation and/or verification (what should exist).*
- ***Condition:*** *The factual evidence that the internal auditor found in the course of the examination (what does exist).*
- ***Cause:*** *The reason for the difference between the expected and actual conditions (why the difference exists).*
- ***Effect:*** *The risk or exposure the organization and/or others encounter because the condition is not consistent with the criteria (the impact of the difference). In determining the degree of risk or exposure, internal auditors should consider the effect their engagement observations and recommendations may have on the organization's operations and financial statements.*

In other words, users of audit reports need to know what should be happening, what is happening, what this means in practice, and why these problems, if any, exist. In addition, they need to know the consequences in terms of increased exposure to risk. This, in turn, allows a consideration of whether there is a reasonable expectation that system objectives will be achieved, and if not, how the recommendations that audit makes will help improve the situation.

We have mentioned the new-look auditor who works closely with the client but is still able to retain professional objectivity. This type of auditor may well want to prepare recommendations that have been developed in conjunction with the client. The blended audit approach we have mentioned earlier may include a workshop event after the auditor has arrived at the main conclusions. In this type of forum, ways forward may be discussed with the work team so that the risk register and action plans can be further developed as a direct result of the audit that has been carried out. Recommendations that are being considered by the internal auditor should pass a number of tests before they are documented, including having been made with an appreciation of the following issues:

- Findings should be linked to the original objectives that had been set for the audit, and some form of commentary should be made regarding each aspect of the terms of reference covered by the audit.
- The audit opinion should be driven by the risk assessment and include a view on whether significant risks are likely to materialize or whether they are mitigated, so far as is possible, by controls and wider risk management strategies.
- If the system that has been audited has a logical flow of activities from start to finish, the findings may be ordered to reflect this logic.
- Findings should flow into recommendations. Where aspects of the system are at risk, this should be commented on and recommendations made, and support for action already being taken by management should also be provided.
- Findings should be balanced and comments made on positive steps taken by management as well as areas where further improvements are possible.

The Old Approach

There are some auditors who find it hard to put together a good audit report and struggle with their files and documentation for many days trying to work out what should go in the report and what may be left out. In the end, the report becomes a hit or miss affair with findings dumped in at random alongside excessive commentary regarding the way the system is working. A poor audit report will result from using the following approach:

1. The auditor turns up at the manager's office with set terms of reference for the audit and engages in an open-ended discussion about the operation being audited. Managers will talk about what's wrong with the system, staffing problems, and other matters that are on their minds at the time of the interview.

2. The auditor will make extensive notes and promise to sort things out if possible. Meanwhile vague terms of reference are set for the audit along the following lines: "to review the adequacy and effectiveness of controls over system x."

3. The auditor returns to the operation and talks to staff about what they do at work and what they think about the operation in question. Again, these are open-ended discussions, and staff will talk about their personal gripes and whether their managers are doing a good job or not.

4. The auditor will then analyze as many files as possible during the time that is assigned to the audit, looking for errors and unusual items.

5. The auditor may run a data interrogation routine of the automated database, again looking for duplicated transactions, and incomplete or "odd" data.

6. The auditor spends the rest of the time talking to staff at random about some of the matters found through examining the files and database and asks staff in confidence whether there is any abuse occurring at work.

7. The auditor will make a final round of the office looking at the state of the files and whether the offices are tidy and well laid out.

8. At the end of the interview, the auditor returns to the audit offices and spends a couple of weeks working through the detailed documentation extracted from files, from the analysis carried out, and the detailed interview records that have been made. These documents are spread out over the auditor's desk, and an intense period of study and concentration ensues as the auditor decides what should go into the audit report.

9. Eventually, a comprehensive report is prepared, setting out how the system works and some of the insider information that has been provided to the auditor. Any errors or inconsistent transactions found by the auditor are listed in the report under the "findings" section.

10. The report makes several recommendations on correcting errors found and reflecting some of the ideas from the manager and staff that are supported by the auditor. Many of the audit recommendations represent actions that are already being carried out by management.

11. The draft report sits around for a while until an audit manager carries out a review and looks at the errors that the auditor has found and the style of the writing before signing it off for publication.

12. The draft report is sent to the manager several weeks after the audit fieldwork, for comments and a deadline of four weeks given for a response.

13. A formal response is provided by the client manager, and this is appended to the report. The draft report is turned into a final audit report with a note against each recommendation saying whether it has been "accepted," "rejected," or "accepted with alteration."

14. The detailed final report is signed off by the chief audit executive.

15. The final report is copied to the director for the area in question, the external auditor, and the board and is noted as available for the audit committee.

16. The auditor starts the next engagement.

The New Approach

The audit described in the example above is not an unusual situation, and audit work may appear similar to putting together a giant jigsaw, where the auditor struggles to put the pieces into place, and sometimes cheats by cutting pieces of the puzzle to suit. Findings in this sense become whatever pops out from the audit, particularly relating to sensitive matters that people have whispered to the auditor on things they do not like at work. There is another way of getting to findings, recommendations, and an audit report that forms a more professional and systematic way of performing assurance work. One version of this improved approach is outlined briefly below:

1. The auditor meets with the client manager and discusses the terms of reference for the audit and best approach that acknowledges the progress that has so far been made in establishing effective risk management arrangements.

2. The system is ascertained and its objectives clarified.

3. Control objectives may also be used to focus the audit on key aspects of the operation.

4. The auditor meets with the manager and staff to agree on the risks that have the most impact on the systems and control objectives. These risks are prioritized again through discussion (or a workshop) with work teams.

5. The evaluation stage comes next, where the controls that are in place are reviewed to assess how far they help manage the risks that have been identified. The results are discussed with the manager, and key controls that are fundamental to the success of the activities are agreed upon.

6. These key controls are tested for compliance, and an assessment is made as to whether there is a good control environment in place that promotes

adherence to standards. The use of control awareness seminars for work teams may be discussed with the manager if there is scope to make improvements in control appreciation among staff.

7. Areas where there are insufficient controls, or where controls are not being applied properly, may be briefly explored to look for evidence of loss, error, abuse, inefficiency, poor information, and so on as a result of poor controls. These findings are discussed with management as they arise.

8. The findings are entered in the working files, using the Internal Control Evaluation Schedule as the pivotal document, and the audit manager may turn up regularly and have a look at the files and progress made. These findings are presented to the management team at the end of the audit fieldwork (wrap-up meeting) and discussions made on ways forward (action plans).

9. The draft audit report and action plan appear quickly after the wrap-up meeting as the report writes itself, including terms of reference (from the opening meeting), brief notes on the system audited and progress made on establishing risk management (ascertainment stage), control weaknesses (evaluation stage), implications (testing stage), and recommendations and tentative action plan (wrap-up meeting). The draft report goes out quickly to management from the operation that was audited.

10. The focus is on the action plan and internal control improvement as part of better risk management, and a formal presentation may be made by the audit manager (and audit team) to the operational manager and senior personnel if the action plan needs to be discussed further.

11. Consulting engagements may be requested to support the action plan that has been developed—for example, CSA workshop facilitation may be adopted by management, and audit may be asked to help develop this initiative.

12. A final report is issued in line with the set distribution policies.

13. The audit work, based on the agreed action plan, is followed up after a set time frame of, say, three to six months.

14. The audit allows the CAE to give a view to the board and audit committee on the state of risk management and control in the areas that have been audited.

The first approach views the audit report as the end product of the audit and a dumping ground for everything that has a passing relevance to the work performed by the auditor. The latter approach provides a better focus on efficiency and gives form to a risk-based audit process. Here, the audit report simply becomes part of the process and a way of facilitating the risk management and control improvement plan, while providing a formal record of audit findings and assurances. Formal audit reports are nonetheless an important aspect of the audit, and the next section provides more detail on this topic.

Developing Findings: A Worked Example

Audit Engagement: The Corporate Antifraud Policy (continued)

The Internal Control Evaluation Schedule (ICE) is the linchpin of the entire audit. The ICE records in summary all that has happened during the audit from ascertaining and evaluation through to detailed testing. The ICE will indicate:

1. What the system is trying to achieve—the systems and control objectives.
2. The operational risks that have been identified and assessed that impact on the ability to achieve these objectives.
3. The test strategy and summary results.
4. The audit opinion and associated recommendations.

Using the continuing example of the audit of the fraud policy, the audit, findings, opinion, and recommendations that will appear in the audit report can be derived by revisiting the ICE, as illustrated in Exhibit 5.17 (Control Objective 2 only). Note that the final column may now be completed, covering the audit opinion and any recommendations.

The key to all good auditing is to conduct the fieldwork in a systematic manner. This is achieved by working to professional standards and focusing on risks as the key driver to the audit. The aim is to verify and improve the risk management system and ensure that effective internal controls are not only in place but also actually working properly. The ICE represents "the audit," and as it is being developed, the client should be kept informed. All that is left is to prepare the formal audit report. In fact, some auditors argue that the ICE can be published as the audit report, simply by adding an extra column to the schedule to cover the management action plan that should have been agreed to with the client. The fraud policy audit continues as a worked example at the end of the next section on audit reporting.

For Further Discussion

What criteria may be used to distinguish between a significant and a nonsignificant audit finding, and in what way does this criteria help the internal auditor arrive at a formal opinion for assurance-based audits?

Exhibit 5.17. Internal Control Evaluation Schedule

Key Risks and Rating	Key Controls	Initial Evaluation	Test Plan	Opinion and Recommendations
2.1 Staff unsure of what action to take if they come across suspicions of wrongdoings (rated 15).	2.1 Response plan within policy contains advice.	Insufficient detail and advice on this matter.	2.1(a) Assess fraud policy for adequate detail on roles. 2.1(b) Include relevant question in staff survey.	Although policy itself covers key areas, many employees have a poor understanding of their roles. **Rec:** Staff awareness seminars should be held across the organization.
2.2 Responsibility for receiving allegations unclear (rated 19).	2.2 Financial controller is nominated officer.	May be inappropriate.	2.2 Check competencies for this role and whether covered by Financial Controller.	Financial controller post is not equipped to take responsibility for fraud policy. **Rec:** Reassign role; could be part of new head of compliance role that is now being developed.
2.3 Culture of nonreporting in place impairs procedure (rated 20).	2.3 No specific controls.	Apparent weakness.	2.3(a) Test views in the survey and carry out interviews. 2.3(b) Review past frauds and assess whether they could have been reported earlier.	Little awareness of whistleblowing procedures and no specific encouragement to use the arrangements. **Rec:** Build this into fraud awareness seminars for staff.
2.4 Evidence damaged due to inappropriate response to allegation (rated 20).	2.4 Fraud policy states that staff should not conduct investigations.	Okay.	2.4 Review recent frauds and assess whether evidence treated properly at the outset.	Once started, fraud investigations are carried out to high standards, from the outset. **Rec:** n/a

—— SECTION 7 ——

AUDIT REPORTING AND FOLLOW-UP

After an audit has been completed and the dust has settled, there should be several products for the client:

- Improved risk management and control.
- An enhanced reputation of internal audit.
- A good working relationship with the client.
- A good understanding of corporate governance and disclosure requirements.
- Formal assurances on the system in question.

This is what internal auditing is all about: making a difference, adding value, and helping get risk management into the business so that stakeholders may take comfort in disclosures about internal control and company performance. These products are intangible in the sense that they support and lift the business, but focus on decisions and judgments made by others on advice from internal audit.

But audit has no executive power to make these decisions and commit resources, only to give help, advice and support, and formal assurances. The mechanism that underpins the audit product is the publication of the formal audit report, which has a degree of permanence and status, making it an important document. If we take the view that the audit product is embodied in support, advice, and information to the extreme, then it may be argued that there is no need for an audit report. At the same time, everyone employed by the organization has a clear responsibility that should be discharged and documented, even where the role is advisory rather than executive. The new thrust from society is on disclosures, and increasingly, regulations and laws relating to business, commerce, and government place a burden on each company to provide numerous official returns and reports. Audit likewise must stand up and be counted, and issue formal reports on all the work that it has been involved in. There are different types of audit reports that may be issued, and these are discussed below.

Preliminary Survey Report

This type of report was mentioned earlier as a way of preparing the terms of reference and audit approach that fit the context of the audit. The preliminary survey report is prepared after meeting with the client and achieving an initial outline of the current risk management arrangements. It may cover:

- The audit in question.
- Source of the audit.

- Previous audit work and results of last follow-up audit.
- Objectives of the audit (and control objectives if appropriate).
- Scope of the audit and what it will focus on.
- A view on whether detection of irregularity forms part of the audit scope.
- Audit guidance on any programs of work that have been prepared at this stage.
- Staff that may be assigned, including any specialists.
- Hours that should be assigned to audit staff.
- Timing of audit and key client contacts.
- Reporting lines internally and to client management.
- Recommendations on whether the audit should be performed at this time.

The report will go to the audit manager and CAE and result in an official approval for the audit to go ahead, if this is the decision. In a fast-changing environment where different sections of the organization may have made different degrees of progress in risk management and controls disclosure reporting, the survey allows a careful consideration of the assignment of audit resources.

Interim Engagement Report

Once the audit assignment plan has been prepared and a start has been made on the audit, consideration should be had to the use of interim audit reporting. We can start with Performance Standard 2400, which sets the first challenge by stating:

Internal auditors should communicate the engagement results promptly.

Timing can be the key to operational success. Decisions made now by busy managers may add much more value than decisions that are pending, waiting for the results of a formal report. There is an inherent inconsistency where the auditor reports the need for urgent action by management but has spent weeks of deliberation before arriving at this report. While it is wrong to send out incomplete reports, or reports that are based on flimsy ideas, there needs to be a balance, where audit reports are not held up unnecessarily. Interim audit reports are useful for longer audits that last more than a week. They can also be applied where the audit itself is broken into clear sections, and results may be reported as each part of the audit is completed. So where an audit covers head office procedures, financial regulations, local office practices, and outreach programs, it may be an idea to prepare interim reports as each part of the audit is covered.

Notwithstanding the use of formal interim reports, the internal auditor should meet with the client at least on a weekly basis to give an update on developments and progress. Any serious issues that arise during the course of the audit should be brought to management's attention as soon as possible. Performance Standard 2410.C1 states:

> *Communication of the progress and results of consulting engagements will vary in form and content depending upon the nature of the engagement and the needs of the client.*

The task is to translate this requirement into a policy to be applied by audit staff. There is further guidance available in the form of Practice Advisory 2410-1, which suggests:

> *Interim reports may be written or oral and may be transmitted formally or informally. Interim reports may be used to communicate information that requires immediate attention, to communicate a change in engagement scope for the activity under review, or to keep management informed of engagement progress when engagements extend over a long period. The use of interim reports does not diminish or eliminate the need for a final report.*

One further policy underpins the use of interim reporting: that is that nothing appearing in the audit report should come as a surprise to the client. The audit process is based on working closely with the client to improve the system and confirm that all is well. Official audit reports can create a barrier to this ideal, as this report will be available to everyone who has an interest in the subject matter and who is authorized to view the report. Interim reporting can help overcome this problem and should form part of in-house standards. The interim report should indicate:

- The audit.
- Terms of reference and any changes that have been made in form and scope.
- Progress to date and whether audit is on-line to finish on time.
- Findings to date and whether there is any action that needs to be taken at this stage.
- Anything else that needs to be addressed.

This report should not be too large and may appear as a slimmed-down version that simply sets out anything of note in as few words as possible. In fact, one effective technique is to update the client at the end of each week and issue a short e-mail confirming what was discussed.

Draft Audit Report

It is part of natural justice that each person should have a right to reply in all assertions that have an impact on their lives. Audit reports must likewise fit into this philosophy. Getting to the final audit report is aided by a constructive wrap-up or closing meeting with the client to go over the findings. There is much guidance available on this subject in Practice Advisory 2440-1, which propounds the following policies:

- *Internal auditors should discuss conclusions and recommendations with appropriate levels of management before issuing final engagement communications.*

- *Discussion of conclusions and recommendations is usually accomplished during the course of the engagement and/or at postengagement meetings (exit interviews). Another technique is the review of draft engagement issues, observations, and recommendations by management of the audited activity. These discussions and reviews help ensure that there have been no misunderstandings or misinterpretations of fact by providing the opportunity for the engagement client to clarify specific items and to express views of the observations, conclusions, and recommendations.*

Facts, views, and possible action required all form part of the agenda for these meetings. It is important that the right people attend the wrap-up. The Practice Advisory also covers this point:

Although the level of participants in the discussions and reviews may vary by organization and by the nature of the report, they will generally include those individuals who are knowledgeable of detailed operations and those who can authorize the implementation of corrective action.

The draft report should go to the client, in the form of the business manager who is most responsible for the system that has been reviewed. It may be an idea to restrict circulation of this report so that factual matters and areas where further clarification may be provided by the client can be addressed and the report corrected to better reflect the circumstances at hand. The final audit report has a formal status and position within the organization, and care must be taken to ensure it is balanced and reliable. Practice Advisory 2440-1 recognizes the importance of the final report, suggesting:

The chief audit executive or designee should review and approve the final engagement communications before issuance and should decide to whom the report will be distributed.

The review process should be built into the entire audit process and should involve a detailed consideration of the draft report. Factual information and quotations should be double-checked before the report is signed off on. The draft report may also be accompanied by correspondence asking that all factual matters be checked and corrected if required. The response to the draft report may be dealt with in various ways. It can be:

- Included as an appendix to the report.
- Noted in sections where the material is relevant.
- Assimilated in an updated version of the report, along with a note to that effect.

Auditors should avoid a "ping-pong" situation whereby the draft report is sent out, response is received from the client, comments on the response are sent back by audit, and observations on the latest comments then appear back from the client. If this is happening, it suggests there was something wrong with the audit, and audit procedures need to be reviewed. However, where the audit dealt with an investigation into negligence or management abuse then, this situation is more likely to happen and may well be unavoidable.

Final Audit Report

This is what most people refer to when talking about internal audit reports—that is, the final report that is published after an audit engagement has been carried out. The final audit report is the responsibility of the CAE. Performance Standard 2440 states:

> The CAE should disseminate results to the appropriate individuals.

This Standard applies to both assurance and consulting engagements. The "appropriate individual" is defined by Performance Standard 2440.A1:

> The CAE is responsible for communicating the final results to individuals who can ensure that the results are given due consideration.

The concept of risk drives internal audit work, and this is also the case for the audit report. The risk-based approach is supported in Practice Advisory 2010-2, which makes clear:

> Management reporting and communication should convey risk management conclusions and recommendations to reduce exposures. For management to fully understand the degree of exposure, it is critical that audit reporting identify the criticality and consequence of the risk activity to achieving objectives.

This is the aim of the report. A process for getting to a high-impact report was described in Section 6. Each audit shop should have a defined standard that covers audit reporting as it helps set a convenient platform for the auditor to present an account of the audit. The structure of the report will vary between audit shops, but the report may contain the following sections:

- *Cover:* This may contain the "audit logo" and design that is known throughout the organization. It is best to reserve this format for final reports only so that draft and interim reports do not get mixed up with the published final version. It is also worthwhile thinking about the image of the audit outfit and what ideas the adopted design conjures up in the mind of the reader.

- *List of contents:* Include page numbers for ready access to parts of the report. For larger reports, the contents may include subheadings as well as the main sections of the report.

- *Executive summary and action plan:* This is perhaps the most important part of the report. It should be capable of being read as a separate document and describe the terms of reference (objectives and scope of work), main conclusions (linked to the scope of work), and audit opinion (crucial for assurance work). Attached to this should be the agreed action plan, setting out the recommendations and who will do what in terms of future action.

- *Main body:* This may be broken down into aspects of the scope of the audit and cover work carried out, detailed findings, and recommendations.

- *Appendixes:* Where anything is an integral part of the report and aids the readers' understanding of the audit, it should appear in the appendix. If it does not pass these tests, it should stay in the working papers file and not clog up the report. It is poor practice to include anything in the appendixes that is not referred to in the report. Some audit shops place the detailed terms of reference and work carried out, people contacted, files examined, and so on in the appendixes. Others leave out such detail altogether.

It normally takes a newly appointed auditor some time to appreciate that users of the audit report will almost always only look at the executive summary. They really have no time at all to browse through a detailed document. We live in the "PC screen" era, and if something needs to be said, it should really fit onto a screen; not many people these days bother to scroll down past one screen of words. This means a single-page executive summary with an attached action plan is probably a good way to get across the key messages, with a more detailed document available on request. The internal control evaluation schedule is a good way to capture all the significant information that the reader needs to get best value from the audit report, and this can be taken straight from the audit working paper files (e.g., the ICES).

The report itself should be a balanced document and not what some call based on "Gotcha" audits, which view success as catching the client with some embarrassing finding. There needs to be some balance, and this is promoted in Practice Advisory 2410-1, which suggests:

> *Observations and recommendations may also include engagement client accomplishments, related issues, and supportive information if not included elsewhere.*

We have mentioned the report distribution and the importance of getting the document to the right people to ensure action happens, and the report may also give comfort to those who are responsible for the operation that has been audited. We have also suggested that audit reporting is about inspiring the appropriate action, which is associated with a better risk and control improvement plan, developed by management. Some auditors do not have a "gotcha" mentality but feel that they must develop many findings in an audit report, uncover a respectable batch of errors, and be able to prepare at least a dozen recommendations, for the audit to be seen as worthwhile. This is a mistaken view. We need to return to the risk management concept and consider the way risk is assessed as significant, and probable or less significant and unlikely; or a variation on these combinations. Managers need to know where the danger spots are and direct resources toward tackling them; they also need to know where comfort zones are located so they can either leave them be, or adopt a more progressive strategy of raising the risk appetite in the area in question and try out new initiatives. Information on where the high- and low-risk areas are to be found is equally useful for a busy manager with limited time and resources. An audit report that files no major findings and gives a positive opinion on the effectiveness of the current risk management and control arrangement gives great information to the client and is not an embarrassment for the auditor to report. Quite the contrary, where the auditor makes up a series of insignificant findings just to fill up the report, this can be misleading, confusing, and annoying to managers who want to know:

- What's going on?
- Where are things okay?
- Where are they not?
- What should I do about this?

They want this information quickly and from a reliable source, for it to be of any use in helping them manage risk better. In terms of reporting lines, guidance is available from Practice Advisory 2440-1, which suggests:

> *Final engagement communications should be distributed to those members of the organization who are able to ensure that engagement results*

are given due consideration. This means that the report should go to those who are in a position to take corrective action or ensure that corrective action is taken. The final engagement communications should be distributed to management of the activity under review. Higher-level members in the organization may receive only a summary communication. Communications may also be distributed to other interested or affected parties such as external auditors and the board.

The audit role in reporting to management may be found in the simple use of the four "As" model, which includes:

1. Provide **assurances** where there are no substantial unmitigated risks, for management, the board, and the audit committee to worry about.
2. Provide **advice** where risk management needs to be improved.
3. Promote real **action** from management in developing better risk management and controls, once the need has been established.
4. Offer **assistance** in making improvements work through, for example, CSA or control awareness events.

It is a good idea to keep these attributes in mind when preparing the final audit report. Detailing the main findings, and making helpful suggestions to the client about ways to develop improvements is also quite rewarding. The difficult part of audit reporting comes from Performance Standard 2410.A1, which states:

The final communication of results should where appropriate, contain the internal auditor's overall opinion.

This short statement represents quite a challenge for the auditor, because in forming the opinion, regard must be had to the best interests of the organization and not just a wish to maintain good working relations with the client. The new auditor will come to appreciate the delicate balance that comes into play when addressing this point as they progress in their chosen field.

Follow-up Report

Performance Standard 2500 says:

The CAE should establish and maintain a system to monitor the disposition of results communicated to management.

This simple requirement has actually seen the demise of many an auditor. How come? This is because the follow-up audit actually verifies the real value-add from the audit process.

> **EXAMPLE** ➤ The auditor turns up at the client's office and is greeted with coffee and doughnuts. After a cheerful chat, where the initial terms of

reference for the audit are agreed upon without comment by the business manager, the real work starts, and the auditor spends two weeks working on the audit. Staff in the office are very busy but always find time to answer the auditor's queries. A brief wrap-up meeting with the manager happens at the end of the audit, and all sides appear to be happy with the findings and direction of the half-dozen recommendations that the auditor proposes. The draft report is accepted by the manager, and the final report contains a list of the six things that the team need to do to implement the auditor's recommendations. Six months later, the auditor returns on a follow-up review and finds out that none of the recommendations has been actioned. The manager is very apologetic and says that they have been so busy doing "real work" that they just have not had time. And since the system is being changed next year, it will probably be best to wait until the new system kicks in, as most of the audit recommendations will become redundant thereafter. Fresh coffee and doughnuts are offered to the auditor by way of apology.

This used not to be a rare situation, and many auditors felt discouraged that their efforts had made no real impact on the business, in terms of creating much needed change. The follow-up audit is only a verification of the success of the original audit if:

- The auditor hit real risks in the audit terms of reference,
- The findings related to real issues facing the client, and
- The auditor made suggestions for improving system controls and getting risk under control.

The audit will not only be well received but also be fully actioned by the client. If any of these factors are missing, then the audit will have less impact. This represents the reality of business life. Performance Standard 2500.A1 goes on to state:

The CAE should establish a follow-up process to monitor and ensure that management actions have been effectively implemented or that senior management has accepted the risk of not taking action.

Note that a similar requirement attaches to consulting work. There is another important consideration that the auditor needs to take on board. That is that management do not have to implement audit recommendations, and it is only agreed ones that should be followed. Where audit and management differ on whether an audit recommendation should be actioned, management have the executive right to accept the situation without making these changes. Performance Standard 2600 addresses this possibility, saying:

When the CAE believes that senior management has accepted a level of residual risk that is unacceptable to the organization, the CAE should discuss the matter with senior management. If the decision regarding residual risk is not resolved, the CAE and senior management should report the matter to the board for resolution.

In terms of following-up audit recommendations that have been agreed and set out in appropriate action plans, there is advice available from Practice Advisory 2500.A1-1, which sets out the factors to be applied when performing such follow-ups:

- *The significance of the reported observation or recommendation.*
- *The degree of effort and cost needed to correct the reported condition.*
- *The impacts that may result should the corrective action fail.*
- *The complexity of the corrective action.*
- *The time period involved.*

The follow-up may be a formal separate audit or a lesser affair. The Advisory provides further advice in this respect:

There may also be instances where the chief audit executive judges that management's oral or written response shows that action already taken is sufficient when weighed against the relative importance of the engagement observation or recommendation. On such occasions, follow-up may be performed as part of the next engagement.

The adopted procedure for following up audit work will be set to fit the context and circumstances. What is clear is that the results will shed light on whether audit is providing a decent service, and the CAE should have a personal interest in seeing the reports from follow-up audits and whether they mean:

- Everything is fine.
  or
- There are good reasons why not all recommendations have been actioned.
  or
- The board should be informed of the situation.
  or
- There is a problem with the way audits are being conducted in the organization.

The key is to consider all four of the above matters before making a snap decision.

Formal Presentations

Some audits have a strategic implication in that they lead to significant change programs. Consulting engagements may be wide-ranging and call for a revamp of current working practices, or the merger of two separate services that have the potential to maximize on inherent synergy. Moreover, a fraud investigation may lead to criminal charges' being brought against a manager for taking bribes from vendors, but may also result in major changes to the way contracts are negotiated and managed.

Where there is a lot at stake, and the implications cover several sections and teams, people need to be convinced that the proposed changes are worthwhile. For "big change" audits, a technique that complements the formal audit report is to perform an oral presentation to management teams and key representatives. Presentations may also be applied to reports made to the board or audit committee, particularly the annual audit report, where there are serious issues concerning the year that has just closed. Formal presentations only work where there is a positive environment with all sides having an interest in attending and contributing to the proceedings. Presentations allow the auditor to explain the background to the work and findings as well as linking ways forward to the wider risk management context and disclosure reporting. Presentations may be set against the Sarbanes-Oxley reporting requirements, particularly Section 404 disclosures on internal controls. When using this technique, it is an idea to consider the following:

- Presentations are useful for delivering draft reports where proposed changes cover several sections in the organization.

- Carefully consider the people involved and the setting to help promote positivity all around.

- Preparation is important where the use of visual aids such as a data projector and diagrams may help in delivering key messages.

- Brief handouts may assist the event but not so as to overload the attendees.

- The question-and-answer part of the presentation is quite important, and sufficient time should be left for this part of the event. Good participation should be encouraged.

- Change has to be justified, and the onus falls on the auditor to explain why it is needed and how it fits into the current risk management and control strategy.

- Presentations should be brief and to the point. Time is money, and it does not take long to present basic points of note.

- One useful formula is to introduce the aim of the presentation, all parties present, the main findings, an overall opinion, and the required actions — or list of options. Then take questions, and close by summarizing what has happened and return to the opening aim of the presentation.

- A more advanced form of presentation involves attaching a short workshop to the end to get the group to work through some of the key questions that have been raised, particularly where there are several options available.
- Make sure the presentation is closed properly, with thanks, summaries, and a note on next steps. Some presenters ask each attendee to provide a short closing comment if this is appropriate.
- Auditors need to practice presentation/facilitation skills and ensure they are confident and equipped to work in this way.

Oral presentations can go either really well or dive badly. It depends on the context, the relationship that has been established by audit, the quality of the audit work, and whether auditors are able to manage this forum with skill and suitable insight.

Audit Committee Activity Report

The final type of audit report is that which is presented to the audit committee whenever it meets. The Sarbanes-Oxley formula and SEC disclosure requirements have placed the audit committee at the forefront of the corporate governance agenda. And the internal audit shop can take much of the strain off the audit committee if it is able to provide top-notch support. The key is to answer questions posed by the committee before they realize that they should be asking them, to do the research and become the first point of contact for vexing issues that face committee members. Reports of the activities of internal audit should cover several key matters:

- What internal audit has been doing since the last report.
- Progress on completing the annual audit plan.
- Any issues concerning the corporate governance, risk management, and control that the audit committee should be made aware of.
- Whether there have been any problems with implementing audit recommendations.
- Progress made on implementing an effective control framework.
- Any matters that the CAE is aware of that affect the role and responsibilities of the audit committee.
- Any major risk exposures that need to be noted, which should also be monitored by the board.
- Performance reports covering key performance indicators for the internal audit function.

- Major changes and issues in internal auditing about which the audit committee should be made aware.
- Formal assurances on systems of internal control for audit areas reviewed during the year.
- And finally, plans for future periods and any changes to the current audit strategy.

The audit committee needs to know what is going on, on the corporate governance front, but it is the board (principal executive and finance officer) who has to make formal attestations and disclosures to the regulatory authorities. As such, the board needs to be appraised by internal audit about relevant matters. Performance Standard 2060 covers the auditor's board-level reporting obligations:

> *The CAE should report periodically to the board and senior management on the internal audit activity's purpose, authority, responsibility, and performance relative to its plan. Reporting should also include significant risk exposures and control issues, corporate governance issues, and other matters needed or requested by the board and senior management.*

It is the annual audit report that is of most importance to the organization and that should contain formal assurance statements, regarding audit areas that have been considered. The annual report should also address the performance of the audit resource and comment on items such as:

- Extent to which the annual audit has been completed.
- Extent of chargeable audit hours as compared to nonchargeable time.
- Level of staff absence due to vacancies, sick leave, and other reasons.
- Number of implemented recommendations.
- Level of requests from clients for consulting and assurance work.
- Extent of involvement in CSA workshops on request from management.
- Number of control awareness seminars delivered during the year.
- Number of audits with time overruns.
- Results of audit customer questionnaires and quality scores.
- Results of any external reviews.

Audit committee reports can make or break an audit shop. If there is a world-class audit team in post and the presentations made to the audit committee are impressive and forward-looking, then the CAE may take comfort in receiving continuing support from top management and the committee. If this is not the case, the skies will eventually fall in on the CAE.

Communicating the Message

Before we leave the topic of audit reporting, one additional checklist should be provided. This checklist consists of five of the attributes for communicating via the audit report, as follows:

1. Audit reports have to make sense, be acceptable, be balanced, and be used to make important management decisions. This is a demanding proposition. Performance Standard 2420 sets out what makes for good communications by listing criteria as follows:

   Communications should be accurate, objective, clear, concise, constructive, complete and timely.

   All published reports should be prepared by applying these criteria. The Practice Advisory for this Standard 2420-1 goes into more detail, and a summary of good quality information includes further attributes covering the following pointers:

   - *Concise communications are to the point and avoid unnecessary elaboration, superfluous detail, redundancy, and wordiness. They are created by a persistent practice of revising and editing a presentation. The goal is that each thought will be meaningful but succinct.*

   - *Constructive communications are helpful to the engagement client and the organization and lead to improvements where needed. The contents and tone of the presentation should be useful, positive, and well-meaning and contribute to the objectives of the organization.*

   - *Complete communications are lacking nothing that is essential to the target audience and include all significant and relevant information and observations to support recommendations and conclusions.*

   - *Timely communications are well-timed, opportune, and expedient for careful consideration by those who may act on the recommendations. The timing of the presentation of engagement results should be set without undue delay and with a degree of urgency and so as to enable prompt, effective action.*

2. There are many different reports that bounce around an organization, and many are written to allow one party to make a decision that they have already decided to make anyway. A report on staff compensation levels written by an employee representative group who are fighting for pay raises will have a different perspective from one written by a consultant who is told that the wage bill is too high. Each one will contain reviews,

analysis, comparisons, and references that will support the overall conclusions and proposals. Each will appear clear, objective, and well-balanced; but they are bound to be miles apart in their final deliberations. Internal auditors sit firmly in the middle and have no ax to grind. It is hoped that the audit report will be entirely reliable, and if this is not the case, there is really little point in having an audit shop at all. Practice Advisory 2420-1 goes into more detail and explains what makes for good communications:

> Objective communications are fair, impartial, and unbiased and are the result of a fair-minded and balanced assessment of all relevant facts and circumstances. Observations, conclusions, and recommendations should be derived and expressed without prejudice, partisanship, personal interests, and the undue influence of others. Clear communications are easily understood and logical. Clarity can be improved by avoiding unnecessary technical language and providing all significant and relevant information.

3. This pretty well sums it up. User friendly reports are written with the reader in mind. The only difficulty is that assurance audit reports have several different users:

   - The process owner may want to read the detailed findings and facts, and extrapolations of test results.
   - The director will want to know about anything that causes embarrassment, and that the operation is more or less on track.
   - The principal executive and chief finance officer (CFO) will be concerned about the impact of the audit of their overall consideration of internal control, particularly relating to financial reporting standards and published disclosures.
   - The external auditor will be interested in any test results that impact the financial statements or suggest that the underlying accounting system is at fault.
   - The board may be concerned about the state of the control framework and in particular any section from the report that comments on the ethical climate around parts of the organization.
   - Senior management for the system in question may be interested only in the executive summary and proposed action plan.
   - The chief finance officer may want to review gaps in controls that could lead to fraud and abuse.
   - Front-line staff may want to look at aspects of the report that relate to staffing issues and working practices in use on a day-to-day basis.

This makes for a whole array of needs and perspectives that have to be addressed by the writer of the report. As a shortcut, we can return to our original proposition that argues the executive summary and action plan are what is most important for an audit engagement report, and it is here that the format and wording should be most carefully considered.

4. Audit reports should be prepared in line with an agreed in-house standard. This standard may be in the form of a report-writing guide that is used by audit staff to ensure consistency in style and format in all documents published by the audit shop. The guide should cover basic points regarding the way reports should be written, including, for example, promoting the use of:

- Short, numbered paragraphs and concise sentences that sum up the point in question in a clear and factual manner. This should also discourage the excessive use of vague phrases, such as "it appeared that," "there is a possibility that a degree of," or "it may be the case that under some circumstances."

- Active rather than passive sentence. For example, "We noted the lack of set procedures in Section X," is preferable to "The lack of set procedures in Section X was noted."

- The use of graphics and diagrams that enhance the reader's appreciation of the points being made. For example, as shown in Exhibit 5.18, a simple bar chart may be used to drive home the point that excessive use of temporary staff with no accounting experience in Team 2 has led to a relatively high rate of financial errors, when compared with Teams 1, 3, and 4 (note: each team is of similar size and performs similar work).

Exhibit 5.18. Reported Errors per Work Team

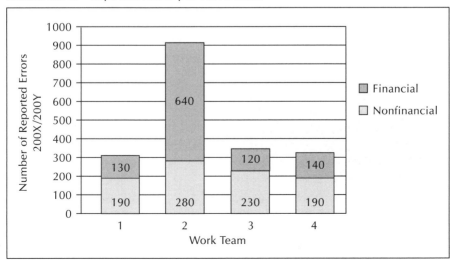

5. The final point to note is that no one is perfect. One mistake by internal audit should not mean it folds entirely. There should be some damage limitation strategy in place, and this is assisted by Performance Standard 2421, which deals with the situation where mistakes have entered into the report and come to light:

> *If a final communication contains significant error or omission, the CAE should communicate corrected information to all individuals who received the original communication.*

Audit Reporting: A Worked Example

Audit Engagement: The Corporate Antifraud Policy (continued)

The auditor needs to report the results of the audit work. In an e-business context, this may consist of a verbal briefing and short schedule (not unlike the ICE) that says what was considered, what risks were assessed, what the auditor found, and what can be done to improve risk management and control. But the traditional approach is to prepare a formal audit report, and this report becomes a published document that is available to all authorized parties. Some public-sector organizations place their internal audit reports on their Web site for all interested parties to access. It is necessary to prepare a formal audit report and, staying with the worked example of the fraud policy audit, Exhibit 5.19 shows one version of the List of Contents, Executive Summary, and Management Action Plan (extracts only for Control Objective 2: "To ensure that all suspicions of fraud and irregularity are reported and properly investigated").

Exhibit 5.19.   Internal Audit Report: Corporate Fraud Policy

---

List of Contents
Executive Summary and Action Plan
Introduction Terms of Reference and Work Carried Out
Detailed Findings and Recommendations
Appendixes
Appendix A: Terms of Reference
Appendix B: Fraud Policy
Appendix C: Fraud Response Plan
Appendix D: Staff Survey

Executive Summary

Introduction

1. A review of the corporate fraud policy was requested by the Audit Committee at their meeting of xx 200x and included in the audit plans for 200x/200y. The audit was carried out by Fred Fredricks during the period xxx–yyy 200x using the risk-based systems approach to assurance audits.

Exhibit 5.19. Internal Audit Report: Corporate Fraud Policy *(Continued)*

2. The terms of reference for the audit were agreed upon with the Financial Controller, who is the process owner for the fraud policy, to review the existing arrangements for ensuring that

   (a) Staff understand the corporate antifraud policy and their roles and responsibilities with respect to fraud prevention, detection, and response.

   (b) There are suitable measures for reporting suspicions of fraud and irregularity.

   (c) There is a capacity to investigate fraud and irregularity to professional standards.

   It was agreed that a formal audit report will be issued to the audit committee, CFO, and Financial Controller.

3. The audit did not include any steps to detect fraud or investigate specific allegations, and only concerned the adequacy and effectiveness of the fraud policy. A description of the work carried out is found in the main body of the report.

4. We extend our thanks to all those staff who assisted us in the performance of the audit.

Findings
(control objective 2 only)

5. The fraud policy is well designed and covers all important aspects of fraud prevention, detection, and response, and is regularly updated by a specialist external consultant.

6. The Financial Controller post is not equipped to take responsibility for fraud policy. The postholder has no available resource that allows him to disseminate the policy to employees, apart from its inclusion in the staff handbook.

7. The fraud policy is not widely publicized, and many employees have a poor understanding of their roles and responsibilities under the policy. This impairs the effectiveness of fraud risk management and the company's whistleblowing procedures.

Audit Opinion
(control objective 2 only)

8. Fraud is seen by the board as one of their top ten risks. Fraud investigations are conducted in a professional manner once problems concerning irregularity have come to light. However, the degree to which the fraud policy is understood by employees across the organization is inadequate. This means the risk of fraud in terms of prevention and detection is not being managed to an acceptable level. The audit recommendations are designed to address the various shortcomings and are attached as part of the action plan that has been agreed to with management.

Audit Recommendations
(control objective 2 only)

9. A program of staff awareness seminars should be established to ensure employees are aware of the fraud policy and build the risk of fraud into their risk assessment workshops where appropriate.

(continues)

Exhibit 5.19.   Internal Audit Report: Corporate Fraud Policy *(Continued)*

10. The responsibility for the fraud policy should be assigned to the post of Compliance Officer that is currently under development. Responsibility for the fraud policy should be shared between the Financial Controller and Legal Officer until the Compliance Officer is appointed.

11. The management action plan based on this audit has been agreed upon by all relevant parties and is attached (see Audit Report Extract: Management Action Plan).

Audit Report Extract: Management Action Plan
Audit of the Corporate Fraud Policy

Audit Recommendations	Management Action	Responsible Person	Evaluation and Target Dates
1. A program of staff awareness seminars should be established to ensure employees are aware of the fraud policy and build the risk of fraud into their risk assessment workshops where appropriate.	1. The chair of the audit committee has asked that internal audit conduct these seminars, the sponsor being the CFO.	CFO and Chief Audit Executive.	The awareness seminars will be developed next month and piloted in the Finance section. They will then be rolled out to the other support services, then operations over the next six months. The staff awareness survey will be repeated in six months' time to reassess the level of awareness after the seminars have been concluded.
2. The responsibility for the fraud policy should be assigned to responsibilities for the post of Compliance Officer (CO) that is currently under development. Responsibility for the fraud policy should be shared between the Financial Controller and Legal Officer until the CO is appointed.	2. Agreed as recommended. The responsibility will become part of the CO job requirement that is currently being prepared.	Head of Personnel and chair of the Appointments Panel for the new CO post.	Director of Human Resources will report progress to the board at next meeting. CO should be appointed and in post by the end of the year.

—— SECTION 8 ——

THE AUDIT MODEL

The Audit Services should flow from the derived audit strategy and follow a defined systematic and professional approach, as illustrated in Exhibit 5.20.

Society and Stakeholders. The audit model is driven primarily by the needs and interests of society—that is, the need for good company performance that contributes to the economy, and both fair and transparent business practices.

Exhibit 5.20. Audit Model 5

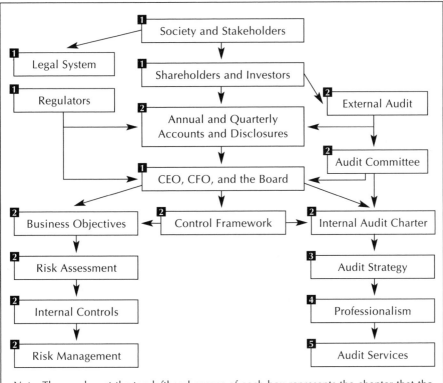

Note: The number at the top lefthand corner of each box represents the chapter that the items relate to.

Stakeholders include all those who have a direct or indirect interest in the way business, commerce, and public services are conducted.

Shareholders and Investors.   Principal stakeholders are the people and institutions who hold shares in listed companies. Banks and investment companies may well have a direct interest that is represented in funds loaned to the company. Meanwhile, *The People* are principal stakeholders in public-sector organizations. Company shareholders should exercise their voting rights with due regard to the need to ensure there is ethical behavior and accountability from company officials.

Legal System.   There are a multitude of federal and state laws that relate to the way private- and public-sector organizations are established, maintained, and extinguished. Many larger organizations have responded by setting up compliance functions to address the variety and magnitude of such legal provisions. Company directors and officials can face severe penalties where specific laws are breached.

Regulators.   Most industries have an associated regulator that sets standards and represents the public in ensuring organizations behave properly. The SEC, American Stock Exchange, New York Stock Exchange, and NASDAQ regulations are some of the more well-known models.

CEO, CFO, and the Board.   Shareholders appoint a CEO and board of directors to direct and oversee the organization on their behalf. These officers have a responsibility to discharge their duties in a professional manner and account for the results to the shareholders. A management team will be appointed in public-sector bodies and have a similar responsibility to the government and general public. The board should adhere to the highest standards of ethics and ensure they conduct their business in an acceptable and documented manner. Moreover, the board should have in place suitable mechanisms through which they may judge their own performance and conduct.

Annual Accounts and Disclosures.   The organization reports to its stakeholders through published financial and performance statements. These reports act as a window to the outside world, and business analysts spend a great deal of time examining the detailed facts and figures in company accounts on behalf of their clients. Listed companies along with many other organizations have to make various disclosures on an annual and quarterly basis, in particular resulting from the Sarbanes-Oxley Act. The published accounts should be reliable and now have to be personally certified by the principal executive and CFO.

External Audit.   The external auditors are appointed by the shareholders to make sure the board has provided a full and reliable account of the company's financial performance over the previous year. The financial statements will be checked by the external auditors before they are formally published. External auditors should ensure they are independent in their audit work and are able to exercise an appropriate degree of professional skepticism at all times. This part of the audit model is a major contribution to governance because material published by the organization is independently verified.

Audit Committee. A further layer of governance that is growing in importance is the audit committee. This forum, established by the board, comprises independent directors who provide an additional oversight role, focusing on the specialist areas of financial accounting, ethics, audit, accountability, risk management, and control. The audit committee is not there to undermine the board, but provides advice and support regarding the specialist areas in question. Moreover, it should ask challenging questions of the board, on the premise that it is better that these tough questions come from an in-house audit committee than from external regulators.

Internal Audit Charter. The internal auditor's role and position in the organization is set by the audit charter that is agreed upon with the board and audit committee. To be of any real use, this charter should be set firmly within the governance, risk management, and control arenas.

Business Objectives. The next stage of the model relates to the setting of formal corporate objectives that document the mission of the organization and what it is there to achieve.

Risk Assessment. Anything that has an impact on the business objectives can be seen as a potential risk. These risks need to be understood, isolated, and weighed in terms of significance. Formal risk assessment gives an organization a head start in understanding where its vulnerabilities lie and where it has scope for advancement. The bottom line is that risks that affect the organization's ability to deliver and achieve its objectives have to be addressed for there to be any real chance of success. Control risk self-assessment and regular risk surveys are good ways to promote risk assessment throughout the organization.

Internal Control. Controls should be in place to address risks that have been assessed as significant. The current climate stresses the importance of controls over financial reporting and disclosures, as well as compliance with various standard regulations. The systems of internal control need to be maintained, updated, and made right as part of the way employees work.

Risk Management. Controls fit into the wider remit of risk management, and managers and their teams need to build risk mitigation into their overall strategies. There are many different potential responses to risks, depending on the nature, significance, and cost of controls. The organization needs to weigh the available measures on a regular basis and ensure the adopted response meets the expectations of the board and stakeholders. In other words, the response to risk needs to fit the risk tolerance levels that have been defined by the board in its risk and control policy.

Control Framework. The entire risk management and control policy should be incorporated within the adopted control framework. Standard models such as COSO sit on a foundation of ethical values and propriety, which may see as the "tone at the top" that is set by the board and top executives.

Audit Strategy. The audit model includes the response from internal audit to the corporate risk policy and approach that is used in the organization. Based on the audit charter, and driven by the corporate risk assessment that the board and management have developed, internal audit should construct a strategy that reflects the future direction of the organization and risks that arise in achieving this strategy.

Professionalism. Having designed a high-impact audit strategy, there needs to be a high-impact audit shop in place to deliver set goals. This is the next part of the audit model, where professionalism is an essential component of the audit model. Professionalism is based on several key factors, including:

- Independence.
- Competent and motivated audit staff.
- Good procedures and documentation.
- Quality assurance mechanisms, including supervision, and internal and external reviews.

Audit Services. A sound strategy and professional staff enables the delivery of good audit services. The audit shop should carefully define its assurance and consulting services and set standards for the way these services are delivered to add value to the business.

—— SECTION 9 ——

SUMMARY: TOP TEN CONSIDERATIONS

A summary of the ten main points covered in the chapter follows:

1. The audit process will depend on the adopted style and approach that best suits the organization and the audits in question. Much will revolve around the state of risk management that is found by the auditor and whether an assurance or consulting approach is most appropriate. The

audit strategy kicks off the audit process, and standards require that "the CAE should establish risk-based plans to determine the priorities of the internal audit activity, consistent with the organization's goals." The audit shop will need to prepare an annual audit plan for the board and audit committee that reflects the risks facing the organization and the current state of risk management. The various audit planning stages may be defined as:

- Board/audit committee agenda
- Audit charter
- Audit strategy
- Annual audit plan
- Quarterly audit plan
- Work program
- Preliminary survey
- Assignment plan
- Audit fieldwork
- Report
- Follow-up

2. The preliminary survey is an important audit technique that seeks to define the terms of reference, approach, and whether the full audit should go ahead. This survey will involve discussions with client management and a consideration of the types of risks that confront the area in question, which will enable the auditor to define a detailed assignment plan.

3. The audit assignment planning stages flow from the preliminary survey and will define:

- Where this system starts
- Where it stops
- Timing issues
- Compliance and fraud aspects
- Information implications
- Response to client requests
- Whether broad brush or narrow detail
- Auditors assigned to the job and time budgets
- Control objectives (where used)
- How the audit will be monitored, reviewed, and controlled
- Reporting lines and supervision of audit staff
- Practical matters regarding travel, accommodation, and so on

4. The audit fieldwork continues after the assignment has been planned and starts with ascertaining the system in question in terms of the:

- Operational objectives
- Strategies and programs
- Control objectives
- Key risks
- System input, process, and output routines
- Procedures and working practices
- How the system fits into the organization
- Important change issues

The system can be recorded using notes, block diagrams, or more formal flowcharts.

5. The next stage of the audit is to assess the adequacy of controls that mitigate key risks. This evaluation will be against set criteria that are based on the adopted control framework and controls that are assessed as important in respect of the risks to the business. The Internal Control Questionnaire is based on the auditor's working through set questions about standard controls that should be considered. The Internal Control Evaluation Schedule is an alternative approach that is more flexible and dynamic, in that it focuses on the actual risk that is found in the system and is developed as the audit progresses.

6. Testing comes next, and this is about confirming the tentative results of the evaluation stage, regarding strong and/or poor controls. Testing consists of compliance tests that check whether key controls are working as intended, while substantive tests check the implication of poor or breached controls. Testing should result in information concerning the state of controls that is:

- Sufficient
- Competent
- Relevant
- Useful

Testing should be used sparingly as it costs time and money to plan and perform and samples can be extracted to represent the entire population. For information-based systems, computer interrogation may be used to examine the integrity of relevant data. Sources of information for testing routines are varied and include:

- Interviews
- Analytical review

- Surveys
- External confirmation
- Examination
- Verification
- Reconciliation
- Observation
- Inspection
- Reperformance
- Vouching
- Anything else that makes sense

7. Having completed the fieldwork, the auditor is in a position to further develop the findings and think about the audit report. Audit standards require that "internal auditors should base conclusions and engagement results on appropriate analysis and evaluations." Meanwhile, audit work should be systematic and properly structured to meet professional standards, and should address the following aspects of each main finding:
   - Criteria
   - Condition
   - Cause
   - Effect

8. Formal audit reports are an important part of the audit process. While the focus is on action that results from an audit, the report is a record of the event. There is a variety of different types of audit reports, including:
   - Preliminary survey report
   - Interim engagement reports
   - Draft audit report
   - Final audit report
   - Follow-up report
   - Formal presentations
   - Audit committee activity report

9. Meanwhile, the final audit assignment report will tend to have the following sections:
   - Cover
   - List of contents
   - Executive summary and action plan

- Main body
- Appendixes

Through the audit report and continual contact with the client, the auditor seeks to:

- Provide assurances
- Provide advice
- Promote real action
- Offer assistance

Effective communications mean working well with the client, but the audit report is also a device for communicating and should contain:

- Short, numbered paragraphs and concise sentences
- Active rather than passive sentences
- Appropriate use of graphics and diagrams

10. The audit model adds a new component of Audit Services. These services will be balanced between assurance and consulting work and, in line with documented standards, should be delivered in a structured and professional manner.

----- SECTION 10 -----

YOUR PERSONAL DEVELOPMENT EXERCISES

Using the terms of reference and internal control evaluation schedule for the audit of performance management that are set out below, please complete the following tasks:

1 Examine the two documents carefully.

2. Make any reasonable assumptions to complement these two documents and list them.

3. Prepare a draft report based on this material and your assumptions, to reflect the results of the audit engagement.

4. Prepare a PowerPoint presentation on the draft report on the basis that the people who would be responsible for implementing the various audit recommendations will attend the presentation.

5. Practice this presentation if possible using the PowerPoint package and the draft report as a handout for each member of the audience. Note that your audit management team may be interested in listening to your presentation as a way of encouraging your report writing and presentation skills.

Performance Management Audit

Terms of reference: To review the adequacy and effectiveness of controls over the:

- Objectives and the way they cascade down throughout the organization
- The performance target-setting process
- Information that supports performance management

The audit involved interviews with the corporate planning officer, directors, budget monitoring officer, and several business managers and support service managers, as well as examination of samples of documentation and information regarding various performance management and monitoring reports.

The control objective and risks to the achievement of these objectives were identified in conjunction with the Corporate Planning, Human Resource, and Business Line Managers. Some of the risks were derived from previous risk assessment exercises undertaken by business managers over the last few months. All samples used to test and confirm the assessment of internal controls were derived at random, and all relevant information to complete the audit was provided by management. The main findings are shown in Exhibit 5.21.

Exhibit 5.21. Control Evaluation

Control Objective: Performance management is based on agreed objectives, realistic targets, reliable information, and timely interventions to ensure good corporate performance is achieved.

Risk	Existing Controls	Initial Evaluation	Tests Carried Out	Conclusion and Recommendations
1. No real definition of corporate objectives in a way that is understood by business and other managers.	Corporate mission statements issued on Web site and discussed by senior management team.	Good statements but no procedure for providing mission to middle management and staff.	Examine mission statement for clarity and impact; Check degree of consideration at levels below senior management team.	Poor understanding of mission statement at more junior management levels and no input to new staff orientation process. **Rec:** Build information on corporate mission into orientation process and staff meetings.
2. No clear linkage between mission statement, objectives, and strategic plans.	Strategic planning process starts with corporate mission.	Okay.	Examine strategic plans for business lines and check links to mission.	Mission is built into strategy but is not fed into many new projects that are under development. **Rec:** Project methodology should be amended to include required links into mission statements.
3. Objectives do not take on board influence of stakeholders and corporate.	Stakeholder analysis is required in the development of all strategic objectives.	Okay.	Examine the use of stakeholder analysis in sample of business lines.	Strong use of stakeholder analysis. **Rec:** N/a

(continues)

Exhibit 5.21. Control Evaluation (*Continued*)

Risk	Existing Controls	Initial Evaluation	Tests Carried Out	Conclusion and Recommendations
4. Objectives set at section level are out of step with overall business line objectives.	Regular business managers' meetings to set cross-section objectives.	Practice is okay, but use of meetings is not documented.	Examine minutes of business managers' meetings for reference to objective setting.	Out of the five business lines, four spend time at managers' meetings on objective setting. **Rec:** Prepare a documented policy on matters to be covered in business managers' meetings.
5. Section objectives do not feed into team and individual objectives and targets.	Performance management system requires all objectives to cascade downward in a logical manner.	Okay.	Examine sets of individual objectives across the business lines and track them up to team, section, and business objectives.	Cascade process working well. **Rec:** N/a
6. Team targets are not set in a way that is challenging but achievable, using a wide range of sources.	Performance management scheme provides a short note on balanced target setting.	Possibly inadequate coverage of balanced and meaningful target setting.	Examine a sample of targets and assess the balance between achievability and challenge, using the guidance from the official performance management scheme and published best practice.	Nearly half of the targets examined had no detail of how they were developed; 25% contained no challenge but simply restated last year's targets; target setting is not done in a systematic, meaningful and transparent manner. **Rec:** Formal training for senior and middle management in performance target setting.

(continues)

Exhibit 5.21. Control Evaluation (*Continued*)

Risk	Existing Controls	Initial Evaluation	Tests Carried Out	Conclusion and Recommendations
7. Information used to support the performance management system is unreliable	The business-performance-monitoring information system is in place and reviewed annually by the board.	Okay.	Examine sample of performance reports to assess reliability using criteria agreed upon with the corporate planning officer and Chief Human Resources Officer.	Performance-reporting information is sound, and reports are issued quarterly but quickly fall out of date when approaching the end of the quarter. **Rec:** Performance reports should be prepared on a monthly (and not quarterly) basis.

6

THE AUDIT PROPOSITION

────── SECTION 1 ──────

IMPACTING CORPORATE GOVERNANCE

We started the book by setting a context for internal auditing and the need for a clear focus and direction to audit work. This context is inherent in the corporate governance, risk management, and control dimensions. We can use the following five-stage model to summarize and bring together these three dimensions, as shown in Exhibit 6.1. Each of the components of the five-stage model is briefly noted below:

1. ***Corporate governance.*** This is the overarching concept that includes the other four elements of the model. Corporate governance is about doing things properly, which depends on a suitable control framework, risk management, good corporate systems of control, and specific controls that work well to promote success.

2. ***Control framework.*** All organizations need to develop a control framework to support their interpretation of good corporate governance. This may be based on the COSO model, as outlined in Section 7 of Chapter 2. The control framework is partly based on the way the board views control and the way employees see this concept. It should be supported by an internal control policy. Added to the COSO model is the external audit role, which checks and verifies the financial reporting aspects of control.

Exhibit 6.1.   Five-Stage Model for
Dimensions of Internal Auditing

1. Corporate governance
2. Control framework
3. Risk management strategy
4. Systems of internal control
5. Effective controls

The Sarbanes-Oxley Act has led to the rebirth of ethical standards as a cornerstone of control and propriety.

3. **Risk management strategy.** Many organizations are turning to a risk-based approach to developing controls. Once risks have been identified and assessed (for impact and likelihood), a suitable risk management strategy may be developed to deal with risk to achieving objectives. The strategy may include contingency plans, insurance coverage, withdrawal from certain activities, acceptance of the risk, and a whole array of alternative courses of action. A principal response to risk is controls to mitigate the risk by decreasing the likelihood that the risk will arise or ensuring that there is an appropriate response if a risk does materialize. This is why we use the term *risk management and control*, although some may argue that risk management incorporates all efforts to mitigate risk—that is, by establishing controls.

4. **Systems of internal control.** After having undertaken risk assessment, the adopted response in terms of internal controls may be reviewed and documented. Senior management should review these systems and ensure they perform so as to mitigate risk to an acceptable level. Much depends on the definition of risk tolerance, in that there should be a shared understanding of the level of risk that is acceptable to the organization. Executives and senior managers may have to prepare formal statements certifying that their systems of internal control have been reviewed and provide a reasonable expectation that goals will be accomplished. This is particularly relevant for areas that require disclosure to regulatory authorities and that have an impact on the integrity of financial reporting.

5. **Effective controls.** The final component of this model is the individual controls that together make up the system of internal control. These controls are inherent in what people do at the front line, as part of their everyday work practices. Just as objectives cascade downward from corporate objectives to departmental objectives, section, team, then individual objectives, so do controls flow upward—from specific controls, to control standards, to corporate procedures, to overall control policies, and then to form the control framework described as the second component above.

As we have said, corporate governance sits at the top of the five-point model. Whenever this term is mentioned, it implicitly incorporates the other four elements as well as board functioning and shareholder rights. The more the auditor researches and understands corporate governance and the way the associated ideals are developing at home and internationally, the better the chance that the audit shop will add real value to the organization. Many organizations are now employing a Corporate Governance Officer, a Chief Risk Officer, or a Chief

Compliance and Disclosures Officer to resource this drive for certification and transparency. This provides tremendous challenges for the new-look internal auditor, who under the consulting arm will advise on setting up these arrangements and in line with the main assurance role will want to check that these developments are actually working. Above and beyond role definition is the need to apply professional internal auditing standards. In fact, internal auditors have also got their burden of disclosure to contend with, and if audit standards have been breached to any extent, they must comply with Performance Standard 2430, which makes clear that:

> *When noncompliance with the Standards impacts a specific engagement, communication of the results should disclose the:*
>
> - *Standard(s) with which full compliance was not achieved,*
> - *Reason(s) for noncompliance, and*
> - *Impact of noncompliance on the engagement.*

For Further Discussion

What impact has the growth of codes of corporate governance had on the internal auditor's work?

—— SECTION 2 ——

SUPPORTING THE BOARD AND THE AUDIT COMMITTEE

There are many career auditors whose party trick is to relay the many hours spent sitting in a dreary basement counting inventories and writing out detailed lists of items that can be checked against the official records. The stories become more exciting when the auditor recounts the strange and often funny surveillance exercises that were carried out as part of the audit role. Stories about standing on a street corner, pretending to read a newspaper that is held upside down, and from time to time peeking at the "subject" can raise a few laughs at these parties. Extensive checking and examining as well as an eye for fine detail used to be the mainstay for the good field auditor. To say that this has altered over the last ten years is an understatement. The auditor has moved from presenting lists of errors to the inventories clerk, to presenting major issues that impact the corporate governance agenda to the board. Practice Advisory 1110-1 reinforces this board-level contact, suggesting:

> *The chief audit executive should have direct communication with the board, audit committee, or other appropriate governing authority. Regular communication with the board helps assure independence and provides*

a means for the board and the chief audit executive to keep each other informed on matters of mutual interest.

The board is seen as:

A board of directors, audit committee of such boards, heads of an agency or legislative body to whom internal auditors report, board of governors or trustees of a nonprofit organization, or any other designated governing bodies of organizations.

Meanwhile, the heightened responsibilities placed on the audit committee by Sarbanes-Oxley have strengthened the reporting line from internal audit to this forum. Practice Advisory 2060-2 describes three key aspects of internal audit's support for the auditor committee:

1. *"Assisting the audit committee to ensure that its charter, activities, and processes are appropriate to fulfill its responsibilities."* The audit committee is set up by the board and has many duties established by legislation and listed companies' regulations. Although they will be served by experienced and mature people, there is still a major gap in the supply of good independent directors to service the growing use of audit committees in all sectors and in all sizes of organizations. The internal auditor is in a good position to advise the audit committee on its coverage and scope of activities. Internal audit can also help the committee work through some of the reporting systems that need to be in place to support listed companies' certification and disclosure requirements. Internal audit is able to drill down into an organization and appreciate the practical implications of establishing signing-off procedures and also linking this with developments such as Control Self-Assessment programs and the use of verified Risk Registers.

2. *"Ensuring that the charter, role, and activities of internal audit are clearly understood and responsive to the needs of the audit committee and the board."* Each CAE should be armed with a well-prepared presentation of the internal audit role and where it fits into the corporate governance jigsaw. It is essential that the real potential from an effective internal audit process be understood by the independent directors and that the audit committee know what it can expect from the CAE. The practice advisories and guidance issued by the IIA contain a wealth of information on what internal audit should be doing in its organization to progress governance. These documents should not become best-kept secrets but rather should be used as the basis of formal presentations to the board, senior management, and the audit committee about turning the guidance into corporate policy. Brochures, Web site material, and key

messages should be designed and made available to explain the role of internal audit. Frequently asked questions can be posted on the internal audit Web site to give clear information on exactly what internal audit stands for and how the audit process operates. All publications and presentations should adhere to a house-style and consistent message that is aligned to audit standards, approaches, and procedures. New audit committee members may be given a presentation led by the CAE, and any change in audit strategy should result in an appropriate presentation to the next audit committee meeting.

3. *"Maintaining open and effective communications with the audit committee and the chairperson."* The CAE really needs to spend time outside the audit offices to market the audit role. This person should be meeting with senior management, board members, and the audit committee chair on a regular basis to sell the audit product. For example, many people do not know about the formal consulting role of internal audit and the fact that engagements may be requested by management (or the board/audit committee) and so long as they fit the published criteria, they may well be accepted. The CAE should meet with the audit committee chair and retain this communication link for private discussions that may be used to support the independence of internal audit. This link has the potential to raise the audit profile tremendously. One caveat: whatever the CAE promises to deliver must be delivered and must be delivered well.

The general availability of internal audit to help the audit committee discharge its responsibilities should be complemented by formal returns made by the CAE to the committee. As well as promoting the audit role, the CAE needs to deliver defined products to the committee, which have been described by Practice Advisory 2060-2 as including the following activities by the CAE:

1. *Provide an annual summary report or assessment on the results of the audit activities relating to the defined mission and scope of audit work.*

2. *Issue periodic reports to the audit committee and management summarizing results of audit activities.*

3. *Keep the audit committee informed of emerging trends and successful practices in internal auditing.*

4. *Together with external auditors, discuss fulfillment of committee information needs.*

5. *Review information submitted to the audit committee for completeness and accuracy.*

6. *Confirm there is effective and efficient work coordination of activities between internal and external auditors. Determine if there is any*

duplication between the work of the internal and external auditors and give the reasons for such duplication.

The Advisory goes on to highlight the point that, ideally, the CAE should be seen by the audit committee as a "trusted advisor." Practice Advisory 2020-1 covers the types of reports and returns that the CAE should make to the audit committee, including audit plans, progress reports, and so on. One interesting point made by the Advisory is that the CAE may ask the committee whether their new members would benefit from risk and controls training developed by internal audit. Meanwhile, the audit committee should be encouraged to review its own performance in comparison with best-practice standards. The CAE should ensure there is good information on the way internal audit coordinates and reviews other control and monitoring information so that the audit committee may rely on the fact that there is a coordinated control reporting process in place. We have called the corporate governance system a jigsaw that needs to be put together by the board and verified by the audit committee. Internal audit is there to help find the pieces, ensure they fit, and help the organization respond when the picture changes and the jigsaw has to be broken up and reworked. The first stage is to make sure everyone associated with the organization is seeing the same picture.

> ### For Further Discussion
> *What would encourage an audit committee to outsource its in-house internal audit shop?*

—— SECTION 3 ——

PROVIDING ASSURANCES ON CONTROLS

Internal audit is a major player in the internal control game. The short answer to the question regarding the audit assurance role is to say that internal audit provides an objective indication of whether controls are adequate or not. Sounds simple? Unfortunately, this proposition has to be explored in some detail before we can arrive at a suitable model of controls assurance. The starting place is to work out what *adequate control* means. The term has been considered by the IIA, which suggests that adequate control is present if:

Management has planned and organized (designed) in a manner that provides reasonable assurance that the organization's risks have been managed effectively and that the organization's goals and objectives will be achieved efficiently and economically.

An objective view on this concept of adequacy depends on what we mean by *objectivity*. This has been defined by the IIA as:

> *An unbiased mental attitude that requires internal auditors to perform engagements in such a manner that they have an honest belief in their work product and that no significant quality compromises are made. Objectivity requires internal auditors not to subordinate their judgment on audit matters to that of others.*

So we have an idea of what good controls look like and the value that comes from a party who reviews these controls in an objective manner. Internal control is now firmly on the board agenda, and for that matter everyone's agenda, because of Section 404 of the Sarbanes-Oxley Act and resultant SEC rules. This means that companies must file an internal control report in their annual report that states:

- Management's responsibility for establishing and maintaining adequate internal controls and procedures for financial reporting for the company.
- Management's conclusions about the effectiveness of those controls and procedures at the end of the company's financial year.
- The external auditors' attestation to and report on management's evaluation of the company's internal controls and procedures for financial reporting.

The SEC's view of internal control focuses on the impact on the financial statements, which is to be expected in light of problems from Enron and World-Com, where financial misstatement and fraud were the main problems. Internal control in this slightly more narrow context covers control that ensures that:

- The company's transactions are properly authorized.
- The company's assets are safeguarded against unauthorized or improper use.
- The company's transactions are properly recorded and reported.
- The financial statements conform with generally accepted accounting principles.

The audit committee also comes into play through a formal report regarding disclosure issues and whether they have reviewed the audited financial statements and discussed the results with management. Meanwhile, the principal executive and financial officers must formally certify the information in the company's quarterly and annual reports. Any changes to internal control must be certified on a quarterly basis. Some argue that internal control reporting should extend beyond financial reporting systems and fraud prevention, and cover business strategy, delivery, and support systems. In other words, they should run across the organization and address business risk generally. This in turn would create additional challenges for both the internal and external auditor. The external audit profession is moving toward this view, by considering integrated audits covering financial statements and internal control reporting on areas such as fraud policies and corporate ethical codes. This development coincides with the growing use of formally appointed Compliance Officers to oversee the implementation of disclosures and regulatory rules (e.g., SEC, NYSE, and NASDAQ requirements) along with the adoption of a suitable code of ethics. Again, there are those who feel this formal code of ethics should be considered for all employees and not just executives and senior finance officers in public companies reporting under Section 13(a) or 15(d) of the amended 1934 Securities and Exchange Act.

Silo Reporting

Internal control arrangements have to be formally reported on. Even though the internal control arrangements are currently set within the financial reporting arena, there is a view that the remit will spread across the organization. The main problem facing the board, audit committee, and, therefore, internal audit is the consequence of "silo" controls reporting, in that different parts of the organization report on their controls in a way that suits them and in a language that they understand. Compliance, inspection, review, and financial control teams likewise review controls and issue an assortment of reports that impact in some shape or form on the topic of internal controls.

The temptation is for internal audit to become just another one of these silo control-reporting teams. The audit work on payroll, business planning, inventory management, budgetary control, e-business programs, sales projects, and so on each results in a short audit report that talks about the system of controls and actions agreed upon with the client to improve these systems. Put together, the individual reports comment on individual controls but cannot be drawn together to form an overall view of "the organization." Each auditor's report will represent that auditor's particular isolated silo. One way around this problem is to create a controls reporting infrastructure based around the risk management process, which is discussed in the next section.

For Further Discussion

Is it feasible for internal audit to form an overall opinion on internal control in an organization by using the aggregation of findings on control from all the audits performed during the year?

—— SECTION 4 ——

MAKING RISK MANAGEMENT WORK

We have discussed risk-based auditing throughout the book. The question facing the audit shop is:

How does it contribute to the establishment of robust but responsive risk management and reporting within the organization?

Another, complementary question asks:

How does the audit shop support the public disclosure requirements on internal control?

Executives have to certify financial information and controls. They will turn to their managers and employees generally and apply a similar pressure that they are under to live up to their tremendous new responsibilities. Meanwhile, these same executives need to set an ethical framework that promotes full and honest reporting, of what's good and what's not so good. This is over and above the old approach of basic box checking, to fulfill minimal legal requirements under the advisement of company lawyers. The new agenda focuses on real and meaningful information that has been verified. Risk assessment is important because it provides a platform for developing good internal controls. Where risk management works well, controls will likewise make sense, and managers can report upward on their efforts in this respect. This reporting infrastructure will then be able to support the annual disclosures on internal control. The internal auditor must understand the risk-reporting system in place and ensure they provide maximum value-add to examining, improving, and verifying this system and resulting information. The internal auditor will be concerned with the way an organization:

- Sets its objectives.
- Develops control objectives on key disclosure elements such as financial reporting, fraud, and ethical standards.
- Defines processes for delivering these control objectives and associated process owner—for example, the financial reporting system.
- Isolates and weighs up risks to the processes.
- Manages these risks through sound internal controls.
- Tests and examines key controls for reliability and compliance.
- Issues certified reports on the above in line with the requirements of specific quarterly regulatory disclosure returns.
- Reviews and updates the above in line with an improvement plan and response-based updates.

This system must run across the organization and feed into board-level reports. The system is not foolproof, and errors, abuse, miscoded accounts, fraud, inconsistency, and inefficiency can creep into any system. Where employees are alert to red flags and embark on a program of continual improvement, these problems should be minimized. The challenge is to get the audit assurance process to fit neatly into risk assessment and reporting, and there is help on hand for the internal auditor, in the form of Practice Advisory 2110-1, where key points include the following summaries:

- Auditors need to provide assurances on the adequacy of risk management that involves forming an opinion on its effectiveness.
- Risk management remains the responsibility of management, while the board and audit committee have oversight roles.
- Internal audit can act as consultants to assist the organization in this respect.
- Corporate risk assessment can be used to drive the audit planning activities.
- The auditor should ensure the adopted risk management process addresses several considerations, including that:

    1. *Risks arising from business strategies and activities are identified and prioritized.*
    2. *Management and the board have determined the level of risks acceptable to the organization, including the acceptance of risks designed to accomplish the organization's strategic plans.*
    3. *Risk mitigation activities are designed and implemented to reduce, or otherwise manage, risk at levels that were determined to be acceptable to management and the board.*
    4. *Ongoing monitoring activities are conducted to periodically reassess risk and the effectiveness of controls to manage risk.*
    5. *The board and management receive periodic reports of the results of the risk management processes.*
    6. *The corporate governance processes of the organization should provide periodic communication of risks, risk strategies, and controls to stakeholders.*

These matters provide a useful framework for the audit effort. Internal audit needs to assess whether there is a process in place that is able to identify and assess key risk across the organization, and whether it is being used by managers and staff properly. This represents the overview, but the practical reality can be much more demanding. Internal audit's ability to report on internal controls has been considered in Practice Advisory 2120.A1-1. Some of the suggestions from this Advisory are:

- Controls are seen as having a wide application and should provide a reasonable expectation that:

  1. *Financial and operational information is reliable and possesses integrity.*
  2. *Operations are performed efficiently and achieve effective results.*
  3. *Assets are safeguarded.*
  4. *Actions and decisions of the organization are in compliance with laws, regulations, and contracts.*

- Internal audit's work over the year should enable an opinion to be formed on the system of internal control.
- The CAE should communicate an overall judgment about the organization's system of internal control to senior management and the audit committee.
- The annual audit plan should be formulated with the reporting requirements in mind, and if the scope of planned work means that it is not possible to form such an opinion, this fact should be made clear.
- The annual audit report on internal control can include information on current control issues and trends and any likely problems in parts of the organization complying with laws and regulations.

The Advisory makes clear the challenge in using an aggregate of results for various audit engagements to provide an overall view on internal control. In fact, this challenge is viewed as part of the expectation gap between what senior management and the board believe internal audit are capable of providing and what is actually feasible. Meanwhile, the risk agenda will focus on the degree of commonality of risk tolerance in that residual risk is understood across the organization, in terms of acceptability or not. The "silo approach" to risk and control suffers from this inconsistency in risk tolerance, and reports that hit the board talk about their exposures in terms that are so incompatible as to be meaningless. Therefore, risk and control reports might use an assortment of classifications, such as:

- Red, yellow, and green risks
- Hot risks
- Growing risks
- Reportable risks
- Key risks
- Principal risks
- Back-burner risks
- Creeping risk

Whatever else is used to classify each type of risk may be quite clear at each local site, but together mean nothing as they are reported up to senior management and the board. It gets worse when different categories of risk are used in different parts of the organization because each has no bearing on the other. Some argue that each organization needs a Chief Risk Officer to bring together some of these potential disparities. It is here that the internal auditor has a key role in looking across the organization and making sure the reports on risk mitigation and control make sense on a corporate level. The executives send down their message on risk and control, while business lines around the organization report up their concerns; it is the task of matching these two sources that creates the challenge. And it is here that audit should insist that there be a mechanism in place to enable this dialogue. A great deal can be achieved through implementing the following three processes:

1. A good risk and control policy developed by the board.

2. An effective control risk self-assessment program.

3. A well-thought-through risk/controls reporting system.

An internal audit effort that is focused on these three processes will be well received. And assurances to the board that they are in place, that they work, and that they can be relied on will provide immense value to the quarterly controls reporting activity. The internal auditor needs to consider how to assist the CEO and CFO of a reporting company in their task to certify in each quarterly or annual report that they are responsible for establishing and maintaining disclosure controls and procedures and that they follow SEC requirements by having:

1. Designed such controls and procedures to ensure that material information relating to the company, including its consolidated subsidiaries, is made known to them by others within the company; and

2. Evaluated the effectiveness of the company's disclosure controls and procedures as of a date within 90 days before the filing date of the report and presented their conclusions in the report.

The CEO and CFO will look to self-certification by senior managers, CSA workshop results, legal counsel reviews on disclosure compliance, external audit reports, audit committee views, whistleblowers' hotline, and most importantly the internal auditor's overall opinion on each of these sources of information.

For Further Discussion

Is there a potential inconsistency between risk tolerance levels of the board, audit committee, internal audit, and senior managers, and if so, what are the implications of this divergence?

——— SECTION 5 ———

PARTNERSHIPS WITH MANAGEMENT

We have talked about the relationship between the board, audit committee, and internal audit. But what makes an organization tick is really its managers and staff, and their needs and expectations should also be considered by the internal auditor. The traditional auditor spent a great deal of time with junior management, in the endless search for errors and irregular transactions. The new-look auditor is spending more time at the "top table" working on strategic issues that present major challenges for senior management.

The problem is that middle managers may get missed from the internal auditor's guest list as the assurance role focuses on the needs of the board and audit committee. The consulting arm tends to swing into action to address this possible imbalance. In terms of risk management and control reporting, it is the self-assessment process (CSA workshops) that may have the most meaning to business managers as they are asked to review and certify their controls, or better still, encourage their work teams to review their controls and then certify this procedure. There is no natural resource in an organization that comes equipped with the insights and skills to help establish these arrangements, and internal audit is well positioned to perform this task. Practice Advisory 2120.A1-2 describes the benefits of CSA as:

> An organization that uses self-assessment will have a formal, documented process that allows management and work teams, who are directly involved in a business unit, function, or process to participate in a structured manner for the purpose of:
> - Identifying risks and exposures.
> - Assessing the control processes that mitigate or manage those risks.
> - Developing action plans to reduce risks to acceptable levels.
> - Determining the likelihood of achieving the business objectives.

This entails a big judgment call on whether to throw the internal audit resource behind the CSA program as part of the consulting role, or to stand back and review whatever management are putting in place to this effect. The value-add equation may point to the former approach, although we should return to the Practice Advisory for a caveat in terms of their advice:

> The primary role of the internal audit activity will continue to include the validation of the evaluation process by performing tests and the expression of its professional judgment on the adequacy and effectiveness of the whole risk management and control systems. . . . As the level of internal audit's involvement in the CSA program and individual workshop deliberations increases, the chief audit executive should monitor the objectivity of the internal audit staff, take steps to manage that objectivity

(if necessary), and augment internal audit testing to ensure that bias or partiality do not affect the final judgments of the staff.

In assurance work, the auditor can also form good working relationships with management. The main difference with assurance work is that there is a third person in the marriage, in the guise of the board/audit committee. The "client concept" is much broader and includes people outside the audit area in question. Against the backdrop of the traditional "police-officer" role that has attached to the auditor for many years, the auditor may take the following steps to get best value from the audit for all client groups:

- Discuss the terms of reference in the opening meeting with the client and try to build any concerns expressed by the client into the scope of the audit. These concerns will probably fall under the category of "risks to the business" and are therefore important when performing risk-based auditing.
- Explore progress made so far by the client in establishing risk management in the business area. The audit aim may be seen as improving the risk management and control strategy and verifying that the result is reliable (or will be reliable).
- Involve staff from the operational area under review, in the audit process. As mentioned in the blended approach, it is possible to facilitate group work on assessing risk, and getting to better controls, and incorporate any reliable aspects of this exercise into an assurance audit.
- Keep working closely with the client during the course of the audit.
- Encourage the client to get involved in developing solutions in terms of improved controls, where appropriate.
- Report fairly and balance good and less desirable practices.
- However, make it clear that the auditor will remain firm in the matter of outright noncompliance or negligence and make sure the audit scope (or access rights) cannot be interfered with to restrict coverage of all relevant aspects of the audit.

The best way to perform assurance and consulting engagements is to get everyone on the side of the auditor. Fraud investigations, however, are different, in that not everyone will want the truth to come out.

For Further Discussion

Is there any difficulty in balancing the need to get on well and work closely with managers in the organization with the need to retain sufficient professional independence to perform reliable and objective internal audit work?

—— SECTION 6 ——

THE GLOBAL AUDIT COMMUNITY

The internal auditor has been asked to look beyond the audit shop to what the organization is trying to achieve in terms of effective risk management and internal control. Meanwhile, the societal expectations in terms of wider corporate governance must also be tracked as various rules and frameworks evolve and develop. This is still not enough. The surge in internal auditing is an international phenomenon. Most corporate governance codes around the world either refer to the important role of internal audit or state that listed companies must have an internal audit process in place. Likewise, government bodies and agencies tend to make internal auditing mandatory. Most developed and many developing countries have Institute of Internal Audit affiliation and run their own IIA local offices or actual organizations. Affiliates are found in many countries outside the United States, including the United Kingdom, Germany, Mexico, China, Chinese Taiwan, Belgium, Italy, Finland, Australia, France, South Africa, Israel, Italy, and Japan. In many other countries, such as Jamaica, the local IIA members have their own IIA Web site. The IIA's global governance plan provides IIA representation throughout the world and has been developing for many years. The stated intention of this plan is to:

- *Enhance the IIA's governance structure.*
- *Enable more participation by affiliates in decision making and direction setting.*
- *Establish a Committee of the Corporation to oversee uniquely North American matters.*
- *Build stronger commitment and consensus.*
- *Provide better attention to managing global financial matters.*
- *Cultivate a greater sense of global mindset in the IIA's volunteer and staff organizations.*

The IIA standards are designed to have global application, although some countries make minor adjustments to fit local contexts and terminology. Nominated representatives are able to sit on a Global Forum or Council to further implement the governance plan and procedures.

Internal auditing is one of the few professions that is attempting to define a global process with standards, best practice, and a research capability. The new auditor should consider joining the international internal auditing community and widen any research, reading, and Web site access to take on board important developments, wherever they arise in the world. Most multinational enterprises have an internal audit presence, and many audit staff spend their time traveling between various countries and regions. Meanwhile, major funding and development agencies have their own internal audit outfit to support the development and reconstruction programs that seek to assist emerging democracies. There is also a tendency for these development agencies to encourage governments to acquire their own internal audit resource or grow their current capacity, in line with professional standards. Even countries where basic essentials top the aid agenda, there is still the recognition of how food and basic supply programs can benefit from effective controls and an audit process to support the development of these controls. Developing countries will have their priorities, and once basic sustenance has been secured, the processes to attend to next include, in order of priority:

1. Sustainable and efficient elected government, public services, and commercial infrastructure.
2. Preparation of suitable accounts.
3. Independent external audit of these accounts.

After these processes have been addressed, most emerging governments start to consider wider aspects of corporate governance, including a professional internal audit capacity. Returning to developed economies, internal auditing around the world has new benchmarks to consider. One such consideration relates to delivering high-impact value to the governance, risk, and control systems. The use of blended audit approaches based on the consulting and assurance audit service models may be one way of making an impact.

For Further Discussion

What is the experience, the perceived role, and value of internal auditing in some of the countries visited over the years?

— SECTION 7 —

FUTURE DIRECTIONS AND CHALLENGES

The new internal auditor will have entered the profession at an exciting time. All types of organizations are involved to some extent in the struggle to balance three major demands from society:

1. To be aware of and understand the implications of all new regulations and laws that impact their sector and to respond appropriately.
2. To perform and achieve success as defined by key stakeholders.
3. To adhere to the highest standards of integrity, accountability, and transparency.

This is what is expected of listed companies, family enterprises, public-sector agencies, government policy-making bodies, politicians, health officials, charities, community groups, local authorities, and all the other organizations and groups that constitute business, commerce, government, and not-for-profit bodies. Companies that impose a great deal of pressure on staff to meet extremely high income targets, yet fail to reinforce ethical standards, will encourage abuse and false accounting.

Shareholders who demand instant returns from companies in highly competitive industries, and ask no questions about where these returns came from, may promote a culture of creative accounting. Sales managers who insist on short-term increases in sales quotas may nurture cutthroat practices based on misrepresentation and pressure selling. A local mayor who demands rapid increases in the cleanup rate for violent crime may be working with a police force that shoots first and asks questions later. In truth, it is very hard to achieve all of the three goals set out above, and it is here that an organization looks for someone to provide a balance and sense to the business, who is reliable, professional, and above all, unbiased. And it is here that internal audit can play a key role in guiding the business through rough seas, and avoiding sharp rocks, sharks, and other threats.

The internal auditor's work has moved away from a tick-box approach to hard controls and procedures covering last year's activities. The audit remit also revolves around the control culture and soft controls that flex to support new strategies being developed for the future. Meanwhile, the business climate has moved from strict compliance with the letter of the law through to an understanding of the spirit of the law, with the aspirations of oversight bodies being assimilated into business working practices. The IIA has developed new competencies to reflect these changes and is continuing to expand this research into ways of responding to the heightened expectation from regulators, customers, investors and other stakeholders, and society in general.

The thrust into Web-based e-business makes corporate reputation all-important. Consumers now have unlimited choice in what they buy and who they buy from, while the responsive organization who can deliver the "best package" to the consumer has more chance of survival. Moving away from traditional business models used to be seen as risky. In fact, it could be argued that risk-taking is a feature of growing businesses, and risk management is really about stretching the limits as far as they will go without breaking the law or breaking the company.

An internal audit shop that cannot understand this basic principle will underperform. Many managers want to know where the low-risk parts of the business are, so they can install new initiatives to exploit this stability, taking more risk in these areas. The auditor's assurances regarding these activities are crucial in helping management decide where there is capacity for expansion. The input from internal audit to formal disclosure requirements should be uppermost in the mind of each CAE. Proactive and positive strategies addressing this matter should supersede the existing audit plans, and close regard should be paid to Practice Advisory 2120.A1-3, important extracts of which are noted below:

a. *The internal auditor's role in such processes may range from initial designer of the process, participant on a disclosure committee, coordinator or liaison between management and its auditors, to independent assessor of the process.*

b. *All internal auditors involved in quarterly reporting and disclosure processes should have a clearly defined role and evaluate responsibilities with appropriate IIA Consulting and Assurance Standards, and with guidance contained in related Practice Advisories.*

c. *Internal auditors should ensure that organizations have a formal policy and documented procedures to govern processes for quarterly financial reports, related disclosures and regulatory reporting requirements. Appropriate review of any policies and procedures by attorneys, external auditors, and other experts can offer additional comfort that policies and procedures are comprehensive and accurately reflect applicable requirements.*

d. *Internal auditors should encourage organizations to establish a "disclosure committee" to coordinate the process and provide oversight to participants. . . . Normally the chief audit executive (CAE) should be a member of the disclosure committee.*

e. *Internal auditors should periodically review and evaluate quarterly reporting and disclosure processes, disclosure committee activities, and related documentation, and provide management and the audit committee with an assessment of the process and assurance concerning overall operations and compliance with policies and procedures. Internal auditors whose independence may be impaired due to their assigned role in the process should ensure that management and the audit committee are able to obtain appropriate assurance about the process from other sources. Other sources can include internal self-assessments as well as third parties such as external auditors and consultants.*

f. *Internal auditors should recommend appropriate improvements to the policies, procedures, and process for quarterly reporting and related disclosures based on the results of an assessment of related activities.*

Another area where there is much interest and growth is enterprise risk management (ERM). This is essentially where risk is seen as an organization-wide concept. Rather than considering pockets of risk management practice from project teams, security staff, health and safety checks, environmental inspections, and so on, risk is assessed throughout the entire business. This cross-activity thinking involves linking risk-based practices and establishing an integrated approach to risk management. The internal auditor, likewise, may consider adopting this corporate position rather than view each audit as a separate engagement or "pocket." This approach encourages the auditor to rise above the detail and think "cross-organization."

ERM[1] is an important decision to make because it allows an internal control reporting system to cover the entire organization. Sarbanes-Oxley really applies to internal control disclosures that support the financial reporting systems and compliance areas, and some feel that a line may be drawn between financial accounting and the main business operations. However, listing rules are still developing, and there is another view that supports a broader definition of internal control reporting. Because good organizations turn to the spirit, and not just the letter of the law, it may be seen as best practice to reach out and widen the adopted disclosure and reporting arrangements and go beyond those specified in regulations. Disclosures must be completed quarterly and whenever there are relevant changes in circumstances. An efficient information system, one that is responsive, quick, and reliable, is now a fundamental aspect of good corporate governance. Internal audit's effort to help promote and also verify this system is time well spent.

Personal liability is another issue that keeps people awake at night. For some, it is the biggest single risk that they face. Having certified the financial returns, the principal executive and financial officer are responsible for the authenticity of those returns or at least for making sure they have not knowingly misrepresented the truth. Executives may place reliance on their management team to prepare and present reliable financial statements and attestations on compliance issues. But it is information from objective sources such as external and internal audit that may be seen as more dependable.

The audit committee is now seen as another source of reliable information in its oversight capacity. But again, there are personal risks, where the committee members—particularly the designated "financial expert"—have an additional burden to review, consider, and report on business matters that they may not have close contact with, as outside directors. The internal auditors are once again a major source of advice for the audit committee in helping it discharge its statutory responsibilities. Audit committees are expected to be tough on promoting the culture and standards that underpin disclosure and compliance obligations. The balance between advising the board on ways forward and insisting that certain steps be actioned by management will develop over time. In one sense, the internal audit stance will mirror that taken by the audit committee, and the balance between consulting and assurance work will likewise depend on the way "carrot and stick" cultures start to emerge.

If all parts of the corporate governance system work well, there is a good chance that the organization will meet its obligations to its stakeholders. We have noted the assurance and review aspects of external audit and their contribution toward sound financial statements. One development that is becoming increasingly important is the support provided by internal audit to the audit committee as it takes on additional responsibilities for ensuring the external audit process works properly. Internal audit can be asked to help this oversight role of the audit committee. Practice Advisory 2050-2 provides an insight into the new and demanding position that many internal audit shops may find themselves in. This Advisory suggests:

> *The internal auditor's participation in the selection, evaluation, or retention of the organization's external auditors may vary from:*
>
> * *No role in the process.*
>   *to*
> * *Advising management or the audit committee.*
>   *to*
> * *Assistance or participation in the process.*
>   *to*
> * *Management of the process.*
>   *to*
> * *Auditing the process.*

There is a decision to be made, and the Advisory goes on to recommend that internal audit assume some kind of role in the selection or retention of external audit and makes the point:

> *Internal auditors should determine how the organization monitors ongoing service activities from external auditors.*

Another aspect of internal auditing that is gaining ground is involvement in the organization's ethical program. The cornerstone of most good control models, including antifraud and compliance programs, is the ethical culture of employees and close associates. If this ethical culture is positive and alert, the main organizational control issues will relate to competence, awareness, resources, and efficiency and not focus on abuse, shortcuts, and inappropriate behavior. Time spent assessing the ethical culture and establishing initiatives to promote the right climate is also time well spent. Enterprise-wide risk management depends on openness and propriety where people are empowered to review their risks and controls. It really only works where communications are efficient and the vast majority of people behave with integrity. Practice Advisory 2130-1 tackles the question of ethics and how audit can contribute to high standards of conduct. We quote two key paragraphs below:

> * *The internal audit activity may assume one of several different roles as an ethics advocate. Those roles include chief ethics officer (ombudsman, compliance officer, management ethics counselor, or ethics expert), member of an internal ethics council, or assessor of the organization's*

ethical climate. In some circumstances, the role of chief ethics officer may conflict with the independence attribute of the internal audit activity.

- *At a minimum, the internal audit activity should periodically assess the state of the ethical climate of the organization and the effectiveness of its strategies, tactics, communications, and other processes in achieving the desired level of legal and ethical compliance.*

This Advisory sets another challenge to the internal auditing profession: determining how far to get involved in the ethics function and how best to meet the minimum suggested input in terms of reviewing the ethical climate. This is the ultimate soft control. In one sense, the two degrees of input—making things happen, or assessing the extent to which they are happening—capture the essence of the opportunities facing the typical internal audit shop. This is akin to the balance between consulting and assurance work, or the provision of a blended audit service that provides the best response to the client, taking on board the context and what will best serve both the organization and its stakeholders. We have mentioned the governance, risk management, and control processes many times throughout the book. It is hoped that the reader will use this material as a springboard for developing an active interest in these three related concepts and how they affect the internal auditor. In fact, the future of internal auditing is difficult to plot as it is largely dependent on the future growth and direction of governance in society.

For Further Discussion

1. *Is enterprisewide risk management the key to a successful organization, or is this just a topical fad?*
2. *If risk-based auditing represents the current focus of internal auditing, will reputation-based auditing take over from this in years to come?*

—— SECTION 8 ——

THE FINAL AUDIT MODEL

By adding the corporate governance, risk register, internal control certificates, internal audit assurances, and a business performance box to the audit model, it is now complete. This model, shown in Exhibit 6.2, may be used to represent the context and role of internal auditing within an organization.

Exhibit 6.2. Final Audit Model

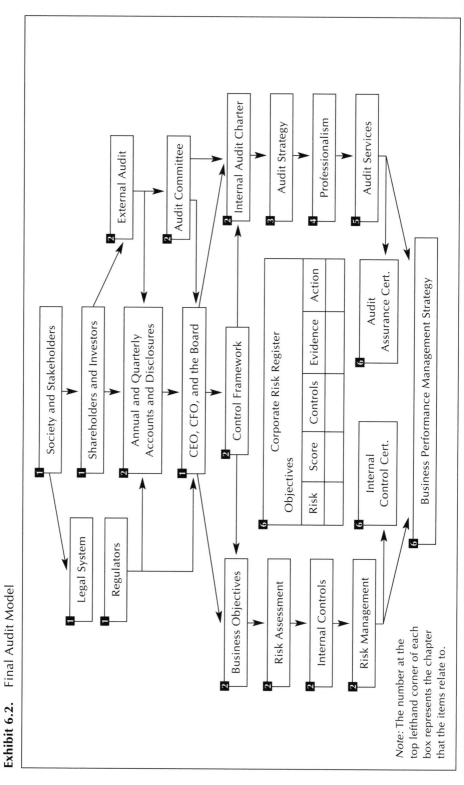

Note: The number at the top lefthand corner of each box represents the chapter that the items relate to.

274

Society and Stakeholders. The audit model is driven primarily by the needs and interests of society—that is, the need for good company performance that contributes to the economy, and both fair and transparent business practices. Stakeholders include all those who have a direct or indirect interest in the way business, commerce, and public services are conducted.

Shareholders and Investors. Principal stakeholders are the people and institutions who hold shares in listed companies. Banks and investment companies may well have a direct interest that is represented in funds loaned to the company. Meanwhile, *The People* are principal stakeholders in public-sector organizations. Company shareholders should exercise their voting rights with due regard to the need to ensure there is ethical behavior and accountability from company officials.

Legal System. There are a multitude of federal and state laws that relate to the way private- and public-sector organizations are established, maintained, and extinguished. Many larger organizations have responded by setting up compliance functions to address the variety and magnitude of such legal provisions. Company directors and officials can face severe penalties where specific laws are breached.

Regulators. Most industries have an associated regulator that sets standards and represents the public in ensuring organizations behave properly. The SEC, American Stock Exchange, New York Stock Exchange, and NASDAQ regulations are some of the more well-known models.

CEO, CFO, and the Board. Shareholders appoint a CEO and board of directors to direct and oversee the organization on their behalf. These officers have a responsibility to discharge their duties in a professional manner and account for the results to the shareholders. A management team will be appointed in public-sector bodies and have a similar responsibility to the government and general public. The board should adhere to the highest standards of ethics and ensure that the organization conducts its business in an acceptable and documented manner. Moreover, the board should have in place suitable mechanisms through which it may judge its own performance and conduct.

Annual Accounts and Disclosures. The organization reports to its stakeholders through published financial and performance statements. These reports act as a window to the outside world, and business analysts spend a great deal of time examining the detailed facts and figures in company accounts on behalf of their clients. Listed companies along with many other organizations have to make various disclosures on an annual and quarterly basis, in particular resulting from the Sarbanes-Oxley Act. The published accounts should be reliable and now have to be personally certified by the principal executive and CFO.

External Audit. The external auditors are appointed by the shareholders to make sure the board has provided a full and reliable account of the company's financial performance over the previous year. The financial statements will be checked by the external auditors before they are formally published. External auditors should ensure they are independent in their audit work and are able to exercise an appropriate degree of professional skepticism at all times. This part of the audit model is a major contribution to governance as material published by the organization is independently verified.

Audit Committee. A further layer of governance that is growing in importance is the audit committee. This forum, established by the board, comprises independent directors who provide an additional oversight role, focusing on the specialist areas of financial accounting, ethics, audit, accountability, risk management, and control. The audit committee is not there to undermine the board but instead provides advice and support regarding the specialist areas in question. Moreover, it should ask challenging questions of the board, on the premise that it is better that these tough questions come from an in-house audit committee than from external regulators.

Internal Audit Charter. The internal auditor's role and position in the organization is set by the audit charter that is agreed upon by the board and the audit committee. To be of any real use, this charter should be set firmly within the governance, risk management, and control arenas.

Business Objectives. The next stage of the model relates to the setting of formal corporate objectives that document the mission of the organization and what it is there to achieve.

Risk Assessment. Anything that has an impact on the business objectives can be seen as a potential risk. These risks need to be understood, isolated, and weighed in terms of significance. Formal risk assessment gives an organization a head start in understanding where its vulnerabilities lie and where it has scope for advancement. The bottom line is that risks that affect the organization's ability to deliver and achieve its objectives have to be addressed for there to be any real chance of success. Control risk self-assessment and regular risk surveys are good ways to promote risk assessment throughout the organization.

Internal Control. Controls should be in place to address risks that have been assessed as significant. The current climate stresses the importance of controls over financial reporting and disclosures, as well as compliance with various standard regulations. The systems of internal control need to be maintained, updated, and made right as part of the way employees work.

Risk Management.   Controls fit into the wider remit of risk management, and managers and their teams need to build risk mitigation into their overall strategies. There are many different potential responses to risks, depending on the nature, significance, and cost of controls. The organization needs to weigh the available measures on a regular basis and ensure the adopted response meets the expectations of the board and stakeholders. In other words, the response to risk should fit the risk tolerance levels that have been defined by the board in its risk and control policy.

Control Framework.   The entire risk management and control policy should be incorporated within the adopted control framework. Standard models such as COSO sit on a foundation of ethical values and propriety, which may be seen as the "tone at the top" that is set by the board and top executives.

Audit Strategy.   The audit model includes the response from internal audit to the corporate risk policy and approach that is used in the organization. Based on the audit charter, and driven by the corporate risk assessment that the board and management have developed, internal audit should construct a strategy that reflects the future direction of the organization and risks that arise in achieving this strategy.

Professionalism.   Having designed a high-impact audit strategy, there needs to be a high impact audit shop in place to deliver set goals. Here, professionalism is an essential component of the audit model. Professionalism is based on several key factors, including:

- Independence.
- Competent and motivated audit staff.
- Good procedures and documentation.
- Quality assurance mechanisms, including supervision and internal and external reviews.

Audit Services.   A sound strategy and professional staff enable the delivery of good audit services. The audit shop should carefully define its assurance and consulting services and set standards for the way these services are delivered to add value to the business.

Corporate Risk Register.   The pivotal component of the audit model is the risk register or corporate risk database, which is the aggregate recording and reporting system that captures key risks and ensures existing controls are complemented by management action to provide a reasonable chance of success. The register is fed by the efforts of directors, senior management, work teams, and employees generally as they attempt to assess and deal with risk in their areas of responsibility (left-hand side of the model). It is the risk register that underpins the board's view on internal controls.

Internal Control Certification.   The risk register records all efforts to ensure controls do the intended job and enable top management to form a view on the effectiveness of their systems of internal control. This allows senior managers to certify their operations, which in turn supports the CEO and CFO's own certifications in this respect.

Audit Assurance Certification.   The other side of the certification equation relates to an independent view from internal audit, who input into the risk register by their own assessment of its reliability. Internal audit's assurances are more objective than statements made by the business managers on whether their controls work well. It is the "evidence" column of the risk register that causes most problems. The controls self-assessment, management reviews, and staff surveys on the left side of the audit model will reveal employee's basic perceptions about controls. It is only the internal audit coverage that results in wholly reliable evidence about whether internal controls are working well to mitigate unacceptable levels of risk. The audit stamp enriches the overall certification process and enhances the credibility of the CEO's own attestations. Note that the auditor's internal control evaluation schedules (see Chapter 5), which forms the basis of assurance auditing work, look remarkably similar to the client's risk register.

Business Performance Management Strategy.   The bottom line of most organizations in whatever sector relates to its business performance. This underpins the certifications since, if there is no real performance to drive the business forward, there will be little interest in various attestations and certificates. The internal audit shop has two arrowed lines in place in the audit model. The first line hits the *Audit Certification box* in terms of assurance work. The second line goes to the *Business Performance box* in the form of consulting services. In practice, this distinction is not always entirely clear, as assurances on what is working well and where there is excessive risk tend to help management focus their performance better. The audit model is based on the premise that the organization needs to perform well and account for its performance correctly and in accordance with the rules. Management and staff are positioned on the left of the model in terms of performing risk assessment and ensuring controls work well. Internal audit is positioned on the right side of the model, in providing an independent assurance and consulting service that checks to ensure risk management and controls make sense and that also helps develop the necessary arrangements wherever possible.

It is by carefully positioning the audit resource within the above model that its real value may be secured, which should lead to a thriving internal audit process and a more successful organization.

—— SECTION 9 ——

SUMMARY: TOP TEN CONSIDERATIONS

A summary of the ten main points covered in the chapter follows:

1. The links between governance, risk management, and control need to be fully understood:

   - Corporate governance is the overarching principle in question.
   - Control frameworks are required to set out how governance will be achieved.
   - Risk management strategy is a way of assessing risks to the organization and ensuring they are addressed.
   - Systems of internal control are the main way of responding to risks that can be controlled to any extent. Contingency plans should contain risks that cannot otherwise be controlled (or where the cost of control would be prohibitive).
   - Effective controls are in place when the overall governance arrangements are sound and the organization is able to perform in line with stakeholders' expectation as well as comply with all relevant rules.

2. The auditor has moved from presenting lists of errors to the inventories clerk, to presenting major issues that have an impact on the corporate governance agenda to the board and audit committee. This means:

   - Assisting the audit committee in understanding its role.
   - Making sure the board and audit committee understand the internal audit role.
   - Communicating well with audit committee members.

3. Internal control is now firmly on the boardroom agenda and, for that matter, everyone's agenda because of Section 404 of the Sarbanes-Oxley Act and resultant SEC rules. The internal auditors have a key role in supporting this reporting process by reviewing controls and providing assurances on whether they are dependable or not. The emphasis on controls over financial reporting is starting to give way to a wider appreciation of controls over the whole business process.

4. Risk assessment is important because it provides a platform for developing good internal controls. Where risk management works well, controls will likewise make sense, and managers can report upward on their efforts in this respect. Silo reporting causes concern where different parts of the business have different perceptions of risk and control report, which can become fragmented and confusing. The appointment of a chief risk officer can help build risk and control profiles, and where

this reaches across the organization it is called enterprise-wide risk management.

5. While internal audit services the board and audit committee, it still has a responsibility to assist management in their efforts to maintain robust controls. Control risk self-assessment workshops and surveys can be applied by internal audit to provide this support to the line. So long as independent assurance work is resourced, the consulting activities are a good way for internal auditors to help senior and middle management.

6. The rapid growth of internal auditing is a worldwide phenomenon, and this point is appreciated by the IIA. The moves by the IIA to enhance its global governance are designed to:

   • Enable more participation by affiliates in decision making and direction setting.

   • Establish a Committee of the Corporation to oversee uniquely North American matters.

   • Build stronger commitment and consensus.

   • Provide better attention to managing global financial matters.

   • Cultivate a greater sense of global mindset in the IIA's volunteer and staff organizations.

7. Another key development in society, corporations, and work teams relates to the enhanced role of ethical codes. This poses a challenge for internal auditors who need to work out their role in supporting these codes. The official guidance suggests that audit may become closely involved with the way the ethics code is developed and implemented in the organization. If not, then at a minimum the auditor will need to review the state of ethics in the organization, as ethics and the way senior and junior staff behave represent the platform for most good control frameworks.

8. There is much to think about in terms of the future direction of internal auditing, which is tied in with enhancing the professional status of practitioners and ensuring each auditor is able to meet heightened expectations. Practice Advisory 2120.A1-3 has a crucial role in this respect and calls for a careful consideration of how audit links into the quarterly reporting and disclosure requirements from Sarbanes-Oxley and the resulting stock exchange rules.

9. Meanwhile, the future of internal audit is closely tied in with the future direction and development of governance standards and codes that are continuing to emerge each year. As governance concepts evolve, so should the internal audit process likewise change to reflect this movement.

10. The final audit model adds four new features to complete the governance and audit jigsaw:

- Corporate risk register.
- Internal control certification by managers and their staff.
- Audit assurance certification by internal audit.
- Business performance management strategy.

Internal audit should fit into this model in a way that enhances its potential to impact the governance arrangements and that adds value to the business.

—— SECTION 10 ——

YOUR PERSONAL DEVELOPMENT EXERCISES

1. Search the Internet and look up the Web sites of large companies like UPS, Disney Corporation, Ford, Texaco, and so on. Review their annual financial statements and look at their coverage and disclosures regarding:

- Corporate governance.
- Risk management.
- Internal control.
- Environmental reporting.
- Corporate ethics.
- Social responsibility.
- Compliance issues.
- Audit committee reports.
- Independent directors.
- Sarbanes-Oxley reporting requirements.

2. Consider the different perspectives, disclosures, commentaries, and information provided by each company and note the common areas that arise from these financial reports.

3. Search for each of the companies looked at above and review the Web site of the company's internal audit function. Consider the published audit charter and any information provided on the adopted audit strategy in terms of any references to:

- The ten topics listed above.
- Value-added services.
- The balance between assurance and consulting work.
- Benefits from internal audit's objectivity.
- Professionalism and quality assurance procedures.

- Involvement in investigating fraud and irregularity.
- Whether internal audit administers the fraud whistleblowing procedure.
- Any mention of the audit role in CSA and control awareness workshops/seminars.
- How internal audit contributes to improved systems of internal control.
- Any unusual services that are provided by the internal audit shop.

4. Make a note of the common areas that appear in your review, and develop a list of important contributions made by various internal audit shops.

5. Ensure that you understand the contents of this orientation book by rereading the summaries at the end of each chapter.

NOTE

1. ERM—The COSO paper on enterprise risk management can be viewed at *www. coso.org.*

INDEX